Ideology

Ideology

An Introduction

TERRY EAGLETON

VERSO
London · New York

First published by Verso 1991
This edition published by Verso 2007
© Terry Eagleton 1991, 2007
All rights reserved

The moral rights of the author have been asserted

1 3 5 7 9 10 8 6 4 2

Verso
UK: 6 Meard Street, London W1F 0EG
USA: 180 Varick Street, New York, NY 10014-4606
www.versobooks.com

Verso is the imprint of New Left Books

ISBN: 978-1-84467-143-4 (pbk)
ISBN: 978-1-84467-136-6 (hbk)

British Library Cataloguing in Publication Data
A catalogue record for this book is available from the British Library

Library of Congress Cataloging-in-Publication Data
A catalog record for this book is available from the Library of Congress

Printed and bound in the USA by Courier Stoughton Inc.

For Norman Feltes

CONTENTS

Consider, as a final example, the attitude of contemporary American liberals to the unending hopelessness and misery of the lives of the young blacks in American cities. Do we say that these people must be helped because they are our fellow human beings? We may, but it is much more persuasive, morally as well as politically, to describe them as our fellow *Americans* – to insist that it is outrageous that an *American* should live without hope.

RICHARD RORTY, *Contingency, Irony, and Solidarity*

On the uselessness of the notion of 'ideology', see
Raymond Geuss, *The Idea of a Critical Theory.*

RICHARD RORTY, *Contingency, Irony, and Solidarity*

INTRODUCTION TO THE 2007 EDITION

They're gaining on us demographically at a huge rate. A quarter of humanity now and by 2025 they'll be a third. Italy's down to 1.1 child per woman. We're just going to be outnumbered . . . There's a definite urge – don't you have it? – to say, 'The Muslim community will have to suffer until it gets its house in order'. What sort of suffering? Not letting them travel. Deportation – further down the road. Curtailing of freedoms. Strip-searching people who look like they're from the Middle East or from Pakistan . . . Discriminatory stuff, until it hurts the whole community and they start getting tough with their children . . .*

Not the ramblings of a British National Party thug, but the reflections of the novelist Martin Amis, leading luminary of the English metropolitan literary world. There might, perhaps, be a genetic excuse for this squalid mixture of bile and hysteria: Amis's father Kingsley, after all, was a racist, anti-Semitic boor, a drink-sodden, self-hating reviler of women, gays and liberals, and Amis *fils* has clearly learnt more from him than how to turn a shapely phrase. Yet sixteen years ago, when *Ideology* was first published, he would almost certainly have treated these barbaric sentiments with the contempt they deserve. At that point, he would no doubt have recognized the folly and ignorance of believing that authoritarianism and injustice can secure the defence of liberty. It is not just that such a policy is morally

* Quoted by Daniel Soar, *London Review of Books*, 4 January 2007, p. 14.

despicable. It is also that it doesn't work. In fact, it makes the situation immeasurably worse. If the ideologist will not listen to reason, maybe the pragmatist will.

What happened in between Amis then and Amis now, of course, was the so-called 'War Against Terror'. It is this which has inspired a cluster of liberals and leftists in his circle, along with a broader range of commentators and intellectuals, to defend Western freedom by actively undermining it, thus validating Nietzsche's dictum about those whose fight against monstrosity turns them into monsters. Not to speak of validating the paranoid Islamic-fundamentalist view of Western freedom as the sheerest hypocrisy. Bin Laden must be gratified to stumble upon such improbable allies. The only flaw in Amis's argument, one might respectfully venture, is that it is far too restricted. Why apply it only to Western societies? Muslim nations, after all, have excellent reason for suspecting people who appear to be from Texas or Twickenham of intending them no good. Indeed, a good many such easily identifiable types are unleashing mayhem and misery on Iraq and Afghanistan as I write. Would it not be prudent for, say, the Saudis or Yemenis to strip-search Westerners on sight, deport them or, failing that, kick their heads in on the spot? We have, after all, slaughtered far more Arabs over the centuries than the number of individuals who perished in the World Trade Center.

If Martin Amis were to have his trousers forcibly removed on the streets of Dhamar or Damqawt, he might justly protest to the authorities that not all Westerners wish the Arab world harm; that only a small minority of them are raving Islamophobes; and that to characterize the lot of them as potential murderers is outright racism. Yet the Yemenis might do well to close their ears to these soft-bellied liberal pleadings. Injustice, after all, is surely a price worth paying for security. It is expedient that one novelist, or even a whole bunch of them, die for the people. Joseph Stalin seems not to be Amis's favourite historical character, yet there is a good dose of Stalinism in the current right-wing notion that a spot of rough stuff may be justified by the end in view. Not just roughing up actual or intending criminals, mind, but the calculated harassment of a whole population. Amis is not recommending such tactics for criminals or suspects only; he is recommending them as a way of humiliating and insulting certain kinds of men and women at random, so that they will return home and teach their children to be nice to the White Man. There seems something mildly defective about this logic.

There is no question that militant bigots of whatever stripe should be forcibly prevented from blowing off other people's heads, and that this entails vigilance and the force of law. What should be questioned is the assumption which underlies this necessity for Amis and his ilk: that civilization and violence are antithetical, and that the couplet can be roughly translated into West and East. Civilization is indeed precious; but the truth is that it was itself established by violence – by fraud, invasion, revolution, extermination and the like – and that this brute force was then sublimated into the very powers which currently protect it: law, armed forces and the like. The point is made rather more effectively by the ancient Greek tragedians. Pentheus, stiff-necked ruler of Thebes in Euripides' *The Bacchae*, refuses to accept Dionysus, god of riot, into the city, and by savagely repressing him not only triggers some atrocious bloodshed, but turns himself into an image of the very terror he abhors. With greater wisdom, Athens at the close of Aeschylus' *Oresteia* welcomes the marauding Furies into the city, transforming them into the *Eumenides* or Kindly Ones who will contribute to its defence.*

The point is not that Osama Bin Laden should be ceremonially escorted into the palace of Westminster. It is rather that civilizations which fail to recognize the violence at their own core – fail to acknowledge that there is that at the heart of human culture which is profoundly antithetical to it – are likely to suffer hubris, overreach themselves in the pursuit of their enemies, and bring themselves to nothing. For the Freud of *Civilization and its Discontents*, violence must be harnessed by civilization to the task of its own creation; yet there is always something excessive and anarchic about this fickle power, which Freud names as *Thanatos* or the death drive; and this excess can be turned against civility itself. What makes for human culture also threatens to mar it. The urge for order is potentially lethal. The very forces that are intended to subdue chaos are secretly in love with it. There is a paranoid rage for order as well as a non-pathological one. The paranoid kind is a grotesque caricature of our natural desire for peace and security, one which spreads havoc around it. This is what we learn from ancient Greek wisdom, not just from modern-day liberals. It is not a matter of being cavalier about one's own security, or of indulging sentimental liberal illusions about one's enemies. It is a question of a secret complicity between order and chaos, civilization and violence, as the very drive to safeguard the realm can kindle an insensate fury which threatens to scupper it.

Those who sunder such a complicity in the case of tragedy are the powerful

* I have discussed these matters more fully in my *Holy Terror* (Oxford, 2005).

insiders who, confronted with the alien and dispossessed, are able to acknowledge this thing of darkness as their own. The theological name for this self-recognition is repentance. It is when the sovereign discerns a terrifying image of himself in those who are cast out or trodden down that the possibility of redemption begins to glimmer. It is on this note that Sophocles' Theban trilogy ends, as Theseus, the king, takes an enormous risk and welcomes the blind, polluted Oedipus into the city. In ancient mythology, the monster on the threshold usually turns out in some way or another to be a frightful version of oneself. This is not to suggest in some bout of liberal self-laceration that we should come to recognize our own image in those who burn innocent children to death, or in bigots who blow up trains packed with commuters. But it does involve accepting that the West's own hands are hardly clean when it comes to the injustices that drive men and women to these moral obscenities, and that to say so is no more to collude with such actions than to enumerate the causes of Nazism is to endorse it.

In one sense, this book has aged very rapidly. For it begins by remarking on the curious fact that the concept of ideology should be out of fashion among intellectuals at just the time when it was flourishing in reality. Islamic fundamentalism is mentioned in the opening lines of the Introduction; but at this point it remained a reassuringly remote phenomenon. Its weapons had not yet razed buildings on US soil, even though they had created a fair amount of havoc elsewhere. It was still possible to maintain that we lived, for better or for worse, in a post-ideological age. Ideologists, as Raymond Williams once remarked of the masses, were other people. The suggestion that the spirit of red-necked Western chauvinists might be lurking within a few vaguely progressivist English novelists, not to speak of *bien pensant* radical journalists, would have seemed at the time absurd.

It was not, however, 9/11 which started it all. The horror story known as the Return of the Ideologists did not begin with Islamic radicalism. While the World Trade Center was still securely standing, a deviant group of far-right-wing US politicians and intellectuals had already hatched their plans for a new American world imperialism, thinly disguised as the gift of sweetness and light to the darker regions of the planet. It was the entry of these dogmatists and fanatics into the White House in the train of George W. Bush which was the vital turning point – almost as bizarre an event, one might claim, as consultant Scientologists entering 10 Downing Street, or Da Vinci Code buffs patrolling the corridors of the Elysée Palace.

None of this was a riposte to Islamic terrorism. It was a response to the long-term failing hegemony of the United States as a global power, rather as Islamic terrorism is for the most part a response to its continuing sovereignty. The most powerful liberal democracy in the world decided to come out as openly ideological, at the very point when its most devoted servant, the United Kingdom (Sancho Panza to its Quixote, as one might say), was drawing in its ideological horns in the wake of Thatcherism and loudly announcing the end, if not of History, then at least of political Left and Right. The contrast was not entirely surprising: this dramatic irruption from the ideological closet is more probable in a society which, like the United States, in any case wears its founding doctrines proudly on its sleeve, as opposed to the British custom of playing them coyly close to one's chest. Political rhetoric is more high-pitched and unabashed, less pragmatic and low-key, in a nation founded on Enlightenment abstractions than in an empiricist culture for which abstractions are more part of the problem than the solution. A British politician could not refer to God without embarrassing most of his listeners; some American ones could not not do so without offending them.

Of course it is true that ideology was alive and kicking all along. But I mean by the term here something akin to the popular sense of the word which I discuss in the book's early pages: a condition in which action is determined by a rigorous system of immutable, oversimplifying doctrine. Or, as the sociologist Emile Durkheim puts it: 'the use of notions to govern the collation of facts rather than deriving notions from them', which is a succinct enough description of the intelligence used to justify the invasion of Iraq in 2003. It is worth noting, however, how very few governments ever actually behave in this way. France for a brief period of its Revolution is a rare exception. Communist states ran their affairs like this in some ways, but then sought surreptitiously for pragmatic ways to get round their own official doctrinaire zeal. The Nazis subordinated reality to ideology to the point of creating the Holocaust; but it would be hard to characterize fascist Germany overall in such unqualified terms. Finding a state which answers in any pure sense to this description is almost as difficult as finding one which has been governed by virtue. There is, mercifully, a shortage of Pol Pots. The sheer complexity of the modern nation-state renders any such political fundamentalism implausible, though there are a number of instances of it in less developed territories.

Durkheim's words, however, constitute an exact description of the current administration in Washington as I write, whose declared aim has been to govern according to 'faith' rather than 'reality'. It is thus among other things the latest outbreak of a long American lineage of idealism, however unlofty its actual conduct may be. Its disdain for anything as prosaic as reality also aligns it, rather oddly, with postmodern culture, for which reality – rather like the body in the cosmetic surgeon's operating theatre – is pliable stuff to be moulded into whatever shape takes your fancy, not recalcitrant material that thwarts your attempts to mould it.

One should not exaggerate the novelty of this development. The reigns of Reagan and Thatcher were scarcely free of stridently doctrinal politics. Yet this could always be justified to some extent by the existence of the Cold War. An enemy who is himself a full-blooded ideologist constrains you to put your own foundational values candidly on the table. This situation, one might innocently assume, was then repeated with the rise of radical Islam: if the West is speaking more piously and noisily of freedom and democracy than it used to, it is because, shamefaced ideologists though we are, we have been forced by the evangelists of terror to confront our own values more head-on, and promote them more robustly. Just as the West, having conquered its Cold War rivals by default, might have sunk relievedly back into its customary pragmatism, Osama Bin Laden came along to prod us rudely out of it again.

But this is not at all how history unfolded. The United States used the end of the Cold War not as an opportunity to speak of jobs and welfare rather than freedom and evil, but to exploit the fact that it was now the only superpower left by re-structuring the rest of the planet in its own national interests. Ironically then, a nakedly ideological politics was enhanced rather than modified by the end of a prolonged period of intense ideological conflict. A new global narrative was launched on the ruins of an old one. This Western brand of zealotry then ran up against an equally lethal Islamic vein of dogmatic absolutism. Ideology, it appeared, was no longer at an end. The credos of modernization and secularization – the belief that a thoroughly technologized world, furnished with a suitably profane, pragmatic, open-ended world-vision, would see off myth, hierarchy, religion and absolutist values – seemed suddenly in ruins. The superstructure was apparently reluctant to conform quite so obediently to the base. Religion was growing stronger, not weaker – at least in the Muslim world and the United States, with sceptical, agnostic Europe squeezed for breath between them.

Whoever would have imagined that theology would prove so central to twenty-first century existence? It is rather like envisaging a mass resurgence of neo-Platonism. Yet it is not exactly without logic either. Late capitalism kicks out the foundations from under men and women, only for some traditional or new-fangled belief-system to slide them back in again. The more ideology is deconstructed, the more ideology is bred – a statement which can be understood among other things as a comment on the relations between the West and the Arab world. The Muslim assault on the West has taken a military form; but the Islamic fundamentalism we are witnessing today has its early twentieth-century roots in ideological rather than in political, military or economic reaction to the hegemony of the West. At its heart lies cultural and religious dissent. In one sense, this is grist to the mill of postmodernism, which has long sought to displace the political and economic with the cultural. Yet postmodernism imagined that in doing so, it was replacing the dogmatism of the natural or metaphysical with the fluid, unfounded relativities of the cultural. It did not quite anticipate that culture itself would become in some quarters a new form of absolutism and foundationalism, one quite as virulent as any more political creed. More virulent in some ways, in fact, since culture is a history and an experience, not a proposition to be rationally endorsed or refuted.

Is the concept of ideology, then, back on the intellectual agenda? Not quite. In far-left circles, to be sure, it never went away. As for some of the currents of post-structuralism or postmodernism which were most nervous of the notion, they have either died of old age or exhaustion, or simply withered on the branch in the new political climate. Even so, it could hardly be claimed that there has been a major resurgence of interest in ideology since this book was first published – if only, perhaps, because theory has not yet had time to catch up with practice. But there is a more weighty reason for this lack of renewed concern. For it is as though the West has not yet quite decided whether it needs to go thoroughly ideological or not, in the sense of engaging in an open battle of rival systems of value. It is an ambiguity mirrored as I write in the Bush/Blair couplet – the former unabashedly ideological, the latter still concealing his penchant for extremist policies under the veil of post-ideological pragmatism. Which of them presages the future of global capitalism?

Or, to put the point another way: is the high moral ground also the low ideological one? Should the West claim that it is superior to its enemies precisely because its actions are determined by reason rather than by doctrine? And would it not constitute a political defeat if it were to allow its antagonists to force it into the kind of ideological straitjacket they themselves are proud to wear? One wants, after all, to advertise one's own values as natural and universal, rather than as one historical way of life pitted against another. Or is this altogether too sanguine an estimation, and the reality is that, pragmatic politics having perished alongside the victims of 9/11, we are now in a post-post-ideological era where, in Tony Blair's phrase, the gloves are off?

Either course holds clear dangers for the West. Ideology, as I suggest in this book, is always most effective when invisible. Yet with natural resources dwindling, rivals to the USA emerging, East-West conflict mounting and fundamentalism growing a-pace, it is hard to see how plausible it will be to claim that we are simply reasonable while our foes are ruthlessly ideological. Martin Amis speaks of the need for a new 'Westernism', which would presumably involve promoting so-called Western values as an aggressive, coherent, self-conscious ideological project. But it is not only that this would in a sense place Us on the same level as Them, rolling back a whole resourceful English conservatism which insists that freedom, democracy and the like cannot be captured in such crude schematic terms. It is also that the West would need to be drastically selective about the sorts of values which characterize its history (genocide? racism? imperialist violence?), and cannot wriggle off this particular hook by defining such phenomena as regrettable aberrations. It is too easy for the Left to counter this move by demonstrating that what is precious and what is obnoxious about the history of the West are to a large extent sides of a single coin. Freedom is certainly a value worth fighting for – as long as one recognizes that when it takes the historically contingent form of private property, it will very quickly escalate into transnational corporations (with the consequent decline of democracy and individual freedom), and internecine global rivalries (with the inevitable corollaries of war, torture, conspiracy, brutality and the like). The problem with the West is not that its governing values are hollow. It is that it cannot help betraying them. To this extent, it resembles those Muslims who pray to Allah while researching into chemical weapons. The best way to preserve one's values is to practise them.

So-called faith-based politics may not survive much longer than George W. Bush. Even so, ideology has returned to our world on a grand scale since this book first saw the light of day, and is likely to be here to stay. Grand narratives have not, after all, ground to a halt. If the conflict between capital and the Koran (or a certain tendentious reading of it) does not constitute such a narrative, it is hard to know what does. At this level, postmodernists and Death-of-History merchants have certainly been routed. At another level, however, postmodernism seems to be validated – for if only both East and West had signed on for its values of pluralism, anti-foundationalism and a respect for cultural difference, surely none of this would have happened? Is not a laid-back postmodern relativism the most effective therapy for both Texan and Taliban absolutisms, rather as a dose of philosophical anti-foundationalism is the surest remedy for religious fundamentalism?

There is something in this case. Postmodern pluralism is doubtless preferable to bombing marketplaces. But postmodernism has also shown itself remarkably inept in dealing with the kinds of political and material realities which underlie the issue of cultural co-existence. On the whole, it has been preoccupied with identity rather than with oil. Pragmatism of this kind may hatch some of the ultimate solutions; but it does not appear to be politically ambitious enough to square up to the problem. One reason why ideology became a suspect concept, which I do not touch on in this study, is that it yielded ground in part to the concept of culture, which seemed capable of doing much the same work in a more flexible way. Culture is on any estimate involved in the war between capital and the Koran. But just as culture does not go all the way down in a general sense, neither does it in this particular instance. The so-called war against terror is a matter of despotisms and democracies, poverty and power, colonialism and neo-imperialism, economic resources and geopolitical realities, failing states and rising ones, with the problem of identity somewhat further down on the agenda. Osama Bin Laden is not fighting to be himself.

This, then, may be another reason for the return of ideology: the fact that culture, which has sought to act as its surrogate, is in the first place no such thing, and in the second place has proved unequal to the global crisis we confront. Cultures are now what are devastated by a set of global forces which have no anchorage in them, and which are utterly indifferent to their specificities. (The other major crisis we confront involves the very opposite of culture: Nature. Humanly manufactured though global warming is, it is not cultural difference or identity which gave rise to it, or which will help to lower the planetary temperature).

One reason why the notion of ideology has returned in practice but less so in theory, then, is that there is still hope in some quarters that postmodern cultural theory may provide the essential antidote to ideology's real-world horrors. The advantage of this is that it forestalls the sterile setting up of one ideology ('Westernism') against another. The disadvantage is that the ideas of culture, anti-foundationalism, difference and the rest are simply too weak and theoreticist a basis on which to mobilize one's political forces. They inherit the traditional political impotence of a *bien-pensant* liberalism. And they now appear more and more like the political baggage of an earlier, less tragic and panic-stricken era.

This, surely, is where the Left can make a decisive intervention. For though it has never abandoned the concept of ideology, and in this sense turns out to be thoroughly up-to-date rather than dismally *passé*, what the Left has traditionally wielded against it is not a system of values such as 'Westernism', but a fundamental material critique. It has not asked how one set of values is to be countered by another, as in the current, drastically reductive talk of democracy versus autocracy (which side are the West's torture camps and prisons on?). Instead, it has sought to expose the material pre-conditions of such values and ideas, and thus to defeat the more deadly brands of them by transforming the conditions which give rise to them. It is this, more than ever, which is surely necessary today.

T.E.
Dublin, 2006

INTRODUCTION

CONSIDER the following paradox. The last decade has witnessed a remarkable resurgence of ideological movements throughout the world. In the
Middle East, Islamic fundamentalism has emerged as a potent political force.
In the so-called Third World, and in one region of the British Isles, revolutionary nationalism continues to join battle with imperialist power. In some
of the post-capitalist states of the Eastern bloc, a still tenacious neo-Stalinism
remains locked in combat with an array of oppositional forces. The most
powerful capitalist nation in history has been swept from end to end by a
peculiarly noxious brand of Christian Evangelicalism. Throughout this
period, Britain has suffered the most ideologically aggressive and explicit
regime of living political memory, in a society which traditionally prefers its
ruling values to remain implicit and oblique. Meanwhile, somewhere on the
left bank, it is announced that the concept of ideology is now obsolete.

How are we to account for this absurdity? Why is it that in a world
racked by ideological conflict, the very notion of ideology has evaporated
without trace from the writings of postmodernism and post-structuralism?[1]
The theoretical clue to this conundrum is a topic that shall concern us in
this book. Very briefly, I argue that three key doctrines of postmodernist
thought have conspired to discredit the classical concept of ideology. The
first of these doctrines turns on a rejection of the notion of representation –
in fact, a rejection of an *empiricist* model of representation, in which the

representational baby has been nonchalantly slung out with the empiricist bathwater. The second revolves on an epistemological scepticism which would hold that the very act of identifying a form of consciousness as ideological entails some untenable notion of absolute truth. Since the latter idea attracts few devotees these days, the former is thought to crumble in its wake. We cannot brand Pol Pot a Stalinist bigot since this would imply some metaphysical certitude about what not being a Stalinist bigot would involve. The third doctrine concerns a reformulation of the relations between rationality, interests and power, along roughly neo-Nietzschean lines, which is thought to render the whole concept of ideology redundant. Taken together, these three theses have been thought by some enough to dispose of the whole question of ideology, at exactly the historical moment when Muslim demonstrators beat their foreheads till the blood runs, and American farmhands anticipate being swept imminently up into heaven, Cadillac and all.

Hegel remarks somewhere that all great historical events happen, so to speak, twice. (He forgot to add: the first time as tragedy, the second as farce.) The current suppression of the concept of ideology is in one sense a recycling of the so-called 'end of ideology' epoch which followed the Second World War; but whereas that movement was at least partially explicable as a traumatized response to the crimes of fascism and Stalinism, no such political rationale underpins the present fashionable aversion to ideological critique. Moreover, the 'end-of-ideology' school was palpably a creation of the political right, whereas our own 'post-ideological' complacency often enough sports radical credentials. If the 'end-of-ideology' theorists viewed all ideology as inherently closed, dogmatic and inflexible, postmodernist thought tends to see all ideology as teleological, 'totalitarian' and meta-physically grounded. Grossly travestied in this way, the concept of ideology obediently writes itself off.

The abandonment of the notion of ideology belongs with a more pervasive political faltering by whole sections of the erstwhile revolutionary left, which in the face of a capitalism temporarily on the offensive has beaten a steady, shamefaced retreat from such 'metaphysical' matters as class struggle and modes of production, revolutionary agency and the nature of the bourgeois state. It is, admittedly, something of an embarrassment for this position that, just at the moment when it was denouncing the concept of revolution as so much metaphysical claptrap, the thing itself broke out where it had been least expected, in the Stalinist bureaucracies of Eastern

Europe. No doubt President Ceausescu spent his last moments on earth reminding his executioners that revolution was an outmoded concept, that there were only ever micro-strategies and local deconstructions, and that the idea of a 'collective revolutionary subject' was hopelessly passé. The aim of this book is in one sense suitably modest – to clarify something of the tangled conceptual history of the notion of ideology. But it also offers itself as a political intervention into these broader issues, and so as a political riposte to this latest treason of the clerks.

A poem by Thom Gunn speaks of a German conscript in the Second World War who risked his life helping Jews to escape the fate in store for them at the hands of the Nazis:

> I know he had unusual eyes,
> Whose power no orders could determine,
> Not to mistake the men he saw,
> As others did, for gods or vermin.

What persuades men and women to mistake each other from time to time for gods or vermin is ideology. One can understand well enough how human beings may struggle and murder for good material reasons – reasons connected, for instance, with their physical survival. It is much harder to grasp how they may come to do so in the name of something as apparently abstract as ideas. Yet ideas are what men and women live by, and will occasionally die for. If Gunn's conscript escaped the ideological conditioning of his fellows, how did he come to do so? Did he act as he did in the name of an alternative, more clement ideology, or just because he had a realistic view of the nature of things? Did his unusual eyes appreciate men and women for what they were, or were his perceptions in some sense as much biased as those of his comrades, but in a way we happen to approve rather than condemn? Was the soldier acting against his own interests, or in the name of some deeper interest? *Is* ideology just a 'mistake', or has it a more complex, elusive character?

The study of ideology is among other things an inquiry into the ways in which people may come to invest in their own unhappiness. It is because being oppressed sometimes brings with it some slim bonuses that we are occasionally prepared to put up with it. The most efficient oppressor is the one who persuades his underlings to love, desire and identify with his power; and any practice of political emancipation thus involves that most difficult of all forms of liberation, freeing ourselves from ourselves. The other side of the story, however, is equally important. For if such dominion fails to yield its victims sufficient gratification over an extended period of time, then it is certain that they will finally revolt against it. If it is rational to settle for an ambiguous mixture of misery and marginal pleasure when the political alternatives appear perilous and obscure, it is equally rational to rebel when the miseries clearly outweigh the gratifications, and when it seems likely that there is more to be gained than to be lost by such action.

It is important to see that, in the critique of ideology, only those interventions will work which make sense to the mystified subject itself. In this sense, 'ideology critique' has an interesting affinity with the techniques of psychoanalysis. 'Criticism', in its Enlightenment sense, consists in recounting to someone what is awry with their situation, from an external, perhaps 'transcendental' vantage-point. 'Critique' is that form of discourse which seeks to inhabit the experience of the subject from inside, in order to elicit those 'valid' features of that experience which point beyond the subject's present condition. 'Criticism' instructs currently innumerate men and women that the acquisition of mathematical knowledge is an excellent cultural goal; 'critique' recognizes that they will achieve such knowledge quickly enough if their wage packets are at stake. The critique of ideology, then, presumes that nobody is ever *wholly* mystified – that those subject to oppression experience *even now* hopes and desires which could only be realistically fulfilled by a transformation of their material conditions. If it rejects the external standpoint of Enlightenment rationality, it shares with the Enlightenment this fundamental trust in the moderately rational nature of human beings. Someone who was entirely the victim of ideological delusion would not even be able to recognize an emancipatory claim upon them; and it is because people do not cease to desire, struggle and imagine, even in the most apparently unpropitious of conditions, that the practice of political emancipation is a genuine possibility. This is not to claim that oppressed individuals secretly harbour some full-blown alternative to their unhappiness; but it is to claim that, once they *have* freed themselves from the causes of that suffering, they must be able to look back, re-write their life-histories and recognize that what they enjoy now is what they would have previously desired, if only they had been able to be aware of it. It is testimony to the fact that nobody is, ideologically speaking, a complete dupe that people who are characterized as inferior must actually learn to be so. It is not enough for a woman or colonial subject to be defined as a lower form of life:

they must be actively *taught* this definition, and some of them prove to be brilliant graduates in this process. It is astonishing how subtle, resourceful and quick-witted men and women can be in proving themselves to be uncivilized and thickheaded. In one sense, of course, this 'performative contradiction' is cause for political despondency; but in the appropriate circumstances it is a contradiction on which a ruling order may come to grief.

Over the past ten years I have discussed the concept of ideology with Toril Moi perhaps more regularly and intensively than any other intellectual topic, and her thoughts on the subject are now so closely interwoven with mine that where her reflections end and mine begin is, as they are fond of saying these days, 'undecidable'. I am grateful to have had the benefit of her keener, more analytic mind. I must also thank Norman Geras, who read the book and gave me the benefit of his valuable judgement; and I am grateful to Ken Hirschkop, who submitted the manuscript of the book to a typically meticulous reading and thus saved me from a number of lapses and lacunae. I am also much indebted to Gargi Bhattacharyya, who generously spared time from her own work to give me valuable assistance with research.

T.E.

1

WHAT IS IDEOLOGY?

NOBODY has yet come up with a single adequate definition of ideology, and this book will be no exception. This is not because workers in the field are remarkable for their low intelligence, but because the term 'ideology' has a whole range of useful meanings, not all of which are compatible with each other. To try to compress this wealth of meaning into a single comprehensive definition would thus be unhelpful even if it were possible. The word 'ideology', one might say, is a *text*, woven of a whole tissue of different conceptual strands; it is traced through by divergent histories, and it is probably more important to assess what is valuable or can be discarded in each of these lineages than to merge them forcibly into some Grand Global Theory.

To indicate this variety of meaning, let me list more or less at random some definitions of ideology currently in circulation:

(a) the process of production of meanings, signs and values in social life;
(b) a body of ideas characteristic of a particular social group or class;
(c) ideas which help to legitimate a dominant political power;
(d) false ideas which help to legitimate a dominant political power;
(e) systematically distorted communication;
(f) that which offers a position for a subject;
(g) forms of thought motivated by social interests;

(*h*) identity thinking;

(*i*) socially necessary illusion;

(*j*) the conjuncture of discourse and power;

(*k*) the medium in which conscious social actors make sense of their world;

(*l*) action-oriented sets of beliefs;

(*m*) the confusion of linguistic and phenomenal reality;

(*n*) semiotic closure;

(*o*) the indispensable medium in which individuals live out their relations to a social structure;

(*p*) the process whereby social life is converted to a natural reality.[1]

There are several points to be noted about this list. First, not all of these formulations are compatible with one another. If, for example, ideology means *any* set of beliefs motivated by social interests, then it cannot simply signify the *dominant* forms of thought in a society. Others of these definitions may be mutually compatible, but with some interesting implications: if ideology is both illusion and the medium in which social actors make sense of their world, then this tells us something rather depressing about our routine modes of sense-making. Secondly, we may note that some of these formulations are pejorative, others ambiguously so, and some not pejorative at all. On several of these definitions, nobody would claim that their own thinking was ideological, just as nobody would habitually refer to them-selves as Fatso. Ideology, like halitosis, is in this sense what the other person has. It is part of what we mean by claiming that human beings are somewhat rational that we would be puzzled to encounter someone who held convic-tions which they acknowledged to be illusory. Some of these definitions, however, are neutral in this respect – 'a body of ideas characteristic of a particular social group or class', for example – and to this extent one might well term one's own views ideological without any implication that they were false or chimerical.

Thirdly, we can note that some of these formulations involve episte-mological questions – questions concerned with our knowledge of the world – while others are silent on this score. Some of them involve a sense of not seeing reality properly, whereas a definition like 'action-oriented sets of beliefs' leaves this issue open. This distinction, as we shall see, is an important bone of contention in the theory of ideology, and reflects a dissonance between two of the mainstream traditions we find inscribed within the term. Roughly speaking, one central lineage, from Hegel and Marx to Georg Lukács and some later Marxist thinkers, has been much preoccupied with ideas of true and false cognition, with ideology as illusion, distortion and mystification; whereas an alternative tradition of thought has been less epistemological than sociological, concerned more with the function of ideas within social life than with their reality or unreality. The Marxist heritage has itself straddled these two intellectual currents, and that both of them have something interesting to tell us will be one of the contentions of this book.

Whenever one is pondering the meaning of some specialized term, it is always useful to get a sense of how it would be used by the person-in-the-street, if it is used there at all. This is not to claim such usage as some final court of appeal, a gesture which many would view as itself ideological; but consulting the person-in-the-street nonetheless has its uses. What, then, would be meant if somebody remarked in the course of a pub conversation: 'Oh, that's just ideological!' Not, presumably, that what had just been said was simply false, though this might be implied; if that was what was meant, why not just say so? It is also unlikely that people in a pub would mean something like 'That's a fine specimen of semiotic closure!' or hotly accuse one another of confusing linguistic and phenomenal reality. To claim in ordinary conversation that someone is speaking ideologically is surely to hold that they are judging a particular issue through some rigid framework of preconceived ideas which distorts their understanding. I view things as they really are; you squint at them though a tunnel vision imposed by some extraneous system of doctrine. There is usually a suggestion that this involves an oversimplifying view of the world – that to speak or judge 'ideologically' is to do so schematically, stereotypically, and perhaps with the faintest hint of fanaticism. The opposite of ideology here, then, would be less 'absolute truth' than 'empirical' or 'pragmatic'. This view, the person-in-the-street might be gratified to hear, has the august support of the sociologist Emile Durkheim, who characterized the 'ideological method' as consisting in 'the use of notions to govern the collation of facts rather than deriving notions from them.'[2]

It is surely not hard to show what is wrong with such a case. Most people would now concede that without preconceptions of some kind – what the philosopher Martin Heidegger calls 'pre-understandings' – we would not even be able to identify an issue or situation, let alone pass judgement upon it. There is no such thing as presuppositionless thought, and to this extent all of our thinking might be said to be ideological. Perhaps *rigid* preconceptions makes the difference: I presume that Paul McCartney has eaten in the last three months, which is not particularly ideological, whereas you presuppose that he is one of the forty thousand elect who will be saved on the Day of Judgement. But one person's rigidity is, notoriously, another's open-mindedness. His thought is red-neck, yours is doctrinal, and mine is deliciously supple. There are certainly forms of thought which simply 'read off' a particular situation from certain pre-established general principles, and the style of thinking we call 'rationalist' has in general been guilty of this error. But it remains to be seen whether all that we call ideological is in this sense rationalistic.

Some of the most vociferous persons-in-the-street are known as American sociologists. The belief that ideology is a schematic, inflexible way of seeing the world, as against some more modest, piecemeal, pragmatic wisdom, was elevated in the post-war period from a piece of popular wisdom to an elaborate sociological theory.[3] For the American political theorist Edward Shils, ideologies are explicit, closed, resistant to innovation, promulgated with a great deal of affectivity and require total adherence from their devotees.[4] What this comes down to is that the Soviet Union is in the grip of ideology while the United States sees things as they really are. This, as the reader will appreciate, is not in itself an ideological viewpoint. To seek some humble, pragmatic political goal, such as bringing down the democratically elected government of Chile, is a question of adapting oneself realistically to the facts; to send one's tanks into Czechoslovakia is an instance of ideological fanaticism.

An interesting feature of this 'end-of-ideology' ideology is that it tends to view ideology in two quite contradictory ways, as at once blindly irrational and excessively rationalistic. On the one hand, ideologies are passionate, rhetorical, impelled by some benighted pseudo-religious faith which the sober technocratic world of modern capitalism has thankfully outgrown; on the other hand they are arid conceptual systems which seek to reconstruct society from the ground up in accordance with some bloodless blueprint. As Alvin Gouldner sardonically encapsulates these ambivalences, ideology is 'the mind-inflaming realm of the doctrinaire, the dogmatic, the im-passioned, the dehumanising, the false, the irrational, and, of course, the "extremist" consciousness'.[5] From the standpoint of an empiricist social engineering, ideologies have at once too much heart and too little, and so can be condemned in the same breath as lurid fantasy and straitjacketing dogma. They attract, in other words, the ambiguous response traditionally accorded to intellectuals, who are scorned for their visionary dreaming at the very moment they are being censured for their clinical remoteness from common affections. It is a choice irony that in seeking to replace an impassioned fanaticism with an austerely technocratic approach to social problems, the end-of-ideology theorists unwittingly re-enact the gesture of those who invented the term 'ideology' in the first place, the ideologues of the French Enlightenment.

An objection to the case that ideology consists in peculiarly rigid sets of ideas is that not every rigid set of ideas is ideological. I may have unusually inflexible beliefs about how to brush my teeth, submitting each individual tooth to an exact number of strokes and favouring mauve toothbrushes only, but it would seem strange in most circumstances to call such views ideological. ('Pathological' might be rather more accurate.) It is true that people sometimes use the word ideology to refer to systematic belief in general, as when someone says that they abstain from eating meat 'for practical rather than ideological reasons'. 'Ideology' here is more or less synonymous with the broad sense of the term 'philosophy', as in the phrase 'The President has no philosophy', which was spoken approvingly about Richard Nixon by one of his aides. But ideology is surely often felt to entail more than just this. If I am obsessional about brushing my teeth because if the British do not keep in good health then the Soviets will walk all over our flabby, toothless nation, or if I make a fetish of physical health because I belong to a society which can exert technological dominion over just about everything but death, then it might make more sense to describe my behaviour as ideologically motivated. The term ideology, in other words, would seem to make reference not only to belief systems, but to questions of *power*.

What kind of reference, though? Perhaps the most common answer is to claim that ideology has to do with *legitimating* the power of a dominant social group or class. 'To study ideology', writes John B. Thompson, '... is to study the ways in which meaning (or signification) serves to sustain relations of domination.'[6] This is probably the single most widely accepted definition of ideology; and the process of legitimation would seem to involve at least six different strategies. A dominant power may legitimate itself by *promoting* beliefs and values congenial to it; *naturalizing* and *universalizing* such beliefs so as to render them self-evident and apparently inevitable; *denigrating* ideas which might challenge it; *excluding* rival forms of thought, perhaps by some unspoken but systematic logic; and *obscuring* social reality in ways convenient to itself. Such 'mystification', as it is commonly known, frequently takes the form of masking or suppressing social conflicts, from which arises the conception of ideology as an imaginary resolution of real contradictions. In any actual ideological formation, all six of these strategies are likely to interact in complex ways.

There are, however, at least two major difficulties with this otherwise persuasive definition of ideology. For one thing, not every body of belief which people commonly term ideological is associated with a *dominant* political power. The political left, in particular, tends almost instinctively to think of such dominant modes when it considers the topic of ideology; but what then do we call the beliefs of the Levellers, Diggers, Narodniks and Suffragettes, which were certainly not the governing value systems of their day? Are socialism and feminism ideologies, and if not why not? Are they non-ideological when in political opposition but ideological when they come to power? If what the Diggers and Suffragettes believed is 'ideological', as a good deal of common usage would suggest, then by no means all ideologies are oppressive and spuriously legitimating. Indeed the right-wing political theorist Kenneth Minogue holds, astoundingly, that *all* ideologies are politically oppositional, sterile totalizing schemes as opposed to the ruling practical wisdom: 'Ideologies can be specified in terms of a shared hostility to modernity: to liberalism in politics, individualism in moral practice, and the market in economics.'[7] On this view, supporters of socialism are ideological whereas defenders of capitalism are not. The extent to which one is prepared to use the term ideology of one's own political views is a reliable index of the nature of one's political ideology. Generally speaking, conservatives like Minogue are nervous of the concept in their own case, since to dub their own beliefs ideological would be to risk turning them into objects of contestation.

Does this mean, then, that socialists, feminists and other radicals should come clean about the ideological nature of their own values? If the term ideology is confined to *dominant* forms of social thought, such a move would be inaccurate and needlessly confusing; but it may be felt that there is need here for a broader definition of ideology, as any kind of intersection between belief systems and political power. And such a definition would be neutral on the question of whether this intersection challenged or confirmed a particular social order. The political philosopher Martin Seliger argues for just such a formulation, defining ideology as 'sets of ideas by which men [*sic*] posit, explain and justify ends and means of organised social action, and specifically political action, irrespective of whether such action aims to preserve, amend, uproot or rebuild a given social order'.[8] On this formation, it would make perfect sense to speak of 'socialist ideology', as it would not (at least in the West) if ideology meant just *ruling* belief systems, and as it would not, at least for a socialist, if ideology referred inescapably to illusion, mystification and false consciousness.

To widen the scope of the term ideology in this style has the advantage of staying faithful to much common usage, and thus of resolving the apparent dilemma of why, say, fascism should be an ideology but feminism should not be. It carries, however, the disadvantage of appearing to jettison from the concept of ideology a number of elements which many radical theorists have assumed to be central to it: the obscuring and 'naturalizing' of social reality, the specious resolution of real contradictions, and so on. My own view is that both the wider and narrower senses of ideology have their uses, and that their mutual incompatibility, descending as they do from divergent political and conceptual histories, must be simply acknowledged. This view has the advantage of remaining loyal to the implicit slogan of Bertolt Brecht – 'Use what you can!' – and the disadvantage of excessive charity.

Such charity is a fault because it risks broadening the concept of ideology to the point where it becomes politically toothless; and this is the second problem with the 'ideology as legitimation' thesis, one which concerns the nature of power itself. On the view of Michel Foucault and his acolytes, power is not something confined to armies and parliaments: it is, rather, a pervasive, intangible network of force which weaves itself into our slightest gestures and most intimate utterances.[9] On this theory, to limit the idea of power to its more obvious political manifestations would itself be an ideological move, obscuring the complex diffuseness of its operations. That we should think of power as imprinting our personal relations and routine activities is a clear political gain, as feminists, for instance, have not been slow to recognize; but it carries with it a problem for the meaning of ideology. For if there are no values and beliefs *not* bound up with power, then the term ideology threatens to expand to vanishing point. Any word which covers everything loses its cutting edge and dwindles to an empty sound. For a term to have meaning, it must be possible to specify what, in particular circumstances, would count as the other of it – which doesn't necessarily mean specifying something which would be *always and everywhere* the other of it. If power, like the Almighty himself, is omnipresent, then the word ideology ceases to single out anything in particular and becomes wholly uninformative – just as if any piece of human behaviour whatsoever, including torture, could count as an instance of compassion, the word compassion shrinks to an empty signifier.

Faithful to this logic, Foucault and his followers effectively abandon the concept of ideology altogether, replacing it with the more capacious 'discourse'. But this may be to relinquish too quickly a useful distinction. The force of the term ideology lies in its capacity to discriminate between those power struggles which are somehow central to a whole form of social life, and those which are not. A breakfast-time quarrel between husband and wife over who exactly allowed the toast to turn that grotesque shade of black need not be ideological; it becomes so when, for example, it begins to engage questions of sexual power, beliefs about gender roles and so on. To say that this sort of contention is ideological makes a difference, tells us something informative, as the more 'expansionistic' senses of the word do not. Those radicals who hold that 'everything is ideological' or 'everything is political' seem not to realize that they are in danger of cutting the ground from beneath their own feet. Such slogans may valuably challenge an excessively narrow definition of politics and ideology, one convenient for a ruling power intent on depoliticizing whole sectors of social life. But to stretch these terms to the point where they become coextensive with everything is simply to empty them of force, which is equally congenial to the ruling order. It is perfectly possible to agree with Nietzsche and Foucault that power is everywhere, while wanting for certain practical purposes to distinguish between more and less central instances of it.

There are those on the political left, however, who feel uneasy about this whole business of deciding between the more and less central. Isn't this merely a surreptitious attempt to marginalize certain power struggles which have been unduly neglected? Do we really want to draw up a hierarchy of such conflicts, thus reproducing a typically conservative habit of thought? If someone actually believes that a squabble between two children over a ball is as important as the El Salvador liberation movement, then you simply have to ask them whether they are joking. Perhaps by dint of sufficient ridicule you might persuade them to become properly hierarchical thinkers. Political radicals are quite as dedicated to the concept of privilege as their opponents: they believe, for example, that the level of food supplies in Mozambique is a weightier issue than the love life of Mickey Mouse. To claim that one kind of conflict is more important than another involves, of course, *arguing* for this priority and being open to disproval; but nobody actually believes that 'power is everywhere' in the sense that any manifestation of it is as significant as any other. On this issue, as perhaps on all others, nobody is in fact a relativist, whatever they may rhetorically assert.

Not everything, then, may usefully be said to be ideological. If there is nothing which is not ideological, then the term cancels all the way through and drops out of sight. To say this does not commit one to believing that there is a kind of discourse which is inherently non-ideological; it just means that in any particular situation you must be able to point to what counts as non-ideological for the term to have meaning. Equally, however, one might claim that there is no piece of discourse which *could* not be ideological, given the appropriate conditions. 'Have you put the cat out yet?' could be an ideological utterance, if (for example) it carried the unspoken implication: 'Or are you being your usual shiftless proletarian self?' Conversely, the statement 'men are superior to women' need not be ideological (in the sense of supporting a dominant power); delivered in a suitably sardonic tone, it might be a way of subverting sexist ideology.

A way of putting this point is to suggest that ideology is a matter of 'discourse' rather than 'language'.[10] It concerns the actual uses of language between particular human subjects for the production of specific effects. You could not decide whether a statement was ideological or not by inspecting it in isolation from its discursive context, any more than you could decide in this way whether a piece of writing was a work of literary art. Ideology is less a matter of the inherent linguistic properties of a pronouncement than a question of who is saying what to whom for what purposes. This isn't to deny that there are particular ideological 'idioms': the language of fascism, for example. Fascism tends to have its own peculiar lexicon (*Lebensraum*, sacrifice, blood and soil), but what is primarily ideological about these terms is the power-interests they serve and the political effects they generate. The general point, then, is that exactly the same piece of language may be ideological in one context and not in another; ideology is a function of the relation of an utterance to its social context.

Similar problems to those of the 'pan-powerist' case arise if we define ideology as any discourse bound up with specific social interests. For, once again, what discourse isn't? Many people outside right-wing academia would nowadays suspect the notion of some wholly disinterested language; and if they are right then it would seem pointless to define ideology as 'socially interested' utterances, since this covers absolutely anything. (The very word 'interest', incidentally, is of ideological interest: as Raymond

Williams points out in *Keywords*, it is significant that 'our most general word for attraction or involvement should have developed from a formal objective term in property and finance ... this now central word for attraction, attention and concern is saturated with the experience of a society based on money relationships'.[11]) Perhaps we could try to distinguish here between 'social' and purely 'individual' kinds of interest, so that the word ideology would denote the interests of specific social groups rather than, say, someone's insatiable hankering for haddock. But the dividing line between social and individual is notoriously problematic, and 'social interests' is in any case so broad a category as to risk emptying the concept of ideology once more of meaning.

It may be useful, even so, to discriminate between two 'levels' of interest, one of which might be said to be ideological and the other not. Human beings have certain 'deep' interests generated by the nature of their bodies: interests in eating, communicating with one another, understanding and controlling their environment and so on. There seems no very useful sense in which these kinds of interest can be dubbed ideological, as opposed, for example, to having an interest in bringing down the government or laying on more childcare. Postmodernist thought, under the influence of Friedrich Nietzsche, has typically conflated these different sorts of interests in an illicit way, fashioning a homogeneous universe in which everything from tying one's shoelaces to toppling dictatorships is levelled to a matter of 'interests'. The political effect of this move is to blur the specificity of certain forms of social conflict, grossly inflating the whole category of 'interests' to the point where it picks out nothing in particular. To describe ideology as 'interested' discourse, then, calls for the same qualification as characterizing it as a question of power. In both cases, the term is forceful and informative only if it helps us to distinguish between those interests and power conflicts which at any given time are fairly central to a whole social order, and those which are not.

None of the argument so far casts much light on the epistemological issues involved in the theory of ideology – on the question, for example, of whether ideology can be usefully viewed as 'false consciousness'. This is a fairly unpopular notion of ideology nowadays, for a number of reasons. For one thing, epistemology itself is at the moment somewhat out of fashion, and the assumption that some of our ideas 'match' or 'correspond to' the way things are, while others do not, is felt by some to be a naive, discreditable theory of knowledge. For another thing, the idea of false consciousness can be taken as implying the possibility of some unequivocally correct way of viewing the world, which is today under deep suspicion. Moreover, the belief that a minority of theorists monopolize a scientifically grounded knowledge of how society is, while the rest of us blunder around in some fog of false consciousness, does not particularly endear itself to the democratic sensibility. A novel version of this elitism has arisen in the work of the philosopher Richard Rorty, in whose ideal society the intellectuals will be 'ironists', practising a suitably cavalier, laid-back attitude to their own beliefs, while the masses, for whom such self-ironizing might prove too subversive a weapon, will continue to salute the flag and take life seriously.[12]

In this situation, it seems simpler to some theorists of ideology to drop the epistemological issue altogether, favouring instead a more political or sociological sense of ideology as the medium in which men and women fight out their social and political battles at the level of signs, meanings and representations. Even as orthodox a Marxist as Alex Callinicos urges us to scrap the epistemological elements in Marx's own theory of ideology,[13] while Göran Therborn is equally emphatic that ideas of false and true consciousness should be rejected 'explicitly and decisively, once and for all'.[14] Martin Seliger wants to discard this negative or pejorative meaning of ideology altogether,[15] while Rosalind Coward and John Ellis, writing in a period when the 'false consciousness' thesis was at the height of its unpopularity, peremptorily dismiss the idea as 'ludicrous'.[16]

To argue for a 'political' rather than 'epistemological' definition of ideology is not of course to claim that politics and ideology are identical. One way one might think of distinguishing them is to suggest that politics refers to the power processes by which social orders are sustained or challenged, whereas ideology denotes the ways in which these power processes get caught up in the realm of signification. This won't quite do, however, since politics has its own sort of signification, which need not necessarily be ideological. To state that there is a constitutional monarchy in Britain is a political pronouncement; it becomes ideological only when it begins to involve beliefs – when, for example, it carries the implicit rider 'and a good thing too'. Since this usually only needs to be said when there are people around who consider it a bad thing, we can suggest that ideology concerns less signification than conflicts within the field of signification. If the members of a dissident political group say to each other, 'We can bring down the government', this is a piece of political discourse; if they say it to the government it becomes instantly ideological (in the expanded sense of the term), since the utterance has now entered into the arena of discursive struggle.

There are several reasons why the 'false consciousness' view of ideology seems unconvincing. One of them has to do with what we might call the moderate rationality of human beings in general, and is perhaps more the expression of a political faith than a conclusive argument. Aristotle held that there was an element of truth in most beliefs; and though we have witnessed enough pathological irrationalism in the politics of our own century to be nervous of any too sanguine trust in some robust human rationality, it is surely hard to credit that whole masses of human beings would hold over some extensive historical period ideas and beliefs which were simply nonsensical. Deeply persistent beliefs have to be supported to some extent, however meagrely, by the world our practical activity discloses to us; and to believe that immense numbers of people would live and sometimes die in the name of ideas which were absolutely vacuous and absurd is to take up an unpleasantly demeaning attitude towards ordinary men and women. It is a typically conservative estimate of human beings to see them as sunk in irrational prejudice, incapable of reasoning coherently; and it is a more radical attitude to hold that while we may indeed be afflicted by all sorts of mystifications, some of which might even be endemic to the mind itself, we nevertheless have some capacity for making sense of our world in a moderately cogent way. If human beings really were gullible and benighted enough to place their faith in great numbers in ideas which were utterly void of meaning, then we might reasonably ask whether such people were worth politically supporting at all. If they are that credulous, how could they ever hope to emancipate themselves?

It follows from this view that if we come across a body of, say, magical or mythological or religious doctrine to which many people have committed themselves, we can often be reasonably sure that there is something in it. What that something is may not be, for sure, what the exponents of such creeds believe it to be; but it is unlikely to be a mere nonsense either. Simply on account of the pervasiveness and durability of such doctrines, we can generally assume that they encode, in however mystified a way, genuine needs and desires. It is false to believe that the sun moves round the earth, but it is not absurd; and neither is it absurd to hold that justice demands sending electric currents through the bodies of murderers. There is nothing ridiculous in claiming that some people are inferior to others, since it is obviously true. In certain definite respects, some individuals are indeed inferior to others: less good-tempered, more prone to envy, slower in the fifty-yard dash. It may be false and pernicious to generalize these particular inequalities to whole races or classes of people, but we can understand well enough the logic by which this comes about. It may be wrong to believe that the human race is in such a mess that it can be saved only by some transcendental power, but the feelings of impotence, guilt and utopian aspiration which such a dogma encapsulates are by no means illusory.

A further point can be made here. However widespread 'false consciousness' may be in social life, it can nevertheless be claimed that most of what people say most of the time about the world must in fact be true. This, for the philosopher Donald Davidson, is a logical rather than an empirical point. For unless, so Davidson argues, we are able to assume that most people's observations are most of the time accurate, there would be an insuperable difficulty in ever getting to understand their language. And the fact is that we *do* seem to be able to translate the languages of other cultures. As one of Davidson's commentators formulates this so-called principle of charity: 'If we think we understand what people say, we must also regard most of our observations about the world we live in as correct.'[17] Many of the utterances in question are of a fairly trivial sort, and we should not under-estimate the power of common illusion: a recent opinion poll revealed that one in three Britons believes that the sun moves round the earth, and one in seven holds that the solar system is larger than the universe. As far as our routine social life goes, however, we just could not in Davidson's view be mistaken most of the time. Our practical knowledge must be mostly accurate, since otherwise our world would fall apart. Whether or not the solar system is bigger than the universe plays little part in our daily social activities, and so is a point on which we can afford to be mistaken. At a fairly low level, individuals who share the same social practices must most of the time understand one another correctly, even if a small minority of them in universities spend their time agonizing over the indeterminacy of discourse. Those who quite properly emphasize that language is a terrain of conflict sometimes forget that conflict presupposes a degree of mutual agreement: we are not politically *conflicting* if you hold that patriarchy is an objection-able social system and I hold that it is a small town in upper New York state. A certain practical solidarity is built into the structures of any shared language, however much that language may be traversed by the divisions of class, gender and race. Radicals who regard such a view as dangerously sanguine, expressive of too naive a faith in 'ordinary language', forget that such practical solidarity and reliability of cognition are testimony to that basic realism and intelligence of popular life which is so unpalatable to the elitist.

What Davidson may be accused of overlooking, however, is that form of 'systematically distorted communication' which for Jürgen Habermas goes by the name of ideology. Davidson argues that when native speakers repeatedly point at a rabbit and utter a sound, this act of denotation must for most of the time be accurate, otherwise we could never come to learn the native word for rabbit, or – by extension – anything else in their language. Imagine, however, a society which uses the word 'duty' every time a man beats his wife. Or imagine an outside observer in our own culture who, having picked up our linguistic habits, was asked by his fellows on returning home for our word for domination, and replied 'service'. Davidson's theory fails to take account of these *systematic* deviations – though it does perhaps establish that in order to be able to decipher an ideological system of discourse, we must already be in possession of the normative, undistorted uses of terms. The wife-beating society must use the word 'duty' a sufficient number of times in an appropriate context for us to be able to spot an ideological 'abuse'.

Even if it is true that most of the ideas by which people have lived are not simply nonsensical, it is not clear that this charitable stance is quite enough to dispose of the 'false consciousness' thesis. For those who hold that thesis do not need to deny that certain kinds of illusion can express real needs and desires. All they may be claiming is that it is false to believe that murderers should be executed, or that the Archangel Gabriel is preparing to put in an appearance next Tuesday, and that these falsehoods are significantly bound up with the reproduction of a dominant political power. There need be no implication that people do not regard themselves as having good grounds for holding these beliefs; the point may simply be that what they believe is manifestly not the case, and that this is a matter of relevance to political power.

Part of the opposition to the 'false consciousness' case stems from the accurate claim that, in order to be truly effective, ideologies must make at least some minimal sense of people's experience, must conform to some degree with what they know of social reality from their practical interaction with it. As Jon Elster reminds us, ruling ideologies can actively shape the wants and desires of those subjected to them;[18] but they must also engage significantly with the wants and desires that people already have, catching up genuine hopes and needs, reinflecting them in their own peculiar idiom, and feeding them back to their subjects in ways which render these ideologies plausible and attractive. They must be 'real' enough to provide the basis on which individuals can fashion a coherent identity, must furnish some solid motivations for effective action, and must make at least some feeble attempt to explain away their own more flagrant contradictions and incoherencies. In short, successful ideologies must be more than imposed illusions, and for all their inconsistencies must communicate to their subjects a version of social reality which is real and recognizable enough not to be simply rejected out of hand. They may, for example, be true enough in what they assert but false in what they deny, as John Stuart Mill considered almost all social theories to be. Any ruling ideology which failed altogether to mesh with its subjects' lived experience would be extremely vulnerable, and its exponents would be well advised to trade it in for another. But none of this contradicts the fact that ideologies quite often contain important propositions which are absolutely false: that Jews are inferior beings, that women are less rational than men, that fornicators will be condemned to perpetual torment.[19] If these views are not instances of false consciousness, then it is difficult to know what is; and those who dismiss the whole notion of false consciousness must be careful not to appear cavalier about the offensiveness of these opinions. If the 'false consciousness' case commits one to the view that ideology is simply unreal, a fantasy entirely disconnected from social reality, then it is difficult to know who, these days at least, actually subscribes to such a standpoint. If, on the other hand, it does no more than assert that there are some quite central ideological utterances which are manifestly false, then it is equally hard to see how anybody could deny this. The real question, perhaps, is not whether one denies this, but what role one ascribes to such falsehood in one's theory of ideology as a whole. Are false representations of social reality somehow constitutive of ideology, or more contingent to it?

One reason why ideology would not seem to be a matter of false consciousness is that many statements which people might agree to be ideological are obviously true. 'Prince Charles is a thoughtful, conscientious fellow, not hideously ugly' is true, but most people who thought it worth saying would no doubt be using the statement in some way to buttress the power of royalty. 'Prince Andrew is more intelligent than a hamster' is also probably true, if somewhat more controversial; but the effect of such a pronouncement (if one ignores the irony) is again likely to be ideological in the sense of helping to legitimate a dominant power. This, however, may not be enough to answer those who hold that ideology is in general falsifying. For it can always be argued that while such utterances are *empirically* true, they are false in some deeper, more fundamental way. It is true that Prince Charles is reasonably conscientious, but it is not true that royalty is a desirable institution. Imagine a management spokesperson announcing that 'If this strike continues, people will be dying in the streets for lack of ambulances.' This might well be true, as opposed to a claim that they will be dying of boredom for lack of newspapers; but a striking worker might nevertheless see the spokesperson as a twister, since the *force* of the observation is probably 'Get back to work', and there is no reason to assume that this, under the circumstances, would be the most reasonable thing to do. To say that the statement is ideological is then to claim that it is powered by an ulterior motive bound up with the legitimation of certain interests in a power struggle. We might say that the spokesperson's comment is true as a piece of language, but not as a piece of discourse. It describes a possible situation accurately enough; but as a rhetorical act aimed at producing certain effects it is false, and this in two senses. It is false because it involves a kind of deception – the spokesperson is not really saying what he or she means; and it carries with it an implication – that getting back to work would be the most constructive action to take – which may well not be the case.

Other types of ideological enunciation are true in what they affirm but false in what they exclude. 'This land of liberty', spoken by an American politician, may be true enough if one has in mind the freedom to practise one's religion or turn a fast buck, but not if one considers the freedom to live without the fear of being mugged or to announce on prime-time television that the president is a murderer. Other kinds of ideological statement involve falsity without either necessarily intending to deceive or being significantly exclusive: 'I'm British and proud of it', for example. Both parts of this observation may be true, but it implies that being British is a virtue in itself, which is false. Note that what is involved here is less deception than self-deception, or delusion. A comment like 'If we allow Pakistanis to live in our street, the house prices will fall' may well be true, but it may involve the assumption that Pakistanis are inferior beings, which is false.

It would seem, then, that some at least of what we call ideological discourse is true at one level but not at another: true in its empirical content but deceptive in its force, or true in its surface meaning but false in its underlying assumptions. And to this extent the 'false consciousness' thesis need not be significantly shaken by the recognition that not all ideological language characterizes the world in erroneous ways. To speak, however, of 'false assumptions' broaches a momentous topic. For someone might argue that a statement like 'Being British is a virtue in itself' is not false in the same sense that it is false to believe that Ghengis Khan is alive and well and running a boutique in the Bronx. Is not this just to confuse two different meanings of the word 'false'? *I* may happen not to believe that being British is a virtue in itself; but this is just my opinion, and is surely not on a level with declarations like 'Paris is the capital of Afghanistan', which everyone would agree to be factually untrue.

What side you take up in this debate depends on whether or not you are a moral realist.[20] One kind of opponent of moral realism wants to hold that our discourse divides into two distinct kinds: those speech acts which aim to describe the way things are, which involve criteria of truth and falsity; and those which express evaluations and prescriptions, which do not. On this view, cognitive language is one thing and normative or prescriptive language quite another. A moral realist, by contrast, refuses this binary opposition of 'fact' and 'value' (which has in fact deep roots in bourgeois philosophical history), and 'denies that we can draw any intelligible distinction between those parts of assertoric discourse which do, and those which do not, genuinely *describe* reality'.[21] On this theory, it is mistaken to think that our language separates out into steel-hard objectivism and soggy subjectivism, into a realm of indubitable physical facts and a sphere of precariously floating values. Moral judgements are as much candidates for rational argumentation as are the more obviously descriptive parts of our speech. For a realist, such normative statements purport to describe what is the case: there are 'moral facts' as well as physical ones, about which our judgements can be said to be either true or false. That Jews are inferior beings is quite as false as that Paris is the capital of Afghanistan; it isn't just a question of my private opinion or of some ethical posture I decide to assume towards the world. To declare that South Africa is a racist society is not just a more imposing way of saying that I happen not to like the set-up in South Africa.

One reason why moral judgements do not seem to us as solid as judgements about the physical world is that we live in a society where there are fundamental conflicts of value. Indeed the only moral case which the liberal pluralist would rule out is one which would interfere with this free market in values. Because we cannot agree at a fundamental level, it is tempting to believe that values are somehow free-floating – that moral judgements cannot be subject to criteria of truth and falsehood because these criteria are as a matter of fact in considerable disarray. We can be reasonably sure about whether Abraham Lincoln was taller than four feet, but not about whether there are circumstances in which it is permissible to kill. The fact that we cannot currently arrive at any consensus on this matter, however, is no reason to assume that it is just a question of some unarguable personal option or intuition. Whether or not one is a moral realist, then, will make a difference to one's assessment of how far ideological language involves false-hood. A moral realist will not be persuaded out of the 'false consciousness' case just because it can be shown that some ideological proposition is empirically true, since that proposition might always be shown to encode a normative claim that was in fact false.

All of this has a relevance to the widely influential theory of ideology proposed by the French Marxist philosopher Louis Althusser. For Althusser, one can speak of descriptions or representations of the world as being either true or false; but ideology is not for him at root a matter of such descriptions at all, and criteria of truth and falsehood are thus largely irrelevant to it. Ideology for Althusser does indeed represent – but what it represents is the way I 'live' my relations to society as a whole, which cannot be said to be a question of truth or falsehood. Ideology for Althusser is a particular organ-ization of signifying practices which goes to constitute human beings as social subjects, and which produces the lived relations by which such subjects are connected to the dominant relations of production in a society. As a term, it covers all the various political modalities of such relations, from an identification with the dominant power to an oppositional stance towards it. Though Althusser thus adopts the broader sense of ideology we have examined, his thinking about the topic, as we shall see later, is covertly constrained by an attention to the narrower sense of ideology as a *dominant* formation.

There is no doubt that Althusser strikes a lethal blow at any purely rationalistic theory of ideology – at the notion that it consists simply of a collection of distorting representations of reality and empirically false propositions. On the contrary, ideology for Althusser alludes in the main to our affective, unconscious relations with the world, to the ways in which we are pre-reflectively bound up in social reality. It is a matter of how that reality 'strikes' us in the form of apparently spontaneous experience, of the ways in which human subjects are ceaselessly *at stake* in it, investing in their relations to social life as a crucial part of what it is to be themselves. One might say that ideology, rather like poetry for the literary critic I.A. Richards, is less a matter of propositions than of 'pseudo-propositions'.[22] It appears often enough on its grammatical surface to be referential (descriptive of states of affairs) while being secretly 'emotive' (expressive of the lived reality of human subjects) or 'conative' (directed towards the achievement of certain effects). If this is so, then it would seem that there is a kind of slipperiness or duplicity built into ideological language, rather of the kind that Immanuel Kant thought he had discovered in the nature of aesthetic judgements.[23] Ideology, Althusser claims, 'expresses a will, a hope or a nostalgia, rather than describing a reality';[24] it is fundamentally a matter of fearing and denouncing, reverencing and reviling, all of which then sometimes gets coded into a discourse which looks as though it is describing the way things actually are. It is thus, in the terms of the philosopher J.L. Austin, 'performative' rather than 'constative' language: it belongs to the class of speech acts which get something done (cursing, persuading, celebrating and so on) rather than to the discourse of description.[25] A pronouncement like 'Black is beautiful', popular in the days of the American civil rights movement, looks on the surface as though it is characterizing a state of affairs, but is in fact of course a rhetorical act of defiance and self-affirmation.

Althusser tries to shift us, then, from a *cognitive* to an *affective* theory of ideology – which is not necessarily to deny that ideology contains certain cognitive elements, or to reduce it to the merely 'subjective'. It is certainly subjective in the sense of being subject-centred: its utterances are to be deciphered as expressive of a speaker's attitudes or lived relations to the world. But it is not a question of mere private whim. To assert that one doesn't like tinkers is unlikely to have the same force as asserting that one doesn't like tomatoes. The latter aversion may just be a private quirk; the former is likely to involve certain beliefs about the value of rootedness, self-discipline and the dignity of labour which are central to the reproduction of a particular social system. On the model of ideology we are examining, a statement like 'Tinkers are a flea-ridden, thieving bunch of layabouts' could be decoded into some such performative utterance as 'Down with tinkers!', and this in turn could be decoded into some such proposition as 'There are reasons connected with our relations to the dominant social order which make us want to denigrate these people.' It is worth noting, however, that if the speaker himself could effect the second decodement, he would already be well on the way to overcoming his prejudice.

Ideological statements, then, would seem to be subjective but not private; and in this sense too they have an affinity with Kant's aesthetic judgements, which are at once subjective and universal. On the one hand, ideology is no mere set of abstract doctrines but the stuff which makes us uniquely what we are, constitutive of our very identities; on the other hand, it presents itself as an 'Everybody knows that', a kind of anonymous universal truth. (Whether *all* ideology universalizes in this way is a question we shall take up later.) Ideology is a set of viewpoints I happen to hold; yet that 'happen' is somehow more than just fortuitous, as happening to prefer parting my hair down the middle is probably not. It appears often enough as a ragbag of impersonal, subjectless tags and adages; yet these shop-soiled platitudes are deeply enough entwined with the roots of personal identity to impel us from time to time to murder or martyrdom. In the sphere of ideology, concrete particular and universal truth glide ceaselessly in and out of each other, by-passing the mediation of rational analysis.

If ideology is less a matter of representations of reality than of lived relations, does this finally put paid to the truth/falsehood issue? One reason to think that it might is that it is hard to see how someone could be mistaken about their lived experience. I may mistake Madonna for a minor deity, but can I be mistaken about the feelings of awe this inspires in me? The answer, surely, is that I can. There is no reason to believe in a post-Freudian era that our lived experience need be any less ambiguous than our ideas. I can be as mistaken about my feelings as I can be about anything else: 'I thought at the time I was angry, but looking back I see that I was afraid.' Perhaps my sensation of awe at the sight of Madonna is just a defence against my unconscious envy of her superior earning-power. That I am experiencing *something* can't be doubted, any more than I can doubt that I am in pain; but what precisely my 'lived relations' to the social order consist in may be a more problematical affair than the Althusserians sometimes seem to think. Perhaps it is a mistake to imagine that Althusser is speaking here primarily of *conscious* experience, since our lived relations to social reality are for him largely unconscious. But if our conscious experience is elusive and indeterminate – a point which those political radicals who appeal dogmatically to 'experience' as some sort of absolute fail to recognize – then our unconscious life is even more so.

There is another, rather different sense in which the categories of truth and falsehood may be said to apply to one's lived experience, which returns us to the issue of moral realism. I really *am* furious that my teenage son has shaved off his hair and dyed his skull a flamboyant purple, but I retain enough shreds of rationality to acknowledge that this feeling is 'false' – in the sense of being, not illusory or a self-misinterpretation, but one based upon false values. My anger is motivated by the false belief that teenagers ought to appear in public like bank managers, that they should be socially conformist and so on. One's lived experience may be false in the sense of 'inauthentic', untrue to those values which can be held to be definitive of what it is for human beings in a particular situation to live well. For a moral realist of radical persuasion, someone who believes that the highest goal in life is to amass as much private wealth as possible, preferably by grinding others into the dust, is just as much in error as someone who believes that Henry Gibson is the name of a Norwegian playwright.

Althusser may be right that ideology is chiefly a question of 'lived relations'; but there are no such relations which do not tacitly involve a set of beliefs and assumptions, and these beliefs and assumptions may themselves be open to judgements of truth and falsehood. A racist is usually someone in the grip of fear, hatred and insecurity, rather than someone who has dispassionately arrived at certain intellectual judgements on other races, but even if his feelings are not *motivated* by such judgements, they are likely to be deeply entwined with them; and these judgements – that certain races are inferior to others, for example – are plainly false. Ideology may indeed be primarily a matter of performative utterances – of imperatives like 'Rule, Britannia!', of optatives like 'May Margaret Thatcher reign for another thousand years!', or interrogatives like 'Is not this nation blessed under heaven?' But each of these speech acts is bound up with thoroughly questionable assumptions: that British imperialism is an excellent thing, that another thousand years of Thatcher would have been a deeply desirable state of affairs, that there exists a supreme being with a particular interest in supervising the nation's progress.

The Althusserian case need not be taken as denying that judgements of truth and falsehood may be at some level applicable to ideological discourse; it may simply be arguing that within such discourse the affective typically outweighs the cognitive. Or – which is a somewhat different matter – that the 'practico-social' takes predominance over theoretical knowledge. Ideologies for Althusser do contain a kind of knowledge; but they are not *primarily* cognitive, and the knowledge in question is less theoretical (which is strictly speaking for Althusser the only kind of knowledge there is) than pragmatic, one which orients the subject to its practical tasks in society. In fact, however, many apologists for this case have ended up effectively denying the relevance of truth and falsehood to ideology altogether. Paramount among such theorists in Britain has been the sociologist Paul Hirst, who argues that ideology cannot be a matter of false consciousness because it is indubitably *real.* 'Ideology ... is not illusion, it is not falsity, because how can something which has effects be false? ... It would be like saying that a black pudding is false, or a steamroller is false.'[26] It is easy enough to see what kind of logical slide is taking place here. There is a confusion between 'false' as meaning 'untrue to what is the case', and 'false' as meaning 'unreal'. (As if someone were to say: 'Lying isn't a matter of falsehood; he really *did* lie to me!') It is quite possible to hold that ideology may sometimes be false in the first sense, but not in the second. Hirst simply collapses the epistemological questions at stake here into ontological ones. It may be that I really did experience a group of badgers in tartan trousers nibbling my toes the other evening, but this was probably because of those strange chemical substances the local vicar administered to me, not because they were actually there. On Hirst's view, one would have no way of distinguishing between dreams, hallucinations and reality, since all of them are actually experienced and all of them can have real effects. Hirst's manoeuvre here recalls the dodge of those aestheticians who, confronted with the knotty problem of how art relates to reality, solemnly remind us that art is indubitably real.

Rather than ditching the epistemological issues altogether *à la* Hirst, it might be more useful to ponder the suggestion that ideological discourse typically displays a certain ratio between empirical propositions and what we might roughly term a 'world view', in which the latter has the edge over the former. The closest analogy to this is perhaps a literary work. Most literary works contain empirical propositions; they may mention, for example, that there is a lot of snow in Greenland, or that human beings typically have two ears. But part of what is meant by 'fictionality' is that these statements are not usually present for their own sake; they act, rather, as 'supports' for the overall world view of the text itself. And the ways in which these empirical statements are selected and deployed is generally governed by this requirement. 'Constative' language, in other words, is harnessed to 'performative' ends; empirical truths are organized as components of an overall *rhetoric.* If that rhetoric seems to demand it, a particular empirical truth may be bent into falsehood: a historical novel may find it more convenient for its suasive strategies to have Lenin live on for another decade. Similarly, a racist who believes that Asians in Britain will outnumber whites by the year 1995 may well not be persuaded out of his racism if he can be shown that this assumption is empirically false, since the proposition is more likely to be a support for his racism than a reason for it. If the claim is disproved he may simply modify it, or replace it with another, true or false. It is possible, then, to think of ideological discourse as a complex network of empirical and normative elements, within which the nature and organization of the former is ultimately determined by the requirements of the latter. And this may be one sense in which an ideological formation is rather like a novel.

Once again, however, this may not be enough to dispose of the truth/falsity issue, relegating it to the relatively superficial level of empirical statements. For there is still the more fundamental question of whether a 'world view' may not itself be considered true or false. The anti-false-consciousness case would seem to hold that it is not possible to falsify an ideology, rather as some literary critics insist that it is not possible to falsify or verify the world view of a work of art. In both cases, we simply 'suspend our disbelief' and examine the proffered way of seeing on its own terms, grasping it as a symbolic expression of a certain way of 'living' one's world. In some senses, this is surely true. If a work of literature chooses to highlight images of human degradation, then it would seem futile to denounce this as somehow incorrect. But there are surely limits to this aesthetic charity. Literary critics do not always accept the world view of a text 'on its own terms'; they sometimes want to say that this vision of things is implausible, distorting, over-simplifying. If a literary work highlights images of disease and degradation to the point where it tacitly suggests that human life is entirely valueless, then a critic might well want to object that this is a drastically partial way of seeing. In this sense, a way of seeing, unlike a way of walking, is not necessarily immune to judgements of truth and falsehood, although some of its aspects are likely to be more immune than others. A world view will tend to exhibit a certain 'style' of perception, which cannot in itself be said to be either true or false. It is not false for Samuel Beckett to portray the world in spare, costive, minimalist terms. It will operate in accordance with a certain 'grammar', a system of rules for organizing its various elements, which again cannot usefully be spoken of in terms of truth or falsehood. But it will also typically contain other sorts of component, both normative and empirical, which may indeed sometimes be inspected for their truth or falsity.

Another suggestive analogy between literature and ideology may be gleaned from the work of the literary theorist Paul de Man. For de Man, a piece of writing is specifically 'literary' when its 'constative' and 'performative' dimensions are somehow at odds with each other.[27] Literary works, in de Man's view, tend to 'say' one thing and 'do' another. Thus, W.B. Yeats's line of poetry, 'How can we know the dancer from the dance?', read literally, asks about how we can draw the distinction in question; but its effect as a rhetorical or performative piece of discourse is to suggest that such a distinction cannot be drawn. Whether this will do as a general theory of the 'literary' is in my view distinctly dubious; but it can be coupled with a certain theory of the workings of ideology, one outlined by Denys Turner. Turner has argued that one notable problem in the theory of ideology turns on the puzzle of how ideological beliefs can be said to be both 'lived' and false. For our lived beliefs are in some sense internal to our social practices; and if they are thus *constitutive* of those practices, they can hardly be said to 'correspond' (or not correspond) to them. As Turner puts its: 'Since, therefore, there seems to be no epistemic space between what is socially lived and the social ideas of it, there seems to be no room for a *false* relationship between the two.'[28]

This, surely, is one of the strongest points which the anti-false-consciousness case has going for it. There cannot be a merely external or contingent relation between our social practices and the ideas by which we 'live' them; so how can these ideas, or some of them, be said to be false? Turner's own answer to this problem resembles de Man's case about the literary text. He claims that ideology consists in a 'performative contradiction', in which what is said is at odds with the situation or act of utterance itself. When the middle class preaches universal freedom from a position of domination, or when a teacher hectors his students at tedious length about the perils of an authoritarian pedagogy, we have 'a contradiction between a meaning conveyed explicitly and a meaning conveyed by the act itself of conveying',[29] which for Turner is the essential structure of all ideology. Whether this in fact covers all that we call ideological practice is perhaps as doubtful as whether de Man's case covers all that we call literature; but it is an illuminating account of a particular kind of ideological act.

So far we have been considering the role within ideology of what might be called *epistemic* falsehood. But as Raymond Geuss has argued, there are two other forms of falsity highly relevant to ideological consciousness, which can be termed *functional* and *genetic*.[30] False consciousness may mean not that a body of ideas is actually untrue, but that these ideas are functional for the maintenance of an oppressive power, and that those who hold them are ignorant of this fact. Similarly, a belief may not be false in itself, but may spring from some discreditable ulterior motive of which those who hold it are unaware. As Geuss summarizes the point: consciousness may be false because it 'incorporates beliefs which are false, or because it functions in a reprehensible way, or because it has a tainted origin'.[31] Epistemic, functional and genetic forms of false consciousness may go together, as when a false belief which rationalizes some disreputable social motive proves useful in promoting the unjust interests of a dominant power; but other permutations are also possible. There may, for example, be no inherent connection between the falsity of a belief and its functionality for an oppressive power; a true belief might have done just as well. A set of ideas, whether true or false, may be 'unconsciously' motivated by the selfish interests of a ruling group, but may in fact prove dysfunctional for the promotion or legitimation of those interests. A fatalistic group of oppressed individuals may not recognize that their fatalism is an unconscious rationalization of their wretched conditions, but this fatalism may well not prove serviceable for their interests. It might, on the other hand, prove functional for the interests of their rulers, in which case a 'genetic' false consciousness on the part of one social class becomes functional for the interests of another. Beliefs functional for a social group, in other words, need not be motivated from within that group, but may, so to speak, just fall into its lap. Forms of consciousness functional for one social class may also prove functional for another whose interests are in conflict with it. As far as 'genetic' falsity goes, the fact that the true underlying motivation of a set of beliefs sometimes *must* be concealed from view is enough to cast doubt on its reputability; but to hold that the beliefs which disguise this motive must be false simply on account of their contaminated origin would be an instance of the genetic fallacy. From a radical political viewpoint, there may be positive kinds of unconscious motivation and positive forms of functionality: socialists will tend to approve of forms of consciousness which, however displacedly, express the underlying interests of the working class, or which actively help to promote those interests. The fact that a motivation is concealed, in other words, is not enough in itself to suggest falsity; the question is rather one of what sort of motivation it is, and whether it is of the kind that *has* to remain hidden from view. Finally, we can note that a body of beliefs may be false but rational, in the sense of internally coherent, consistent with the available evidence and held on what appear to be plausible grounds. The fact that ideology is not at root a matter of reason does not license us to equate it with irrationality.

Let us take stock of some of the argument so far. Those who oppose the idea of ideology as false consciousness are right to see that ideology is no baseless illusion but a solid reality, an active material force which must have at least enough cognitive content to help organize the practical lives of human beings. It does not consist primarily in a set of propositions about the world; and many of the propositions it *does* advance are actually true. None of this, however, need be denied by those who hold that ideology often or typically involves falsity, distortion and mystification. Even if ideology is largely a matter of 'lived relations', those relations, at least in certain social conditions, would often seem to involve claims and beliefs which are untrue. As Tony Skillen scathingly inquires of those who reject this case: 'Sexist ideologies do not (distortingly) represent women as naturally inferior? Racist ideologies do not confine non-whites to perpetual savagery? Religious ideologies do not represent the world as the creation of gods?'[32]

It does not follow from this, however, that *all* ideological language necessarily involves falsehood. It is quite possible for a ruling order to make pronouncements which are ideological in the sense of buttressing its own power, but which are in no sense false. And if we extend the term ideology to include oppositional political movements, then radicals at least would want to hold that many of their utterances, while ideological in the sense of promoting their power-interests, are nonetheless true. This is not to suggest that such movements may not also engage in distortion and mystification. 'Workers of the world, unite; you have nothing to lose but your chains' is in one sense obviously false; workers have a good deal to lose by political militancy, not least, in some cases, their lives. 'The West is a paper tiger', Mao's celebrated slogan, is dangerously misleading and triumphalist.

Nor is it the case that all commitment to the dominant social order involves some sort of delusion. Someone might have a perfectly adequate understanding of the mechanisms of capitalist exploitation, but conclude that this kind of society, while unjust and oppressive, is on the whole preferable to any likely alternative. From a socialist viewpoint, such a person is mistaken; but it is hard to call them deluded, in the sense of systematically misinterpreting the real situation. There is a difference between being mistaken and being deluded: if someone lifts a cucumber and announces his telephone number we may conclude that he has made a mistake, whereas if he spends long evenings chatting vivaciously into a cucumber we might have to draw different conclusions. There is also the case of the person who commits himself to the ruling social order on entirely cynical grounds. Someone who urges you to get rich quick may be promoting capitalist values; but he may not necessarily be *legitimating* these values. Perhaps he simply believes that in a corrupt world you might as well pursue your own self-interest along with everyone else. A man might appreciate the justice of the feminist cause, but simply refuse to surrender his male privilege. It is unwise, in other words, to assume that dominant groups are always victims of their own propaganda; there is the condition which Peter Sloterdijk calls 'enlightened false consciousness', which lives by false values but is ironically aware of doing so, and so which can hardly be said to be mystified in the traditional sense of the term.[33]

If dominant ideologies very often involve falsity, however, it is partly because most people are not in fact cynics. Imagine a society in which everybody was either a cynic or a masochist, or both. In such a situation there would be no need for ideology, in the sense of a set of discourses concealing or legitimating injustice, because the masochists would not mind their suffering and the cynics would feel no unease about inhabiting an exploitative social order. In fact, the majority of people have a fairly sharp eye to their own rights and interests, and most people feel uncomfortable at the thought of belonging to a seriously unjust form of life. Either, then, they must believe that these injustices are *en route* to being amended, or that they are counterbalanced by greater benefits, or that they are inevitable, or that they are not really injustices at all. It is part of the function of a dominant ideology to inculcate such beliefs. It can do this either by falsifying social reality, suppressing and excluding certain unwelcome features of it, or suggesting that these features cannot be avoided. This last strategy is of interest from the viewpoint of the truth/falsity problem. For it may be true of the *present* system that, say, a degree of unemployment is inevitable, but not of some future alternative. Ideological statements may be true to society as at present constituted, but false in so far as they thereby serve to block off the possibility of a transformed state of affairs. The very truth of such statements is also the falsehood of their implicit denial that anything better could be conceived.

If ideology is sometimes falsifying, then, it is for what are on the whole rather hopeful reasons: the fact that most people react strongly to being unjustly treated, and that most people would like to believe that they live in reasonably just social conditions. It is strange in this light for some radicals to argue that deception and concealment play no part in a dominant ideological discourse, since to be a political radical commits one to the view that the current social order is marked by serious injustices. And no ruling class concerned with preserving its credibility can afford to acknowledge that these injustices could only be rectified by a political transformation which would put it out of business. If, then, ideology sometimes involves distortion and mystification, it is less because of something inherent in ideological language than because of something inherent in the social structure to which that language belongs. There are certain kinds of interests which can secure their sway only by practising duplicity; but this is not to claim on the other hand that *all* of the statements used to promote those interests will be duplicitous. Ideology, in other words, is not inherently constituted by distortion, especially if we take the broader view of the concept as denoting any fairly central conjuncture between discourse and power. In an entirely just society, there would be no need for ideology in the pejorative sense since there would be nothing to explain away.

It is possible to define ideology in roughly six different ways, in a progressive sharpening of focus. We can mean by it, first, the general material process of production of ideas, beliefs and values in social life. Such a definition is both politically and epistemologically neutral, and is close to the broader meaning of the term 'culture'. Ideology, or culture, would here denote the whole complex of signifying practices and symbolic processes in a particular society; it would allude to the way individuals 'lived' their social practices, rather than to those practices themselves, which would be the preserve of politics, economics, kinship theory and so on. This sense of ideology is wider than the sense of 'culture' which confines itself to artistic and intellectual work of agreed value, but narrower than the anthropological definition of culture, which would encompass all of the practices and institutions of a form of life. 'Culture' in this anthropological sense would include, for example, the financial infrastructure of sport, whereas ideology would concern itself more particularly with the signs, meanings and values encoded in sporting activities.

This most general of all meanings of ideology stresses the social determination of thought, thus providing a valuable antidote to idealism; but otherwise it would seem unworkably broad and suspiciously silent on the question of political conflict. Ideology means more than just, say, the signifying practices associated by a society with food; it involves the relations between these signs and processes of political power. It is not coextensive with the general field of 'culture', but lights up this field from a particular angle.

A second, slightly less general meaning of ideology turns on ideas and beliefs (whether true or false) which symbolize the conditions and life-experiences of a specific, socially significant group or class. The qualification 'socially significant' is needed here, since it would seem odd to speak of the ideas and beliefs of four regular drinking companions or of the Sixth Form at Manchester Grammar School as an ideology all of its own. 'Ideology' is here very close to the idea of a 'world view', though it can be claimed that world views are usually preoccupied with fundamental matters such as the meaning of death or humanity's place in the universe, whereas ideology might extend to such issues as which colour to paint the mail-boxes.

To see ideology as a kind of collective symbolic self-expression is not yet to see it in relational or conflictive terms; so there might seem to be a need for a third definition of the term, which attends to the *promotion* and *legitimation* of the interests of such social groups in the face of opposing interests. Not all such promotions of group interests are usually dubbed ideological: it is not particularly ideological for the army to request the Ministry of Defence to supply it on aesthetic grounds with flared trousers rather than with straight ones. The interests in question must have some relevance to the sustaining or challenging of a whole political form of life. Ideology can here be seen as a discursive field in which self-promoting social powers conflict and collide over questions central to the reproduction of social power as a whole. This definition may entail the assumption that ideology is a peculiarly 'action-oriented' discourse, in which contemplative cognition is generally subordinated to the futherance of 'arational' interests and desires. It is doubtless for this reason that to speak 'ideologically' has sometimes in the popular mind a ring of distasteful opportunism about it, suggesting a readiness to sacrifice truth to less reputable goals. Ideology appears here as a suasive or rhetorical rather than veridical kind of speech, concerned less with the situation 'as it is' than with the production of certain useful effects for political purposes. It is ironic, then, that ideology is regarded by some as too pragmatic and by others as not pragmatic enough, as too absolutist, otherworldly and inflexible.

A fourth meaning of ideology would retain this emphasis on the promotion and legitimation of sectoral interests, but confine it to the activities of a dominant social power. This may involve the assumption that such dominant ideologies help to *unify* a social formation in ways convenient for its rulers; that it is not simply a matter of imposing ideas from above but of securing the complicity of subordinated classes and groups, and so on. We shall be examining these assumptions more closely later on. But this meaning of ideology is still epistemologically neutral and can thus be refined further into a fifth definition, in which ideology signifies ideas and beliefs which help to legitimate the interests of a ruling group or class specifically by distortion and dissimulation. Note that on these last two definitions, not all of the ideas of a ruling group need be said to be ideological, in that some of them may not particularly promote its interests, and some of them may not do so by the use of deception. Note also that on this last definition it is hard to know what to call a politically oppositional discourse which promotes and seeks to legitimate the interests of a subordinate group or class by such devices as the 'naturalizing', universalizing and cloaking of its real interests.

There is, finally, the possibility of a sixth meaning of ideology, which retains an emphasis on false or deceptive beliefs but regards such beliefs as arising not from the interests of a dominant class but from the material structure of society as a whole. The term ideology remains pejorative, but a class–genetic account of it is avoided. The most celebrated instance of this sense of ideology, as we shall see, is Marx's theory of the fetishism of commodities.

We can return finally to the question of ideology as 'lived relations' rather than empirical representations. If this is true, then certain important political consequences follow from this view. It follows, for instance, that ideology cannot be substantially transformed by offering individuals true descriptions in place of false ones – that it is not in this sense simply a *mistake*. We would not call a form of consciousness ideological just because it was in factual error, no matter how deeply erroneous it was. To speak of 'ideological error' is to speak of an error with particular kinds of causes and functions. A transformation of our lived relations to reality could be secured only by a material change in that reality itself. To deny that ideology is primarily a matter of empirical representations, then, goes along with a materialist theory of how it operates, and of how it might be changed. At the same time, it is important not to react so violently against a rationalistic theory of ideology as to abstain from trying to put people right on matters of fact. If someone really does believe that all childless women are thwarted and embittered, introducing him to as many ecstatic childfree women as possible might just persuade him to change his mind. To deny that ideology is fundamentally an affair of reason is not to conclude that it is immune to rational considerations altogether. And 'reason' here would mean something like: the kind of discourse that would result from as many people as possible actively participating in a discussion of these matters in conditions as free as possible from domination.

2

IDEOLOGICAL
STRATEGIES

BEFORE advancing any further, it may be as well to ask whether the topic of ideology really merits the attention we are lavishing upon it. Are ideas really so important for political power? Most theories of ideology have arisen from within the materialist tradition of thought, and it belongs to such materialism to be sceptical of assigning any very high priority to 'consciousness' within social life. Certainly, for a materialist theory, consciousness alone cannot initiate any epochal change in history; and there may therefore be thought to be something self-contradictory about such materialism doggedly devoting itself to an inquiry into signs, meanings and values.

A good example of the limited power of consciousness in social life is the so-called Thatcherite revolution. The aim of Thatcherism has been not only to transform the economic and political landscape of Britain, but to effect an upheaval in ideological values too. This consists in converting the moderately pleasant people who populated the country when Thatcher first arrived in Downing Street into a thoroughly nasty bunch of callous, self-seeking oafs. Unless most of the British have become completely hideous and disgusting characters, Thatcherism has failed in its aims. Yet all the evidence would suggest that the Thatcherite revolution has not occurred. Opinion polls reveal that most of the British people stubbornly continue to adhere to the vaguely social democratic values they espoused before Thatcher assumed office. Whatever it was that kept her in Downing Street, then, it cannot primarily have been ideology. Thatcher was not where she was because the British people loyally identified with her values; she was where she was *despite* the fact that they did not. If there is indeed a 'dominant ideology' in contemporary Britain, it does not appear to be particularly successful.

How then *did* Thatcher secure her power? The true answers may be a good deal more mundane than any talk of 'hegemonic discourses'. She was Prime Minister partly on account of the eccentricities of the British electoral system, which can put a government rejected by most of the electorate into power. She set out from the beginning to break the power of organized labour by deliberately fostering massive unemployment, thus temporarily demoralizing a traditionally militant working-class movement. She succeeded in winning the support of an electorally crucial skilled stratum of the working class. She traded upon the weak, disorganized nature of the political opposition, exploited the cynicism, apathy and masochism of some of the British people, and bestowed material benefits on those whose support she required. All of these moves are caught up in ideological hectoring of one kind or another; but none of them is *reducible* to the question of ideology.

If people do not actively combat a political regime which oppresses them, it may not be because they have meekly imbibed its governing values. It may be because they are too exhausted after a hard day's work to have much energy left to engage in political activity, or because they are too fatalistic or apathetic to see the point of such activity. They may be frightened of the consequences of opposing the regime; or they may spend too much time worrying about their jobs and mortgages and income tax returns to give it much thought. Ruling classes have at their disposal a great many such techniques of 'negative' social control, which are a good deal more prosaic and material than persuading their subjects that they belong to a master race or exhorting them to identify with the destiny of the nation.

In advanced capitalist societies, the communications media are often felt to be a potent means by which a dominant ideology is disseminated; but this assumption should not go unquestioned. It is true that many of the British working class read right-wing Tory newspapers; but research indicates that a good proportion of these readers are either indifferent or actively hostile to the politics of these journals. Many people spend most of their leisure time watching television; but if watching television *does* benefit the ruling class, it may not be chiefly because it helps to convey its own ideology to a docile populace. What is politically important about television is probably less its ideological content than the act of watching it. Watching television for long stretches confirms individuals in passive, isolated, privatized roles, and consumes a good deal of time that could be put to productive political uses. It is more a form of social control than an ideological apparatus.

This sceptical view of the centrality of ideology in modern society finds expression in *The Dominant Ideology Thesis* (1980), by the sociologists N. Abercrombie, S. Hill and B.S. Turner. Abercrombie and his colleagues are not out to deny that dominant ideologies exist; but they doubt that they are an important means for lending cohesion to a society. Such ideologies may effectively unify the dominant class; but they are usually much less successful, so they argue, in infiltrating the consciousness of their subordinates. In feudalist and early capitalist societies, for example, the mechanisms for transmitting such ideologies to the masses were notably weak; there were no communications media or institutions of popular education, and many of the people were illiterate. Such channels of transmission do of course flourish in late capitalism; but the conclusion that the subaltern classes have thus been massively incorporated into the world view of their rulers is one which Abercrombie, Hill and Turner see fit to challenge. For one thing, they argue, the dominant ideology in advanced capitalist societies is internally fissured and contradictory, offering no kind of seamless unity for the masses to internalize; and for another thing the culture of dominated groups and classes retains a good deal of autonomy. The everyday discourses of these classes, so the authors claim, is formed largely outside the control of the ruling class, and embodies significant beliefs and values at odds with it.

What then *does* secure the cohesion of such social formations? Abercrombie *et al.*'s first response to this query is to deny that such cohesion exists; the advanced capitalist order is in no sense a successfully achieved unity, riven as it is by major conflicts and contradictions. But in so far as the consent of the dominated to their masters is won at all, it is achieved much more by economic than by ideological means. What Marx once called 'the dull compulsion of the economic' is enough to keep men and women in their places; and such strategies as reformism – the ability of the capitalist system to yield tangible benefits to some at least of its underlings – are more crucial in this respect than any ideological complicity between the workers and their bosses. Moreover, if the system survives, it is more on account of social divisions between the various groups it exploits than by virtue of some overall ideological coherence. There is no need for those groups to endorse or internalize dominant ideological values, as long as they do more or less

35

what is required of them. Indeed most oppressed peoples throughout history have signally not granted their rulers such credence: governments have been more endured than admired.

The Dominant Ideology Thesis represents a valuable corrective to a left idealism which would overestimate the significance of culture and ideology for the maintenance of political power. Such 'culturalism', pervasive throughout the 1970s, was itself a reaction to an earlier Marxist economism (or economic reductionism); but in the view of Abercrombie and his co-authors it bent the stick too far in the other direction. When one emphasizes, as Jacques Derrida once remarked, one always overemphasizes. Marxist intellectuals trade in ideas, and so are always chronically likely to overrate their importance in society as a whole. There is nothing crudely economistic in claiming that what keeps people politically quiescent is less transcendental signifiers than a concern over their wage packets. By contrast with the patrician gloom of the late Frankfurt School, this case accords a healthy degree of respect to the experience of the exploited: there is no reason to assume that their political docility signals some gullible, full-blooded adherence to the doctrines of their superiors. It may signal rather a coolly realistic sense that political militancy, in a period when the capitalist system is still capable of conceding some material advantages to those who keep it in business, might be perilous and ill-advised. But if the system ceases to yield such benefits, then this same realism might well lead to revolt, since there would be no large-scale internalization of the ruling values to stand in the way of such rebellion. Abercrombie *et al.* are surely right too to point out that subaltern social groups often have their own rich, resistant cultures, which cannot be incorporated without a struggle into the value-systems of those who govern them.

Even so, they might have bent the stick too far in their turn. Their claim that late capitalism operates largely 'without ideology' is surely too strong; and their summary dismissal of the dissembling, mystificatory effects of a ruling ideology has an implausible ring to it. The truth, surely, is that the diffusion of dominant values and beliefs among oppressed groups in society has *some* part to play in the reproduction of the system as a whole, but that this factor has been typically exaggerated by a long tradition of Western Marxism for which 'ideas' are allotted too high a status. As Gramsci argued, the consciousness of the oppressed is usually a contradictory amalgam of values imbibed from their rulers, and notions which spring more directly from their practical experience. By lending too little credence to the potentially incorporative functions of a dominant ideology, Abercrombie and his fellow-authors are sometimes as much in danger of over-simplifying this mixed, ambiguous condition as are the left Jeremiahs who peddle the illusion that all popular resistance has now been smoothly managed out of existence.

There are other grounds on which to question the importance of ideology in advanced capitalist societies. You can argue, for example, that whereas rhetorical appeals to such public values played a central role in the 'classical' phase of the system, they have now been effectively replaced by purely technocratic forms of management. A case of this kind is urged by the German philosopher Jürgen Habermas, in his *Towards a Rational Society* (1970) and *Legitimation Crisis* (1975); but one needs to distinguish here between the view that 'ideology' has yielded to 'technology', and the thesis that the more 'metaphysical' forms of ideological control have now given ground to 'technocratic' ones. Indeed we shall see later that, for many theorists of ideology, the very concept of ideology is synonymous with the attempt to provide rational, technical, 'scientific' rationales for social domination, rather than mythic, religious or metaphysical ones. On some such views, the system of late capitalism can be said to operate 'all by itself', without any need to resort to *discursive* justification. It no longer, so to speak, has to pass through consciousness; instead, it simply secures its own reproduction by a manipulative, incorporative logic of which human subjects are the mere obedient effects. It is not surprising that the theoretical ideology known as structuralism should have grown up in just this historical epoch. Capitalist society no longer cares whether we believe in it or not; it is not 'consciousness' or 'ideology' which welds it together, but its own complex systemic operations. This case thus inherits something of the later Marx's insistence on the commodity as automatically supplying its own ideology: it is the routine material logic of everyday life, not some body of doctrine, set of moralizing discourses or ideological 'superstructure', which keeps the system ticking over.

The point can be put in a different way. Ideology is essentially a matter of meaning; but the condition of advanced capitalism, some would suggest, is one of pervasive *non*-meaning. The sway of utility and technology bleach social life of significance, subordinating use-value to the empty formalism of exchange-value. Consumerism by-passes meaning in order to engage the subject subliminally, libidinally, at the level of visceral response rather than reflective consciousness. In this sphere, as in the realms of the media and everyday culture, form overwhelms content, signifiers lord it over signifieds, to deliver us the blank, affectless, two-dimensional surfaces of a post-modernist social order. This massive haemorrhaging of meaning then triggers pathological symptoms in society at large: drugs, violence, mindless revolt, befuddled searches for mystical significance. But otherwise it fosters widespread apathy and docility, so that it is no longer a question of whether social life has meaning, or whether this particular signification is preferable to that, than of whether such a question is even intelligible. To talk about 'significance' and 'society' in the same breath just becomes a kind of category mistake, rather like hunting for the hidden meaning of a gust of wind or the hoot of an owl. From this viewpoint, it is less meaning that keeps us in place than the lack of it, and ideology in its classical sense is thus superfluous. Ideology, after all, requires a certain depth of subjectivity on which to go to work, a certain innate receptiveness to its edicts; but if advanced capitalism flattens the human subject to a viewing eye and devouring stomach, then there is not even enough subjectivity around for ideology to take hold. The dwindled, faceless, depleted subjects of this social order are not up to ideological meaning, and have no need of it. Politics is less a matter of preaching or indoctrination than technical management and manipulation, form rather than content; once more, it is as though the machine runs itself, without needing to take a detour through the conscious mind. Education ceases to be a question of critical self-reflection and becomes absorbed in its turn into the technological apparatus, providing certification for one's place within it. The typical citizen is less the ideological enthusiast shouting 'Long live liberty!' than the doped, glazed telly viewer, his mind as smooth and neutrally receptive as the screen in front of him. It then becomes possible, in a cynical 'left' wisdom, to celebrate this catatonic state as some cunning last-ditch resistance to ideological meaning – to revel in the very spiritual blank-ness of the late bourgeois order as a welcome relief from the boring old humanist nostalgia for truth, value and reality. The work of Jean Baudrillard is exemplary of this nihilism. 'It is no longer a question', Baudrillard writes, 'of a false representation of reality (ideology), but of concealing the fact that the real is no longer real ...'.[1]

The case that advanced capitalism expunges all traces of 'deep' subject-ivity, and thus all modes of ideology, is not so much false as drastically partial. In a homogenizing gesture ironically typical of a 'pluralistic' post-modernism, it fails to discriminate between different spheres of social exist-ence, some of which are rather more open to this kind of analysis than others. It repeats the 'culturalist' error of taking television, supermarket, 'life style' and advertising as *definitive* of the late capitalist experience, and passes in silence over such activities as studying the bible, running a rape crisis centre, joining the territorial army and teaching one's children to speak Welsh. People who run rape crisis centres or teach their children Welsh also tend to watch television and shop in supermarkets; there is no question of a *single* form of subjectivity (or 'non-subjectivity') at stake here. The very same citizens are expected to be at one level the mere function of this or that act of consumption or media experience, and at another level to exercise ethical responsibility as autonomous, self-determining subjects. In this sense, late capitalism continues to require a self-disciplined subject responsive to ideological rhetoric, as father, juror, patriot, employee, houseworker, while threatening to undercut these more 'classical' forms of subjecthood with its consumerist and mass-cultural practices. No individual life, not even Jean Baudrillard's, can survive entirely bereft of meaning, and a society which took this nihilistic road would simply be nurturing massive social disruption. Advanced capitalism accordingly oscillates between meaning and non-meaning, pitched from moralism to cynicism and plagued by the embarrassing discrepancy between the two.

That discrepancy suggests another reason why ideology is sometimes felt to be redundant in modern capitalist societies. For ideology is supposed to deceive; and in the cynical milieu of postmodernism we are all much too fly, astute and streetwise to be conned for a moment by our own official rhetoric. It is this condition which Peter Sloterdijk names 'enlightened false consciousness' – the endless self-ironizing or wide-awake bad faith of a society which has seen through its own pretentious rationalizations. One can picture this as a kind of progressive movement. First, a disparity sets in between what society does and what it says; then this performative contradiction is rationalized; next, the rationalization is made ironically self-conscious; and finally this self-ironizing itself comes to serve ideological ends. The new kind of ideological subject is no hapless victim of false consciousness, but knows exactly what he is doing; it is just that he continues to do it even so. And to this extent he would seem conveniently insulated against 'ideology critique' of the traditional kind, which presumes that agents are not fully in possession of their own motivations.

There are several objections to this particular 'end of ideology' thesis. For one thing, it spuriously generalizes to a whole society what is really a highly specific mode of consciousness. Some yuppie stockbrokers may be cynically aware that there is no real defence for their way of life, but it is doubtful that Ulster Unionists spend much of their time being playfully ironic about their commitment to keeping Ulster British. For another thing, such irony is more likely to play into the hands of the ruling powers than to discomfort them, as Slavoj Žižek observes: 'in contemporary societies, democratic or totalitarian, … cynical distance, laughter, irony, are, so to speak, part of the game. The ruling ideology is not meant to be taken seriously or literally.'[2] It is as though the ruling ideology has already accommodated the fact that we will be sceptical of it, and reorganized its discourses accordingly. The government spokesman announces that there is no truth in the charges of widespread corruption within the Cabinet; nobody believes him; he knows that nobody believes him, we know that he knows it, and he knows this too. Meanwhile the corruption carries on – which is just the point that Žižek makes against the conclusion that false consciousness is therefore a thing of the past. One traditional form of ideology critique assumes that social practices are real, but that the beliefs used to justify them are false or illusory. But this opposition, so Žižek suggests, can be reversed. For if ideology is illusion, then it is an illusion which structures our social practices; and to this extent 'falsity' lies on the side of what we *do*, not necessarily of what we say. The capitalist who has devoured all three volumes of *Capital* knows exactly what he is doing; but he continues to behave as though he did not, because his activity is caught up in the 'objective' fantasy of commodity fetishism. Sloterdijk's formula for enlightened false consciousness is: 'they know very well what they are doing, but they carry on doing it even so'. Žižek, by contrast, suggests a crucial adjustment: 'they know that, in their activity, they are following an illusion, but still, they are doing it'. Ideology, in other words, not just a matter of what I think about a situation; it is somehow inscribed in that situation itself. It is no good my reminding myself that I am opposed to racism as I sit down on a park bench marked 'Whites Only'; by the acting of sitting on it, I have supported and perpetuated racist ideology. The ideology, so to speak, is in the bench, not in my head.

In much deconstructive theory, the view that interpretation consists in an abyssal spiral of ironies, each ironizing the other to infinity, is commonly coupled with a political quietism or reformism. If political practice takes place only within a context of interpretation, and if that context is notoriously ambiguous and unstable, then action itself is likely to be problematic and unpredictable. This case is then used, implicitly or explicitly, to rule out the possibility of radical political programmes of an ambitious kind. For if the complex effects of such practices are impossible to calculate in advance, then the logic of such a radical programme of action is ultimately unmasterable, and may easily get out of hand. It is a case which the post-structuralist critic Jonathan Culler, among others, has several times argued. One would, then, be singularly ill-advised to attempt any very 'global' sort of political activity, such as trying to abolish world hunger; it would seem more prudent to stick to more local political interventions, such as making sure every one in five professors you hire is an orphan from Liverpool 8. In this sense too, irony is no escape from the ideological game: on the contrary, as an implicit disrecommendation of large-scale political activity, it plays right into the hands of Whitehall or the White House.

It is in any case important not to underestimate the extent to which people may *not* feel ironic about their performative contradictions. The world of big business is rife with the rhetoric of trust; but research reveals that this principle is almost never acted upon. The last thing businessmen actually do is put their trust in their customers or each other. A corporation executive who claims this virtue may not, however, be a cynic or a hypocrite; or at least his hypocrisy may be 'objective' rather than subjective. For the ethical values which capitalism lauds, and its actual cut-throat practices, simply move in different spheres, much like the relationship between religious absolutes and everyday life. I still believe that profanity is a sin, even though my conversation is blue with it much of the time. The fact that I employ a team of six hard-pressed servants around the clock does not prevent me from believing in some suitably nebulous way that all men and women are equal. In an ideal world I would employ no servants at all, but there are pressing pragmatic reasons just at the moment why I am unable to live up to my burningly held beliefs. I object to the idea of private education, but if I were to place my daughter with all her airs and graces in a comprehensive school, the other children might bully her. Such rationalizations are well-nigh limitless, and this is one reason to doubt the suggestion that in modern capitalist society cold-eyed cynicism has entirely ousted genuine self-deception.

We have seen that the importance of ideology can be questioned on several grounds. It can be claimed that there *is* no coherent dominant ideology, or that if there is then it is much less effective in shaping popular experience than has sometimes been thought. You can argue that advanced capitalism is a self-sustaining 'game' which keeps us in place much less through ideas than by its material techniques; and that among these techniques the coercion of the economic is far more effective than any sort of sermonizing. The system, so it is suggested, maintains itself less through the imposition of ideological meaning than through destroying meaning altogether; and what meanings the masses *do* entertain can be at odds with those of their rulers without any serious disruption ensuing. Finally, it may be that there *is* a dominant ideology at work, but nobody is gullible enough to fall for it. All of these cases have their kernel of truth – not least the claim that material factors play a more vital role in securing submission than ideological ones. It is also surely true that popular consciousness is far from being some obedient 'instantiation' of ruling ideological values, but runs counter to them in significant ways. If this gap looms sufficiently wide, then a crisis of legitimacy is likely to ensue; it is unrealistic to imagine that as long as people do what is required of them, what they think about what they are doing is neither here nor there.

Taken as a whole, however, this end–of–ideology thesis is vastly implausible. If it were true, it would be hard to know why so many individuals in these societies still flock to church, wrangle over politics in the pubs, care about what their children are being taught in school and lose sleep over the steady erosion of the social services. The dystopian view that the typical citizen of advanced capitalism is the doped telly viewer is a myth, as the ruling class itself is uncomfortably aware. The doped telly viewer will soon enough join a picket line if her wage-packet is threatened, or become politically active if the government contemplates driving a motorway through his back garden. The 'left' cynicism of a Baudrillard is insultingly complicit with what the system would *like* to believe – that everything now 'works all by itself', without regard to the way social issues are shaped and defined in popular experience. If that experience really was entirely two-dimensional, then the consequences for the system would be grim. For the result, as we have seen, would be an accelerated outbreak of 'pathological' symptoms in society as a whole, as a citizenry deprived of meaning sought to create it in violent, gratuitous ways. Any ruling order must throw its underlings enough meaning to be going on with; and if the logic of consumerism, bureaucracy, 'instant' culture and 'managed' politics is to sap the very resources of social significance, then this is in the long run exceedingly bad news for the governing order. Advanced capitalist society still requires the dutiful, self-disciplined, intelligently conformist subjects which some see as typical only of capitalism's 'classical' phase; it is just that these particular modes of subjectivity are locked in conflict with the quite different forms of subjecthood appropriate to a 'postmodernist' order, and this is a contradiction which the system itself is quite powerless to resolve.

Raymond Geuss has suggested a useful distinction between 'descriptive', 'pejorative' and 'positive' definitions of the term ideology.[3] In the descriptive or 'anthropological' sense, ideologies are belief-systems characteristic of certain social groups or classes, composed of both discursive and non-discursive elements. We have seen already how this politically innocuous meaning of ideology comes close to the notion of a 'world view', in the sense of a relatively well-systematized set of categories which provide a 'frame' for the belief, perception and conduct of a body of individuals.

In its pejorative meaning, ideology is a set of values, meanings and beliefs which is to be viewed critically or negatively for any of the following reasons. True or false, these beliefs are sustained by the (conscious or un-conscious) motivation of propping up an oppressive form of power. If the motivation is unconscious, then this will involve a degree of self-deception on the part of those who adhere to the beliefs. Ideology in this sense means ideas contaminated at root, genetically flawed; and we shall see that this was the meaning of ideology embraced by the later Frederick Engels. Alternatively, ideology may be viewed critically because the ideas and beliefs in question, whether true or not, discreditably or deceptively motivated or not, breed effects which help to legitimate an unjust form of power. Finally, ideology may be thought to be objectionable because it generates ideas which either because of their motivation or their function or both are in fact false, in the sense of distorting and dissimulating social reality. This is objectionable not only because it contributes to shoring up a dominative power, but because it is contrary to the dignity of somewhat rational creatures to live in a permanent state of delusion.

Ideology in this negative sense is objectionable either because it gives birth to massive social illusion, or because it deploys true ideas to un-palatable effect, or because it springs from some unworthy motivation. This *genetic* fact is sometimes thought enough to render the beliefs in question *epistemically* false: since the beliefs have their root in the life-experience of a particular group or class, the partiality of that experience will bend them out of true. They will persuade us to see the world as our rulers see it, not as it is in itself. Lurking in the background here is the assumption that the truth resides only in some form of totalization which would transcend the confines of any particular group's perspective.

What is sometimes felt to be primarily ideological about a form of consciousness, however, is not how it comes about, or whether it is true or not, but the fact that it is functional for legitimating an unjust social order. From this standpoint, it is not the *origin* of the ideas which makes them ideological. Not all of the ideas which originate in the dominant class are necessarily ideological; conversely, a ruling class may take over ideas which have germinated elsewhere and harness them to its purposes. The English middle class found the mystique of monarchy ready-made for it by a previous ruling class, and adapted it efficiently to its own ends. Even forms of consciousness which have their root in the experience of oppressed classes may be appropriated by their masters. When Marx and Engels comment in *The German Ideology* that the ruling ideas of each epoch are the ideas of the ruling class, they probably intend this as a 'genetic' observation, meaning that these ideas are ones actually *produced* by the ruling class; but it is possible that these are just ideas which happen to be in the possession of the rulers, no matter where they derive from. The ideas in question may be true or false; if they are false, they may be considered to be contingently so, or their falsehood may be seen as the effect of the functional work they have to do in promoting shady interests, or as a kind of buckling they undergo in straining to rationalize shabby social motives.

But ideologies can also be viewed in a more positive light, as when Marxists like Lenin speak approvingly of 'socialist ideology'. Ideology means here a set of beliefs which coheres and inspires a specific group or class in the pursuit of political interests judged to be desirable. It is then often in effect synonymous with the positive sense of 'class consciousness' – a dubious equation, in fact, since one could speak of those aspects of a class's consciousness which are in this sense ideological, and those which are not. Ideology might still be viewed here as ideas importantly shaped by an underlying motivation, and functional in achieving certain goals; it is just that these goals and motivations are now approved, as they were not in the case of a class regarded as unjustly oppressive. One can use the term ideology to signify a certain elevation of the pragmatic or instrumental over a theoretical concern for the truth of ideas 'in themselves', while not necessarily holding this to be a *negative* judgement. Indeed radical thinkers as divergent as Georges Sorel and Louis Althusser, as we shall see, have both approvingly seen 'socialist ideology' in this pragmatic light.

The broad definition of ideology as a body of meanings and values encoding certain interests relevant to social power is plainly in need of some fine tuning. Ideologies are often thought, more specifically, to be *unifying, action-oriented, rationalizing, legitimating, universalizing* and *naturalizing*. Whether these features apply to oppositional ideologies as well as to dominant ones is a question we shall have to consider. Let us examine each of these assumptions in turn. Ideologies are often thought to lend coherence to the groups or classes which hold them, welding them into a unitary, if internally differentiated, identity, and perhaps thereby allowing them to impose a certain unity upon society as a whole. Since the idea of a coherent identity is these days somewhat unfashionable, it is worth adding that such unity, in the shape of political solidarity and comradely feeling, is quite as indispensable to the success of oppositional movements as it is part of the armoury of dominant groups.

How unified ideologies actually are, however, is a matter of debate. If they strive to homogenize, they are rarely homogeneous. Ideologies are usually internally complex, differentiated formations, with conflicts between their various elements which need to be continually renegotiated and resolved. What we call a dominant ideology is typically that of a dominant social bloc, made up of classes and fractions whose interests are not always at one; and these compromises and divisions will be reflected in the ideology itself. Indeed it can be claimed that part of the strength of bourgeois ideology lies in the fact that it 'speaks' from a multiplicity of sites, and in this subtle diffuseness presents no single target to its antagonists. Oppositional ideologies, similarly, usually reflect a provisional alliance of diverse radical forces.

If ideologies are not as 'pure' and unitary as they would like to think themselves, this is partly because they exist only in relation to other ideologies. A dominant ideology has continually to negotiate with the ideologies of its subordinates, and this essential open-endedness will prevent it from achieving any kind of pure self-identity. Indeed what makes a dominant ideology powerful – its ability to intervene in the consciousness of those it subjects, appropriating and reinflecting their experience – is also what tends to make it internally heterogeneous and inconsistent. A successful ruling ideology, as we have seen, must engage significantly with genuine wants, needs and desires; but this is also its Achilles heel, forcing it to recognize an 'other' to itself and inscribing this otherness as a potentially disruptive force within its own forms. We might say in Bakhtinian terms that for a governing ideology to be 'monological' – to address its subjects with authoritarian certitude – it must simultaneously be 'dialogical'; for even an authoritarian discourse is addressed *to* another and lives only in the other's response. A dominant ideology has to recognize that there are needs and desires which were never simply generated or implanted by itself; and the dystopian vision of a social order which is capable of containing and controlling all desires because it created them in the first place is thus unmasked as a fiction. Any ruling power requires a degree of intelligence and initiative from its subjects, if only for its own values to be internalized; and this resourcefulness is at once essential for the smooth reproduction of the system and a permanent possibility of reading its edicts 'otherwise'. If the oppressed must be alert enough to follow the rulers' instructions, they are therefore conscious enough to be able to challenge them.

For thinkers like Karl Mannheim and Lucien Goldmann, ideologies would seem to display a high degree of internal unity. But there are those like Antonio Gramsci who would view them as complex, uneven formations, and theorists like Pierre Macherey for whom ideology is so ambiguous and amorphous that it can hardly be spoken of as having a significant structure at all. Ideology for Macherey is the invisible colour of daily life, too close to the eyeball to be properly objectified, a centreless, apparently limitless medium in which we move like a fish in water, with no more ability than a fish to grasp this elusive environment as a whole. One cannot for Macherey speak in classical Marxist style of 'ideological contradictions', for 'contradiction' implies a definitive structure, of which ideology in its 'practical' state is entirely bereft. One can, however, *put* ideology into contradiction by imbuing it with a form which highlights its hidden limits, thrusts it up against its own boundaries and reveals its gaps and elisions, thus forcing its necessary silences to 'speak'. This, for Macherey, is the work upon ideology which is accomplished by the literary text.[4] If Macherey's theory underestimates the extent to which an ideology is significantly structured, one might claim that Georg Lukács's notion of the revolutionary subject overestimates the coherence of ideological consciousness.

A similar overestimation, this time of the dominant ideology, is to be found in the work of the later Frankfurt School. For Herbert Marcuse and Theodor Adorno, capitalist society languishes in the grip of an all-pervasive reification, all the way from commodity fetishism and speech habits to political bureaucracy and technological thought.[5] This seamless monolith of a dominant ideology is apparently devoid of contradictions – which means, in effect, that Marcuse and Adorno take it at face value, judging it as it would *wish* to appear. If reification exerts its sway everywhere, then this must presumably include the criteria by which we judge reification in the first place – in which case we would not be able to identify it at all, and the late Frankfurt School critique becomes an impossibility. The final alienation would be not to know that we were alienated. To characterize a situation as reified or alienated is implicitly to point to practices and possibilities which suggest an alternative to it, and which can thus become criterial of our alienated condition. For Jürgen Habermas, as we shall see later, these possibilities are inscribed in the very structures of social communication; while for Raymond Williams they spring from the complexity and contradictoriness of all social experience. 'No mode of production', Williams argues, 'and therefore no dominant social order and therefore no dominant culture ever in reality includes or exhausts all human practice, human energy, and human intention.'⁶ Every social formation is a complex amalgam of what Williams terms 'dominant', 'residual' and 'emergent' forms of consciousness, and no hegemony can thus ever be absolute. No sharper contrast could be found than with the later work of Michel Foucault, for whom regimes of power constitute us to our very roots, producing just those forms of subjectivity on which they can most efficiently go to work. But if this is so, what is there 'left over', so to speak, to find this situation so appalling? What, including one Michel Foucault, could conceivably protest against this condition, given that all subjectivity is merely the effect of power in the first place? If there is nothing beyond power, then there is nothing that is being blocked, categorized and regimented, and therefore absolutely no need to worry. Foucault does indeed speak of resistances to power; but what exactly is doing the resisting is an enigma his work does not manage to dispel.

Ideologies are often seen as peculiarly *action-oriented* sets of beliefs, rather than speculative theoretical systems. However abstrusely metaphysical the ideas in question may be, they must be translatable by the ideological discourse into a 'practical' state, capable of furnishing their adherents with goals, motivations, prescriptions, imperatives and so on. Whether this will do as an account of all ideology is perhaps doubtful: the kind of idealist ideology under fire in *The German Ideology* is lambasted by Marx and Engels precisely for its *im*practicality, its lofty remoteness from the real world. What is ideological about these beliefs for Marx and Engels is not that they pragmatically orientate men and women to objectionable political actions, but that they distract them from certain forms of practical activity altogether.

A successful ideology must work both practically and theoretically, and discover some way of linking these levels. It must extend from an elaborated system of thought to the minutiae of everyday life, from a scholarly treatise to a shout in the street. Martin Seliger, in his *Ideology and Politics*, argues that ideologies are typically mixtures of analytic and descriptive statements on the one hand, and moral and technical prescriptions on the other. They combine in a coherent system factual content and moral commitment, and this is what lends them their action-guiding power. At the level of what Seliger calls 'operative ideology' we find 'implements' (rules for carrying out the ideology's commitments) which may conflict with the ideology's fundamental principles. We are thus likely to find within an ideological formation a process of compromise, adjustment and trade-off between its overall world view and its more concrete prescriptive elements. Ideologies for Seliger blend beliefs and disbeliefs, moral norms, a modicum of factual evidence and a set of technical prescriptions, all of which ensures concerted action for the preservation or reconstruction of a given social order.

The Soviet philosopher V.N. Voloshinov distinguishes between 'behavioural' ideology and 'established systems' of ideas. Behavioural ideology concerns 'the whole aggregate of life experiences and the outward expressions directly connected with it'; it signifies 'that atmosphere of unsystematised and unfixed inner and outer speech which endows our every instance of behaviour and action and our every "conscious" state with meaning'.[7] There is some relation between this conception and Raymond Williams's celebrated notion of a 'structure of feeling' – those elusive, impalpable forms of social consciousness which are at once as evanescent as 'feeling' suggests, but nevertheless display a significant configuration captured in the term 'structure'. 'We are talking', Williams writes, 'about characteristic elements of impulse, restraint, and tone: specifically affective elements of consciousness and relationship: not feeling against thought, but thought as felt and feeling as thought: practical consciousness of a present kind, in a living and interrelating continuity.'[8]

What such a notion seeks to deconstruct is the familiar opposition between ideology as rigid, explicit doctrine on the one hand, and the supposedly inchoate nature of lived experience on the other. This opposition is itself ideologically eloquent: from what kind of social standpoint does lived experience appear utterly shapeless and chaotic? Virginia Woolf may well have experienced her life in this way, but her servants are less likely to have regarded their days as deliciously fluid and indeterminate. The doctrine goes hand in hand with the modernist banality that the purpose of art is to 'impose order upon chaos'. Against this, the concept of behavioural ideology or structure of feeling reminds us that lived experience is always tacitly shaped already, if only in ambiguous, provisional ways. Theoretically elaborate ideologies of art, science and ethics are for Voloshinov 'crystallizations' of this more fundamental level of existence, but the relationship between the two is dialectical. Formal ideological systems must draw vital sustenance from behavioural ideology, or risk withering away; but they also react back powerfully upon it, setting, as Voloshinov remarks, its 'tone'.

Even within behavioural ideology, different strata can be distinguished. What Voloshinov calls the lowest, most fluid stratum of such consciousness is made up of vague experiences, idle thoughts and random words which flash across the mind. But the upper levels are more vital and substantial, and these are the ones linked with ideological systems. They are more mobile and sensitive than an 'established' ideology, and it is in this subliminal region that those creative energies through which a social order may be restructured first germinate. 'Newly emerging social forces find ideological expression and take shape first in these upper strata of behavioural ideology before they can succeed in dominating the arena of some organised, official ideology.'[9] As these fresh ideological currents infiltrate the established belief systems, they will tend to take on something of their forms and colourings, incorporating into themselves notions already 'in stock'. Once again, Voloshinov's thought runs parallel here to Williams's 'structure of feeling'; for what Williams is seeking to define by that phrase is very often the stirring of 'emergent' forms of consciousness, ones which are struggling to break through but which have not yet attained the formalized nature of the belief systems they confront. As Williams writes, 'there is always, though in varying degrees, practical consciousness, in specific relationships, specific skills, specific perceptions, that is unquestionably social and that the specifically dominant social order neglects, excludes, represses, or simply fails to recognise.'[10] These social experiences still 'in solution', active and pressing but not yet fully articulated, may of course always suffer incorporation at the hands of the dominant culture, as Voloshinov acknowledges too; but both thinkers recognize a potential conflict between 'practical' and 'official' forms of consciousness, and the possibility of variable relations between them: compromise, adjustment, incorporation, outright opposition.

They reject, in other words, those more monolithic, pessimistic conceptions of ideology which would see 'practical consciousness' as no more than an obedient instantiation of ruling ideas.

There is a clear affinity between this distinction and what we shall see later in Antonio Gramsci as a discrepancy between official and practical consciousness – between those notions which the oppressed classes derive from their superiors, and those which arise from their 'life situations'. There is a similar opposition in the work of Louis Althusser between 'theoretical ideologies' (the work of the bourgeois political economists, for example) and what he calls 'ideology in a practical state'. Pierre Bourdieu's concept of 'habitus', which we shall be examining later, is an equivalent to 'practical ideology', focusing upon the way ruling imperatives are actually transmuted into forms of routine social behaviour; but like Voloshinov's 'behavioural ideology' it is a creative, open-ended affair, in no sense a simple 'reflection' of dominant ideas.

To study an ideological formation, then, is among other things to examine the complex set of linkages or mediations between its most articulate and least articulate levels. Organized religion might provide a useful example. Such religion stretches from highly abstruse metaphysical doctrines to meticulously detailed moral prescriptions governing the routines of everyday life. Religion is just a way of bringing to bear the most fundamental questions of human existence on a uniquely individual life. It also contains doctrines and rituals to rationalize the discrepancy between the two – to account for why I fail to live up to these cosmic truths, and (as in confession) to adjust my daily behaviour to their demands. Religion consists of a hierarchy of discourses, some of them elaborately theoretical (scholasticism), some ethical and prescriptive, others exhortatory and consolatory (preaching, popular piety); and the institution of the church ensures that each of these discourses meshes constantly with the others, to create an unbroken continuum between the theoretical and the behavioural.

It is sometimes claimed that if ideologies are action-oriented sets of beliefs, then this is one reason for their false, partial or distorting nature. A connection can be made here, in other words, between the 'sociological' character of ideology – the fact that it concerns ideas geared fairly directly to social practice – and the epistemological issue of these ideas' falsity. On this viewpoint, a true cognition of the world buckles under the pressure of certain pragmatic interests, or is warped by the limits of the class situation from which it springs. To say that the language of bourgeois political economy is ideological is to claim that at certain key points it betrays an 'interference' from the insistence of practical bourgeois interests. It need not be just a 'higher' encodement of those interests, as Marx himself appreciated; it is not just some spurious theoretical reflection of bourgeois behavioural ideology. But at certain points its genuinely cognitive discourse becomes blocked, forced up against certain conceptual limits which mark the real historical frontiers of bourgeois society itself. And these theoretical problems could then only be resolved by a transformation of that form of life.

Ideology, on this view, is thought rendered false by its social determinations. The trouble with this formulation, of course, is that there is no thought which is *not* socially determined. So it must be a question of the *kind* of social determinants under consideration. There is no need to hold that the only alternative to ideology is then some 'non-perspectival', socially disinterested knowledge; you can simply argue that at any given historical point certain socially determined standpoints will yield more of the truth than others. Someone, as they say, may be 'in a position to know', while others may not be. The fact that all viewpoints are socially determined does not entail that all viewpoints are equal in value. A prisoner is more likely to recognize the oppressive nature of a particular juridical system than a judge. Interests may interfere with our knowledge, in the sense, for example, that to understand the situation truly may not be in my interests. But someone else may risk starving to death unless they *do* get to understand the real situation, in which case their knowledge is by no means disinterested.

An ideology may be seen not simply as 'expressing' social interests but as *rationalizing* them. Those who believe that there will be no air left to breathe in Britain if we allow more immigration are probably rationalizing a racist attitude. Rationalization is at root a psychoanalytic category, defined by J. Laplanche and J.-B. Pontalis as a 'procedure whereby the subject attempts to present an explanation that is either logically consistent or ethically acceptable for attitudes, ideas, feelings, etc., whose true motives are not perceived'.[11] To call ideologies 'rationalizing' is already to imply that there is something discreditable about them – that they try to defend the indefensible, cloaking some disreputable motive in high-sounding ethical terms.

Not all ideological discourse need be of this kind, however, either because a group may not regard its own motives as particularly shameful, or because in fact they are not. Ancient society did not consider slave-owning to be reprehensible, and saw no need to rationalize it as we would need to now. Extreme right-wingers see no need to justify the free market by claiming that it will finally benefit everyone; for them, the weakest can simply go to the wall. If what the Diggers and Suffragettes held can be described as ideological, it is not because it betrays concealed and dubious motives. Ruling groups and classes may have some good motives and some shady ones: Western anti-Communism is often enough a self-interested apologia for Western property rights, but sometimes a genuine protest against the repressiveness of the post-capitalist societies. For psychoanalytic theory, the true motive in the act of rationalization is necessarily concealed from the subject, since did she but know it she would seek to change it; but this may or may not be so in the case of ideology. Some Americans really do believe that throwing their military weight around is in the interests of global freedom, whereas others perceive more cynically that it is in the interests of protecting American property. Ruling classes are not always self-deluded, not always utter dupes of their own propaganda.

On this view, then, ideologies can be seen as more or less systematic attempts to provide plausible explanations and justifications for social behaviour which might otherwise be the object of criticism. These apologias then conceal the truth from others, and perhaps also from the rationalizing subject itself. If all social interests are viewed in the manner of the sociologist Pareto as largely affective and irrational, then all theoretical ideology becomes a kind of elaborate rationalization, substituting supposedly rational belief for irrational or arational emotions and opinions. The structure of rationalization is thus metaphorical: one set of conceptions stands in for another.

Oppressed groups in society may rationalize just as thoroughly as their rulers. They may perceive that their conditions leave a lot to be desired, but rationalize this fact on the grounds that they deserve to suffer, or that everyone else does too, or that it is somehow inevitable, or that the alternative might be a good deal worse. Since these attitudes will generally benefit the rulers, it might be claimed that ruling classes sometimes allow those they subjugate to do much of their rationalizing for them. Dominated groups or classes can also rationalize their situation to the point of self-deception, persuading themselves that they are not unhappy at all. It is worth noting here that if we discovered that they really *were* happy, it is hard to know why we should press for their conditions to be changed; we would have to hold instead that they were not in fact happy but were for ideological reasons unaware of this. If it is in one sense clearly not in the interests of an oppressed group to deceive itself about its situation, there is another sense in which it often is, since such self-deception may render its conditions more tolerable. It is not simply a matter of the group's beliefs being at odds here with its interests, but of its having conflicting kinds of interests.

Rationalization may help to promote interests, but there are ways of promoting interests which do not particularly involve rationalization. One may help to promote one's interests precisely by *not* rationalizing them, as in the case of a self-confessed hedonist who wins our sympathies by his disarming candour. A stoical or fatalistic ideology may rationalize the wretched conditions of some social group, but it need not necessarily advance its interests, other than in the sense of supplying it with an opiate. An exception to this case is Nietzsche's celebrated doctrine of *ressentiment*, whereby a downtrodden people deliberately infect their rulers with their own self-castigating nihilism and so cunningly curtail their power.

The mechanism of rationalization is usually thought to be at the root of self-deception, on which there is now a rich, suggestive literature.[12] Self-deception is the condition in which one has wants or desires which one denies or disavows, or of which one is simply unaware. Denys Turner finds this whole conception deeply problematical on two grounds: first, because it would seem to deny the reality of the state of self-deception. The self-deceived person really *is* self-deceived, rather than harbouring some authentic desire overlaid by a layer of false consciousness. Secondly, Turner can make no real sense of the idea of having a desire of which one is unaware, or which one systematically misinterprets to oneself.[13] The problem here may turn partly on the kinds of wants and desires in question. It would seem reasonable to argue that an exploited social group may be profoundly dissatisfied with the regime which profits from it, without fully acknowledging this in a conscious way. It may show up instead in the form of a 'performative contradiction' between what the members of the group do and what they say: they may officially accord loyalty to the regime while demonstrating their indifference to it by, say, massive absenteeism from work. Where those who question the concept of self-deception are surely right is that it would not make sense to say that this group had a burning desire to socialize industry under workers' control, dismantle the structures of patriarchy and withdraw from NATO in four months' time, and not be aware of it. Nobody can entertain aspirations as precise as that and still be unconscious of them, just as a dog may be vaguely expecting its master's return, but cannot be expecting him to return at 2.15 pm on Wednesday.

Ideas and beliefs may spring from underlying desires, but they are also partly constitutive of them. A member of some 'lost' tribe in the Amazon basin cannot desire to be a brain surgeon, since he has no such concept. Rationalization involves a conflict between conscious belief and unconscious or unavowed motivation, but there are problems in regarding ideology in general as a question of repression in the Freudian sense. To be mystified is less to have repressed some piece of knowledge than not to have known something in the first place. There is also the question of whether ideology sometimes involves holding mutually contradictory ideas at the same time, as opposed to being caught in a contradiction between conscious belief and unconscious attitude. It is hard to see how someone could declare that children were in all respects delightful and denounce them in the very next breath as repulsive little beasts, as opposed to observing that children were delightful in some ways but not in others. But a manservant might swing with such bewildering rapidity between admiring his master and betraying withering contempt for him that we might conclude that he held, in effect, two mutually contradictory beliefs at one and the same time. The admiration no doubt belongs to his 'official' ideology, whereas the contempt arises from his 'practical consciousness'. When Othello declares that he believes Desdemona to be faithful to him and yet does not believe it, he may not mean that he sometimes thinks the one thing and sometimes the other, or that part of him trusts in her and part does not, or that he really hasn't a clue what he believes and is totally confused. He may mean that at one level he finds it utterly inconceivable that she has betrayed him, while at another level he has ample evidence to suggest that she has. One aspect of Othello's patriarchal ideology – his complacent faith in his security of sexual posses- sion – is in deadlock with another: his paranoid suspicion of women.

The concept of rationalization is closely allied to that of *legitimation*. Legit- imation refers to the process by which a ruling power comes to secure from its subjects an at least tacit consent to its authority, and like 'rationalization' it can have something of a pejorative smack about it, suggesting the need to make respectable otherwise illicit interests. But this need not always be so: legitimation can simply mean establishing one's interests as broadly accept- able, rather than lending them a spurious wash of legality. Social interests we regard as just and valid may have to fight hard to win credibility from society as a whole. To legitimate one's power is not necessarily to 'naturalize' it, in the sense of making it appear spontaneous and inevitable to one's subordinates: a group or class may well perceive that there could be kinds of authority other than that of their masters, but endorse this authority even so. A mode of domination is generally legitimated when those subjected to it come to judge their own behaviour by the criteria of their rulers. Someone with a Liverpool accent who believes he speaks incorrectly has legitimated an established cultural power.

There is a significant distinction between ideas which *serve* and which help to *legitimate* social interests. A dominant class may promote its ends by preaching that most of its underlings are of subhuman intelligence, but this is hardly likely to legitimate it in the eyes of its subjects. The belief that the highest spiritual value is to put one over on one's competitors would probably need to be rationalized to secure legitimacy for itself. Many of the beliefs of an oppressed group – that their sufferings are unavoidable, or that rebellion will be brutally punished – serve the interests of their masters, but do not particularly legitimate them. The *absence* of certain beliefs may serve one's own interests, or those of another group: it aids the bourgeoisie that they do not hold that the upshot of cutting wages is eternal torment, just as it helps them if those whose wages are cut reject the doctrines of dialectical materialism. A set of false beliefs may further a class's interests, as Marx argues of middle-class revolutionaries in *The 18th Brumaire of Louis Bonaparte*, who delude themselves productively about the splendour of their project. Just as true ideas may prove dysfunctional for advancing social interests, so false ones may prove functional for it; indeed for Friedrich Nietzsche truth is just any illusion which turns out to be life-enhancing. A group, for example, may overestimate its own political strength, but the fruit of this miscalculation may be some successful course of action it would not otherwise have embarked on. As far as ruling classes go, the illusion that they are acting in the common interest may buttress their self-esteem and thus, along with it, their power. Note also that a belief may be *explicable* in terms of one's social position, but may not significantly advance it; and that to claim that a belief is functional for social interests is not necessarily to deny that it is rationally grounded. The holder of the belief may have arrived at it anyway, despite the fact that it is in his or her interests to do so.[14]

It is sometimes thought that some actions of the state are legitimate, whereas others are not. The state has licit powers, but occasionally kicks over the traces. For a Marxist, however, the bourgeois state is illegitimate *in se*, however it may succeed in legitimating itself in the eyes of its subordinates, since it is essentially an organ of unjustifiable class rule. We should remember, however, that such legitimation is never simply an *ideological* affair: ruling classes have material means at their disposal for eliciting the consent of their subordinates, such as raising their wages or providing them with free health care. And as we saw in discussing *The Dominant Ideology Thesis*, it is rash to suppose that a legitimated power is always one successfully internalized by those who are its targets. We need to distinguish between such 'normative' acceptance, and what is probably the more widespread condition of 'pragmatic' acceptance, in which subaltern groups endorse the right of their rulers to govern because they can see no realistic alternative.

An important device by which an ideology achieves legitimacy is by *universalizing* and 'eternalizing' itself. Values and interests which are in fact specific to a certain place and time are projected as the values and interests of all humanity. The assumption is that if this were not so, the sectoral, self-interested nature of the ideology would loom too embarrassingly large, and so would impede its general acceptance.

The *locus classicus* of this view can be found in *The German Ideology*, where Marx and Engels argue that 'each new class which puts itself in the place of one ruling before it, is compelled, merely in order to carry through its aim, to represent its interest as the common interest of all the members of society, that is, expressed in ideal form: it has to give its ideas the form of universality, and represent them as the only rational, universally valid ones.'[15] We should not dismiss such universalization as a mere sleight of hand: Marx and Engels go on instantly in this passage to remark that the interests of an emergent revolutionary class really *are* likely to be connected to the common interests of all other non-ruling classes. The revolutionary proletariat has traditionally sought to rally to its banner other disaffected groups and classes: poor peasants, intellectuals, elements of the petty bourgeoisie and so on, who have their own interests in toppling the ruling bloc. And radical popular movements of one kind or another have traditionally clung to the shirt-tails of the revolutionary bourgeoisie, only, typically, to be sold out once that class has assumed power. When a social class is still emergent, it has had as yet scant time to consolidate its own sectional interests, and bends its energies instead to winning as broad support as possible. Once ensconced in power, its selfish interests will tend to become more obvious, causing it to lapse from universal to particular status in the eyes of some erstwhile supporters. For some Marxist theorists, it is only at this point that ideology proper takes hold: on this view, class consciousness is not ideological when a class is still in its revolutionary phase, but becomes so when it needs later to conceal contradictions between its own interests and those of society as a whole.[16] A false universalization, in short, becomes necessary once a true one has failed.

Universalization, then, is not always a speciously rationalizing mechanism. It is indeed ultimately in the interests of all individuals that women should emancipate themselves; and the belief that one's values are finally universal may provide some significant impetus in gaining legitimacy for them. If a social group or class needs to universalize its beliefs and values to win support for them, then this will make a difference to the beliefs and values in question. It is not just a matter of that class persuading others that its interests are in fact at one with theirs, but of framing these interests in the first place in ways which make this plausible. It is a question, in other words, of how the group or class describes itself to itself, not just of how it sells itself to others. Framing one's interests in this style may run against one's immediate interests, or even against one's longer-term ones. The universal values of the revolutionary bourgeoisie – freedom, justice, equality and so on – at once promoted its own cause and occasioned it grave embarrassment when other subordinated classes began to take these imperatives seriously.

If I am to convince you that it is really in your interests for me to be self-interested, then I can only be effectively self-interested by becoming less so. If my interests have to take yours into account in order to flourish, then they will be redefined on the basis of your own needs, thus ceasing to be identical with themselves. But your interests will not remain self-identical either, since they have now been reworked as achievable only within the matrix of mine. A useful example of this process is the political state. The state for Marxism is fundamentally an instrument of ruling-class power; but it is also an organ by which that class must fashion the general consensus within which its own interests might best thrive. This latter requirement then typically involves the ruling bloc in negotiating with antagonistic forces within the arena of the state in ways which are not always compatible with its own short-term interests.

A class which succeeds in universalizing its aims will cease to appear as a sectional interest at all; at the acme of its power, that power will effectively vanish. It is for this reason that 'universalization' is commonly a pejorative term for radicals. On this view, ideologies are always driven by global ambitions, suppressing the historical relativity of their own doctrines. 'Ideology', announces Louis Althusser, 'has no outside.'[17] This global reach encompasses time as well as space. An ideology is reluctant to believe that it was ever born, since to do so is to acknowledge that it can die. Like the oedipal child, it would prefer to think of itself as without parentage, sprung parthenogenetically from its own seed. It is equally embarrassed by the presence of sibling ideologies, since these mark out its own finite frontiers and so delimit its sway. To view an ideology from the outside is to recognize its limits; but from the inside these boundaries vanish into infinity, leaving the ideology curved back upon itself like cosmic space.

It is not clear, however, that all ideological discourse needs to conceal its frontiers in this way. 'I know I speak as a Western liberal, but I just do believe that Islam is a barbaric creed': such coyly self-referential pronouncements should alert us against the now fashionable belief that for the subject to reckon himself into his own utterances is inevitably a progressive move. On the contrary, as with the disarming candour of the self-declared hedonist, it might actually lend conviction to his viewpoint. Now all ideologists obtusely insist that everyone from Adam to the Chief Druid has shared their opinions – which brings us to the doctrine of '*naturalization*'.

Successful ideologies are often thought to render their beliefs natural and self-evident – to identify them with the 'common sense' of a society so that nobody could imagine how they might ever be different. This process, which Pierre Bourdieu calls *doxa*, involves the ideology in creating as tight a fit as possible between itself and social reality, thereby closing the gap into which the leverage of critique could be inserted. Social reality is redefined by the ideology to become coextensive with itself, in a way which occludes the truth that the reality in fact generated the ideology. Instead, the two appear to be spontaneously bred together, as indissociable as a sleeve and its lining. The result, politically speaking, is an apparently vicious circle: the ideology could only be transformed if the reality was such as to allow it to become objectified; but the ideology processes the reality in ways which forestall this possibility. The two are thus mutually self-confirming. On this view, a ruling ideology does not so much combat alternative ideas as thrust them beyond the very bounds of the thinkable. Ideologies exist because there are things which must at all costs not be thought, let alone spoken. How we could ever *know* that there were such thoughts is then an obvious logical difficulty. Perhaps we just feel that there is *something* we ought to be thinking, but we have no idea what it is.

Ideology, on this view, offers itself as an 'Of course!', or 'That goes without saying'; and from Georg Lukács to Roland Barthes this has figured as a central assumption of 'ideology critique'. Ideology freezes history into a 'second nature', presenting it as spontaneous, inevitable and so unalterable. It is essentially a *reification* of social life, as Marx would seem to argue in his famous essay on the fetishism of commodities. Naturalizing has an obvious link with universalizing, since what is felt to be universal is often thought to be natural; but the two are not in fact synonymous, since one could regard some activity as universal without necessarily judging it to be natural. You might concede that all human societies to date have displayed aggression, while looking eagerly to a future order in which this would no longer be so. But there is clearly a strong implication that what has been true always and everywhere is innate to human nature, and so cannot be changed. One just has to accept that twelfth-century French peasants were really capitalists in heavy disguise, or that the Sioux have always secretly wanted to be stock-brokers.

Like universalization, naturalization is part of the *dehistoricizing* thrust of ideology, its tacit denial that ideas and beliefs are specific to a particular time, place and social group. As Marx and Engels recognize in *The German Ideology*, to conceive of forms of consciousness as autonomous, magically absolved from social determinants, is to uncouple them from history and so convert them into a natural phenomenon. If some feudalist ideologues denounced early capitalist enterprise, it was because they regarded it as unnatural – meaning, of course, untrue to feudal definitions of human nature. Later on, capitalism would return the compliment to socialism. It is interesting, incidentally, that the concept of naturalization itself rests upon a particular *ideology* of Nature, which takes it in the manner of William Wordsworth to be massively immutable and enduring; and it is ironic that this view of Nature should prevail in an historical epoch where the stuff is continually being hacked into human shape, technologically dominanted and transformed. Thomas Hardy opens *The Return of the Native* by speaking of the barren, unchanging landscape of Egdon heath, a tract of land which was planted from end to end by the Forestry Commission not long after his death. Perhaps it is *human* nature which the ideologists have in mind, which is similarly assumed to be immutable. To deny this, as the political left properly does, is not to assert that there is nothing whatsoever about the human species which is natural and unchanging. It is natural that human beings should be born, eat, engage in sexual activity, associate with one another, transform their environments, die and so on; and the fact that all of these practices are, culturally speaking, highly variable is no rebuttal of their naturalness. Karl Marx believed strongly in a human nature, and was surely quite right to do so.[18] There are many crucial aspects of human societies which follow from the material nature of our bodies, a nature which has altered only negligibly in the history of the race. Appeals to nature and the natural are by no means necessarily reactionary: a social order which denies warmth, nourishment and shelter to its members is unnatural, and should be politically challenged on these grounds. When the rulers of the *anciens régimes* in eighteenth-century Europe heard the dread word 'nature', they reached for their weapons.

Many forms of ideology do indeed naturalize their own values; but as with universalization one may take leave to doubt whether this is universally true. The case that ideology converts the controversial into the obvious has itself become so obvious that it is ripe for interrogating. The well-named doctrine of the Assumption of the Blessed Virgin into heaven is certainly ideological, but it is hardly obvious even to many of its pious adherents. It is hard to imagine it springing spontaneously from our casual experience of the world. Many people revere the monarchy; but it is not always self-evident to them that there *must* be a monarch, and they may be well aware that there are societies in reasonable working order which lack such an institution. Someone may be ferociously committed to capitalism in the perfect knowledge that it is a fairly recent historical system, one way of organizing society among many.

The supposed obviousness of ideology goes along with its presumed lack of self-reflexiveness. The assumption here is that it would be impossible for somebody to hold ideological views and be simultaneously aware that they were ideological. Ideologies are discourses unable to curve back critically upon themselves, blinded to their own grounds and frontiers. If ideology knew itself to be such it would instantly cease to be so, just as if a pig knew it was a pig it would not be. 'Ideology', observes Louis Althusser, 'never says: "I am ideological".'[19] Though this may be true much of the time, that 'never' is surely an overstatement. 'I know I'm a terrible sexist, but I just can't stand the sight of a woman in trousers'; 'Sorry to be so bourgeois, but would you mind spitting in the sink rather than in the food mixer?': such utterances may be little more than attempts to forestall criticism by their arch frankness, but they indicate a limited degree of ironic self-awareness which a full-blooded

'naturalization' theory fails to take into account. I may have some consciousness of the social origin and function of my beliefs, without on that score
ceasing to hold them. A novelist like E.M. Forster is perfectly capable of
discerning something of the exploitative conditions on which his own
liberal humanism rests, without thereby ceasing to be a liberal humanist.
Indeed a guilt-stricken insight into the sources of his own privilege is *part* of
his middle-class liberalism; a true liberal must be liberal enough to suspect
his own liberalism. Ideology, in short, is not always the utterly self-blinded,
self-deluded straw target its theorists occasionally make it out to be – not
least in the cynical, infinitely regressive self-ironizing of a postmodernist
age. On the contrary, it can rise from time to time to 'metalinguistic' status
and name itself, at least partially, without abandoning its position. And such
partial self-reflectiveness may tighten rather than loosen its grip. That
ideologies should be thought always naturalizing and universalizing natural-
izes and universalizes the concept of ideology, and gives its antagonists too
easy a political ride.

Finally, we may ask how far the various mechanisms we have examined
are displayed by oppositional ideologies as well as by dominant ones.
Oppositional ideologies often seek to unify a diverse array of political forces,
and are geared to effective action; they also strive to legitimate their beliefs
in the eyes of society as a whole, so that some socialists, for example, speak of
the need to create a 'socialist common sense' in the consciousness of
ordinary men and women. When the middle class was still an emergent
political force, its revolutionary rallying cry of liberty was certainly, among
other, finer things, a rationalization of the freedom to exploit; and it was
intent on both universalizing its values (appealing to an abstract 'mankind'
against the parochialism of the traditional order), and naturalizing them
(invoking 'natural rights' as against mere custom and privilege). Political
radicals today are properly wary of repeating this gesture, and would of
course reject the view that their beliefs merely rationalize some specious
ulterior motive; but they are implicitly committed to universalizing their
values, in that it would make no sense to argue that socialist feminism was
appropriate for California but not for Cambodia. Those on the political left
who feel nervous of such grandly global gestures, fearing that they
necessarily implicate some oppressively abstract notion of 'Man', are simply
liberal pluralists or cultural relativists in radical clothing.

3

FROM THE
ENLIGHTENMENT TO THE
SECOND INTERNATIONAL

THERE is a peculiar feature about words which end in 'ology': '-ology' means the science or study of some phenomenon; but by a curious process of inversion 'ology' words often end up meaning the phenomenon studied rather than the systematic knowledge of it. Thus 'methodology' means the study of method, but is commonly used nowadays to mean method itself. To say you are examining Max Weber's methodology probably means you are considering the methods he uses, rather than his ideas about them. To say that human biology is not adapted to large doses of carbon monoxide means that our bodies are not so adapted, not the study of them. 'The geology of Peru' can refer to the physical features of that country as much as to the scientific examination of them. And the American tourist who remarked to a friend of mine on the 'wonderful ecology' of the West of Ireland just meant that the scenery was beautiful.

Such an inversion befell the word ideology not long after its birth. 'Ideology' originally meant the scientific study of human ideas; but fairly soon the object took over from the approach, and the word rapidly came to mean systems of ideas themselves. An ideologist was then less someone who analysed ideas than someone who expounded them. It is interesting to speculate on at least one of the ways in which this reversal came about. An ideologist, as we shall see in a moment, was initially a philosopher intent on revealing the material basis of our thought. The last thing he believed was that ideas were mysterious things in themselves, quite independent of external conditioning. 'Ideology' was an attempt to put ideas back in their place, as the products of certain mental and physiological laws. But to carry through this project meant lavishing a good deal of attention on the realm of human consciousness; and it is then understandable, if ironic, that such theorists should be taken to believe that ideas were all there was. It is as though one should tag as a 'religious philosopher' some agnostic rationalist who spent a lifetime deep in mysticism and mythology for the purpose of demonstrating that these were illusions bred by certain social conditions. In fact, the early French ideologues *did* believe that ideas were at the root of social life, so that to accuse them of inflating the importance of human consciousness is not simply a mistake; but if they were idealists in this sense, they were materialists in their view of where ideas actually derived from.

Ideology in our own time has sometimes been sharply counterposed to science; so it is ironic to recall that ideology began life precisely *as* a science, as a rational enquiry into the laws governing the formation and development of ideas. Its roots lie deep in the Enlightenment dream of a world entirely transparent to reason, free of the prejudice, superstition and obscurantism of the *ancien régime*. To be an 'ideologist' – a clinical analyst of the nature of consciousness – was to be a critic of 'ideology', in the sense of the dogmatic, irrational belief systems of traditional society. But this critique of ideology was in fact an ideology all of itself, and this in two different senses. For one thing, the early ideologues of the French eighteenth century drew heavily on John Locke's empiricist philosophy in their war against metaphysics, insisting that human ideas were derived from sensations rather than from some innate or transcendental source; and such empiricism, with its image of individuals as passive and discrete, is itself deeply bound up with bourgeois ideological assumptions. For another thing, the appeal to a disinterested nature, science and reason, as opposed to religion, tradition and political authority, simply masked the power interests which these noble notions secretly served. We might risk the paradox, then, that ideology was born as a thoroughly ideological critique of ideology. In illuminating the obscurantism of the old order, it cast upon society a dazzling light which blinded men and women to the murky sources of this clarity.

The aim of the Enlightenment ideologues, as spokesmen for the revolutionary bourgeoisie of eighteenth-century Europe, was to reconstruct society from the ground up on a rational basis. They inveighed fearlessly against a social order which fed the people on religious superstition in order to buttress its own brutally absolutist power, and dreamt of a future in which the dignity of men and women, as creatures able to survive without opiate and illusion, would be cherished. Their case, however, contained one crippling contradiction. For if they held on the one hand that individuals were the determined products of their environment, they insisted on the other hand that they could rise above such lowly determinants by the power of education. Once the laws of human consciousness were laid bare to scientific inspection, that consciousness could be transformed in the direction of human happiness by a systematic pedagogical project. But what would be the determinants of *that* project? Or, as Karl Marx put it, who would educate the educators? If all consciousness is materially conditioned, must not this apply also to the apparently free, disinterested notions which would enlighten the masses out of autocracy into freedom? If everything is to be exposed to the pellucid light of reason, must not this include reason itself?

The ideologues could offer no solution to this quandary; but they persevered nonetheless in their pursuit of the essence of mind. Social and political institutions must be rescued from the sway of metaphysical delusion; but is not this project fatally incomplete unless it extends itself to the most distinctive aspect of humanity, consciousness itself? How can a rational society be constructed if the mind itself, supposedly the very basis of social existence, remains inscrutable and elusive? The programme of an 'ideology' is accordingly to bring this most complex, impalpable of phenomena within the province of scientific research, in a way scandalous to the metaphysical dualists for whom mind is one thing and materiality quite another. The new science of ideology was thus as subversive in its day as psychoanalysis in our own time: if even the soul or psyche could be shown to work by certain determinate mechanisms, then the last bastion of mystery and transcendence in a mechanistic world would be finally toppled. Ideology is a revolutionary strike at the priests and kings, at the traditional custodians and technicians of the 'inner life'. Knowledge of humanity is wrested from the monopoly of a ruling class and invested instead in an elite of scientific theorists.[1]

That scientific reason should penetrate to the inmost recesses of the human psyche is not only theoretically logical but politically essential. For social institutions can be rationally transformed only on the basis of the most exact knowledge of human nature; and justice and happiness lie in the adaptation of such institutions to these unchanging laws, rather than in the arbitrary forcing of human nature into 'artificial' social forms. Ideology, in short, belongs with a full-blooded programme of social engineering, which will remake our social environment, thus alter our sensations, and so change our ideas. Such is the well-meaning fantasy of the great Enlightenment ideologists, of Holbach, Condillac, Helvetius, Joseph Priestley, William Godwin and the younger Samuel Coleridge, that a direct line could be traced from the material conditions of human beings to their sensory experience and then to their thoughts, and that this whole trajectory could be diverted by radical reform towards the goal of spiritual progress and ultimate perfection.[2] Ideology, which in the hands of Marx and Engels will shortly come to denote the illusion that ideas are somehow autonomous of the material world, starts life as exactly the reverse: as one branch of a mechanical materialism which clings to the faith that the operations of the mind are as predictable as the laws of gravity. This science of ideas, as the inventor of the term ideology Destutt de Tracy commented, is a part of zoology, one region within a more general science of the human animal.

The career of Antoine Destutt de Tracy is a fascinating, strangely unsung story.[3] Born an aristocrat, he deserted his own class to become one of the most combative spokesmen of the revolutionary French bourgeoisie. He is thus a classic case of what we shall see later as the Gramscian transition from 'traditional' to 'organic' intellectual. He fought as a soldier during the French revolution and was imprisoned during the Terror; in fact he first hatched the concept of a science of ideas in his prison cell. The notion of ideology was thus brought to birth in thoroughly ideological conditions: ideology belonged to a rational politics, in contrast to the irrationalist barbarism of the Terror. If men and women were truly to govern themselves, then the laws of their nature must first be patiently scrutinized. What was needed, Tracy declared, was a 'Newton of the science of thought', and he himself was a clear candidate for the post. Since all science rests upon ideas, ideology would oust theology as the queen of them all, guaranteeing their unity. It would reconstruct politics, economics and ethics from the ground up, moving from the simplest processes of sensation to the loftiest regions of spirit. Private property, for example, is based upon a distinction between 'yours' and 'mine', which can be tracked in turn to a fundamental perceptual opposition between 'you' and 'me'.

With the revolution still at its height, Tracy became a prominent member of the *Institut Nationale*, the elite group of scientists and philosophers who constituted the theoretical wing of the social reconstruction of

France. He worked in the Institute's Moral and Political Sciences division, in the Section of Analysis of Sensations and Ideas, and was engaged in creating for the *écoles centrales* of the civil service a new programme of national education which would take the science of ideas as its basis. Napoleon was at first delighted by the Institute, proud to be an honorary member, and invited Tracy to join him as a soldier in his Egyptian campaign. (Perhaps this was a calculated backhanded compliment, since a move from *savant* to soldier would surely have been somewhat regressive.)

Tracy's fortunes, however, were soon on the wane. As Napoleon began to renege on revolutionary idealism, the ideologues rapidly became his *bête noir*, and the concept of ideology itself entered the field of ideological struggle. It stood now for political liberalism and republicanism, in conflict with Bonapartist authoritarianism. Napoleon claimed to have invented the derogatory term 'ideologue' himself, as a way of demoting the men of the Institute from scientists and *savants* to sectarians and subversives. Tracy and his kind, so he complained, were 'windbags' and dreamers – a dangerous class of men who struck at the roots of political authority and brutally deprived men and women of their consolatory fictions. 'You ideologues', he grumbled, 'destroy all illusions, and the age of illusions is for individuals as for peoples the age of happinesss.'[4] Before long he was seeing ideologues under every bed, and even blamed them for his defeat in Russia. He closed down the Moral and Political Sciences section of the *Institut Nationale* in 1802, and its members were assigned instead to teach history and poetry. One year before, Tracy had begun publishing his *Projet d'éléments d'idéologie*, in what can only have been a calculated act of defiance of the new milieu of religiose reaction. The continuation of the title of his work reads: '*à l'usage des écoles centrales de la République*' – a clear enough indication of its practical, political character, its role within what Althusser would later call the 'ideological state apparatuses'. 'Ideology' is simply the theoretical expression of a pervasive strategy of social reconstruction, in which Tracy himself was a key functionary. His fight to retain ideology in the *écoles centrales* failed, however, and it was replaced as a discipline by military instruction.

In 1812, in the wake of his Russian debacle, Napoleon rounded upon the ideologues in a now celebrated speech:

> It is to the doctrine of the ideologues – to this diffuse metaphysics, which in a contrived manner seeks to find the primary causes and on this foundation would erect the legislation of peoples, instead of adapting the laws to a

knowledge of the human heart and of the lessons of history – to which one must attribute all the misfortunes which have befallen our beloved France.[5]

In a notable irony, Napoleon contemptuously brackets the ideologues with the very metaphysicians they were out to discredit. That there is some truth in his accusation is surely clear: Tracy and his colleagues, true to their rationalist creed, ascribed a foundational role to ideas in social life, and thought a politics could be deduced from a priori principles. If they waged war on the metaphysical idealism which viewed ideas as spiritual entities, they were at one with its belief that ideas were the basis upon which all else rested. But Napoleon's irritation strikes a note which was to resound throughout the modern period: the impatience of the political pragmatist with the radical intellectual, who would dare to theorize the social formation as a whole. It is the quarrel in our own time between neo-pragmatists such as Stanley Fish and Richard Rorty – unlikely candidates, otherwise, for Napoleon – and the political left. The ideologues' commitment to a 'global' analysis of society is inseparable from their revolutionary politics, and at loggerheads with Bonaparte's mystificatory talk of the 'human heart'. In other terms, it is the eternal enmity between humanist and social scientist – an early instance of Roland Barthes's dictum that 'System is the enemy of "Man".' If Napoleon denounces the ideologues it is because they are the sworn foes of ideology, intent on demystifying the sentimental illusions and maundering religiosity with which he hoped to legitimate his dictatorial rule.

In the teeth of Bonaparte's displeasure, Tracy continued work on a second volume of his *Éléments*, and snatched time to work on a *Grammar*. His approach to language was too abstract and analytic for Napoleon's taste, enraging the latter still further: Tracy insisted on raising questions of the origins and functions of language, while Napoleon favoured the study of language through the teaching of the French literary classics. Once more, 'theorist' and 'humanist' were locked in combat, in a philological dispute which encoded a political antagonism between radical and reactionary. Suspected of involvement in a plot to assassinate the Emperor, Tracy opposed him as a senator and produced the final volume of his life's work, devoted to the science of economics. Like Marx, he believed that economic interests were the final determinants of social life; but he finds in these interests a recalcitrance which threatens to undermine his rationalist politics. What use is reason, he complains, in persuading the idle rich that they are good for nothing? (Tracy was himself one of France's largest landed proprietors, and an absentee landlord at that). The final volume of the *Éléments* thus presses up against a material limit which it will be left to Marx to cross; and the tone of its Conclusion is accordingly defeatist. In turning his eyes to the economic realm, Tracy has been forced to confront the radical 'irrationality' of social motivations in class-society, the rootedness of thought in selfish interests. The concept of ideology is beginning to strain towards its later, pejorative meaning; and Tracy himself acknowledges that reason must take more account of feeling, character and experience. A month after finishing the work, he wrote an article defending suicide.

Late in his life, Tracy published a work on – of all things – love, which was devoured by his admiring disciple Stendhal. Tracy spoke up for the complete freedom of young women to select their own marriage partners, pleaded the cause of unmarried mothers and championed sexual liberty. (His proto-feminism had its limits, however: women were to be fully educated but not allowed the vote.) Thomas Jefferson had him elected to the American Philosophical Society, and Tracy in his turn was deluded enough to declare the United States 'the hope and example of the world'. When the French revolution of 1830 broke out almost literally on his doorstep, the elderly Tracy strolled from his house and threw himself on the barricades.

Marx described Destutt de Tracy as a light among the vulgar economists, though he attacked him in both *The German Ideology* and *Capital*, dubbing him a 'cold-blooded bourgeois-doctrinaire' in the latter work. Emmet Kennedy, in his excellent study of Tracy, makes the perceptive point that the only volume of his treatise on ideology that Marx probably read is the one devoted to economics, and that the appearance of this work of bourgeois political economy as part of a general science of ideology might have firmed up in Marx's mind the connection between the two. In other words, it might have helped to shift Marx from his view of ideology as mere abstract ideas to his sense of it as political apologia.

The emergence of the concept of ideology, then, is no mere chapter in the history of ideas. On the contrary, it has the most intimate relation to revolutionary struggle, and figures from the outset as a theoretical weapon of class warfare. It arrives on the scene inseparable from the material practices of the ideological state apparatuses, and is itself as a notion a theatre of contending ideological interests. But if ideology sets out to examine the sources of human consciousness, what is to be said of the consciousness which performs this operation? Why should that particular mode of reason be immune from its own propositions about the material foundations of thought? Perhaps the whole concept of ideology is just some biologically determined reflex in the head of a French *philosophe* called Destutt de Tracy, with no more objective validity than that. Reason would appear able to monitor the whole of reality; but is it able to monitor itself? Or must it be the one thing which falls outside the scope of its own analysis? The science of ideas would seem to allot itself transcendental status; but it is exactly such a claim which its own doctrines put into question. So it is that Hegel, in the *Phenomenology of Spirit*, will induce reason to curve back upon itself, tracing its stately progress towards the Absolute all the way from its humble germination in our routine sense-data.

The kernel of Napoleon's criticism of the ideologues is that there is something irrational about excessive rationalism. In his eyes, these thinkers have pressed through their enquiry into the laws of reason to the point where they have become marooned within their own sealed systems, as divorced from practical reality as a psychotic. So it is that the term ideology gradually shifts from denoting a sceptical scientific materialism to signifying a sphere of abstract, disconnected ideas; and it is this meaning of the word which will then be taken up by Marx and Engels.

Karl Marx's theory of ideology is probably best seen as part of his more general theory of alienation, expounded in the *Economic and Philosophical Manuscripts* (1844) and elsewhere.[6] In certain social conditions, Marx argues, human powers, products and processes escape from the control of human subjects and come to assume an apparently autonomous existence. Estranged in this way from their agents, such phenomena then come to exert an imperious power over them, so that men and women submit to what are in fact products of their own activity as though they are an alien force. The concept of alienation is thus closely linked to that of 'reification' – for if social phenomena cease to be recognizable as the outcome of human projects, it is understandable to perceive them as material things, and thus to accept their existence as inevitable.

The theory of ideology embodied in Marx and Engels's *The German Ideology* (1846) belongs with this general logic of inversion and alienation. If human powers and institutions can undergo this process, then so can consciousness itself. Consciousness is in fact bound up with social practice; but for the German idealist philosophers whom Marx and Engels have in their sights, it becomes separated from these practices, fetishized to a thing-in-itself, and so, by a process of inversion, can be misunderstood as the very source and ground of historical life. If ideas are grasped as autonomous entities, then this helps to naturalize and dehistoricize them; and this for the early Marx is the secret of all ideology:

> Men are the producers of their conceptions, ideas, etc. – real, active men, as they are conditioned by a definite development of their productive forces and of the intercourse corresponding to these, up to its furthest forms. Consciousness can never be anything else than conscious existence, and the existence of men is their actual life-process. If in all ideology men and their circumstances appear upside-down as in a *camera obscura*, this phenomenon arises just as much from their historical life-process as the inversion of objects on the retina does from their physical life-process.
>
> In direct contrast to German philosophy which descends from heaven to earth, here we ascend from earth to heaven. This is to say, we do not set out from what men say, imagine, conceive, nor from men as narrated, thought of, imagined, conceived, in order to arrive at men in the flesh. We set out from real, active men, and on the basis of their real life-process we demonstrate the development of the ideological reflexes and echoes of this life-process.... Life is not determined by consciousness, but consciousness by life.[7]

The advance here over the Enlightenment *philosophes* is plain. For those thinkers, an 'ideology' would help to dispel errors bred by passion, prejudice and vicious interests, all of which blocked the clear light of reason. This strain of thought passes on to nineteenth-century positivism and to Emile Durkheim, in whose *Rules of Sociological Method* (1895) ideology means among other things allowing preconceptions to tamper with our knowledge of real things. Sociology is a 'science of facts', and the scientist must accordingly free himself of the biases and misconceptions of the layperson in order to arrive at a properly dispassionate viewpoint. These ideological habits and predispositions, for Durkheim as for the later French philosopher Gaston Bachelard, are innate to the mind; and this positivist current of social thought, true to its Enlightenment forebears, thus delivers us a *psychologistic* theory of ideology. Marx and Engels, by contrast, look to the historical causes and functions of such false consciousness, and so inaugurate the major modern meaning of the term whose history we are tracing. They arrive at this view hard on the heels of Ludwig Feuerbach, whose *The Essence of Christianity* (1841) sought for the sources of religious illusion in humanity's actual life conditions, but in a notably dehistoricizing way. Marx and Engels were not in fact the first thinkers to see consciousness as socially determined: in different ways, Rousseau, Montesquieu and Condorcet had arrived at this view before them.

If ideas are at the very source of historical life, it is possible to imagine that one can change society by combatting false ideas with true ones; and it is this combination of rationalism and idealism which Marx and Engels are rejecting. For them, social illusions are anchored in real contradictions, so that only by the practical activity of transforming the latter can the former be abolished. A materialist theory of ideology is thus inseparable from a revolutionary politics. This, however, involves a paradox. The critique of ideology claims at once that certain forms of consciousness are false and that this falsity is somehow structural and necessary to a specific social order. The falsity of the ideas, we might say, is part of the 'truth' of a whole material condition. But the theory which identifies this falsehood therefore under-cuts itself at a stroke, exposing a situation which simply as a theory it is powerless to resolve. The critique of ideology, that is to say, is at the same moment the critique of the critique of ideology. Moreover, it is not as though ideology critique proposes to put something true in place of the falsity. In one sense, this critique retains something of a rationalist or Enlightenment structure: truth, or theory, will shed light on false conceptions. But it is anti-rationalist in so far as what it then proposes is not a set of true conceptions, but just the thesis that all ideas, true or false, are grounded in practical social activity, and more particularly in the contradictions which that activity generates.

More problems then inevitably follow. Does this mean that true ideas would be ideas faithful to practical social activity? Or can their truth or falsehood be ascertained independently of this? Are not the illusions of bourgeois society in some sense actually true to its practices? If they are rationalizations of contradictions to which those practices give rise, are not such misconceptions indeed rooted in the 'real life-process', rather than idly autonomous of it? Or is the point that their very autonomy is itself socially determined? Is this autonomy merely *apparent* – a misperception on the part of human subjects – or is it real? Would true ideas be not just those which corresponded to actual practices, but those which corresponded to 'true' practices? And what would it mean to say of a *practice*, as opposed to a meaning, that it was true or false?

There are several difficulties with the formulations in the passage quoted from *The German Ideology*. For one thing, the whole vocabulary of 'reflexes' and 'echoes' smacks strongly of mechanical materialism. What distinguishes the human animal is that it moves in a world of meaning; and these meanings are constitutive of its activities, not secondary to them. Ideas are internal to our social practices, not mere spin-offs from them. Human existence, as Marx recognizes elsewhere, is purposive or 'intentional' existence; and these purposive conceptions form the inner grammar of our practical life, without which it would be mere physical motion. The term 'praxis' has been often enough used by the Marxist tradition to capture this indissolubility of action and significance. In general, Marx and Engels recognize this well enough; but in their zeal to worst the idealists they risk ending up here simply inverting them, retaining a sharp duality between 'consciousness' and 'practical activity' but reversing the causal relations between them. Whereas the Young Hegelians whom they are assailing regard ideas as the essence of material life, Marx and Engels just stand this opposition on its head. But the antithesis can always be partly deconstructed, since 'consciousness' figures, so to speak, on both sides of the equation. Certainly there can be no 'real life-process' without it.

The problem may spring from the fact that the term 'consciousness' here is being pressed into double service. It can mean 'mental life' in general; or it can allude more specifically to particular historical systems of beliefs (religious, juridical, political and so on), of the kind Marx will later come to ascribe to the so-called 'superstructure' in contrast to the economic 'base'. If one is thinking of consciousness in this second sense, as well-articulated structures of doctrine, its opposition to 'practical activity' becomes rather more plausible. It belongs to the Marxist case that such superstructures are indeed estranged from their practical, productive 'base', and the causes of this estrangement inhere in the very nature of that material activity. This, however, will not entirely meet the point, since for all their alienated character such ideological discourses still powerfully condition our real-life practices. Political, religious, sexual and other ideological idioms are part of the way we 'live' our material conditions, not just the bad dream or disposable effluence of the infrastructure. But the case holds even less if we keep to the broader sense of consciousness, since without it there would be no distinctively human activity at all. Factory labour is not a set of material practices plus a set of notions about it; without certain embodied intentions, meanings, interpretations, it would not count as factory labour at all.

It is necessary, then, to distinguish two rather different cases which *The German Ideology* threatens to conflate. On the one hand, there is a general materialist thesis that ideas and material activity are inseparably bound up together, as against the idealist tendency to isolate and privilege the former. On the other hand, there is the *historical* materialist argument that certain historically specific forms of consciousness become separated out from productive activity, and can best be explained in terms of their functional role in sustaining it. In *The German Ideology*, it is occasionally as though Marx and Engels illicitly fold the latter case into the former, viewing 'what men and women actually do' as a kind of 'base', and their ideas about what they do as a sort of 'superstructure'. But the relation between my act of frying an egg and my conceptions about it is not the same as the relation between the economic activities of capitalist society and the rhetoric of parliamentary democracy. One might add that thinking, writing and imagining are of course just as much part of the 'real life-process' as digging ditches and subverting military juntas; and that if the phrase 'real life-process' is in this sense disablingly narrow in Marx and Engels's text it is also unhelpfully amorphous, undifferentiatedly spanning the whole of 'sensuous practice'.

At one point in their work, Marx and Engels would seem to conjure a chronological difference out of this distinction between two meanings of 'consciousness', when they remark that 'the production of ideas, of conceptions, of consciousness, is *at first* directly interwoven with the material activity and the material intercourse of men, the language of real life.'[8] What they have in mind here is the momentous historical event of the division of mental and manual labour. Once an economic surplus permits a minority of 'professional' thinkers to be released from the exigencies of labour, it becomes possible for consciousness to 'flatter' itself that it is in fact independent of material reality. 'From now on', Marx and Engels observe, 'consciousness is in a position to emancipate itself from the world and to proceed to the formation of "pure" theory, theology, philosophy, ethics, etc."[9] So it is as though one epistemological case holds true for societies predating the division of mental and manual labour, while another is appropriate to all subsequent history. This cannot of course be what they mean: the 'practical' consciousness of priests and philosophers will continue to be 'directly interwoven' with their material activity, even if the theoretical doctrines they produce are loftily aloof from it. The important point, however, is that the schism between ideas and social reality explored by the text is, so to speak, a dislocation internal to social reality itself, in specific historical conditions. It may be an illusion to believe that ideas are the essence of social life; but it is not an illusion to believe that they are relatively autonomous of it, since this is itself a material fact with particular social determinations. And once this condition has set in, it provides the real material basis for the former ideological error. It is not just that ideas have floated free of social existence, perhaps on account of the hubris of a handful of intellectuals; on the contrary, this 'externality' of ideas to the material life-process is itself *internal* to that process.

The German Ideology appears at once to argue that consciousness is indeed always 'practical' consciousness, so that to view it in any other light is an idealist illusion; *and* that ideas are sheerly secondary to material existence. It therefore needs a kind of imagery which equivocates between seeing consciousness as indissociable from action, and regarding it as separable and 'inferior'; and it finds this in the language of 'reflexes', 'echoes' and 'sublimates'. A reflex is in one sense part of what it reflects, as my image in the mirror is in some sense me, and at the same time a secondary, 'second best' phenomenon. *Why* Marx and Engels want to relegate consciousness to this second-hand status is clear enough; for if what we think we are doing is actually constitutive of what we are doing, if our conceptions are internal to our practice, what room does this leave for false consciousness? Is it enough to ask George Bush what he thinks he is doing to arrive at a satisfactory account of his role within advanced capitalism? Marx and Engels see well enough that human agents are often for good historical reasons self-deceived as to the significance of their own actions; I have no unfailingly privileged access to the meaning of my own behaviour, and you can sometimes supply me with a more cogent explanation of it than I can produce myself. But it does not follow from this that there is something called 'what we do' which is independent of meanings altogether. For an action to be a human practice, it must incarnate meaning; but its more general significance is not necessarily the one the agent ascribes to it. When Marx and Engels speak of setting out from 'real, active men' rather than from what these 'men' say, imagine and conceive, they sail perilously close to a naive sensuous empiricism which fails to grasp that there is no 'real life-process' without interpretation. To attempt to 'suspend' this realm of meaning in order the better to examine 'real' conditions would be like killing a patient to examine more conveniently the circulation of her blood. As Raymond Williams has commented, this 'objectivist fantasy' presumes that real life conditions 'can be known independently of language and of historical records'. It is not, Williams observes, as though there is '*first* material social life and *then*, at some temporal or spatial distance, consciousness and "its" products ... consciousness and its products are always, though in variable forms, parts of the material social process itself'.[10] Marx and Engels's hypnotic insistence on terms like 'real', 'sensuous, 'actual', 'practical', briskly and scornfully contrasted with mere 'ideas', makes them a sound a little like F.R. Leavis on a bad day. And just as they cannot ignore interpretation in the case of the men and women they discuss, neither can they overlook it in their own case. For although they claim in empiricist vein to have no premisses of their own other than that of starting from 'real men', it is of course clear enough that what counts for them as real is by no means innocent of theoretical assumptions. In this sense too, the 'real life-process' is bound up with 'consciousness': that of the analysts themselves.

We need, however, to look rather more closely at the metaphor of 'inversion' which controls much of this account of ideology. It should be noted first of all that to invert a polarity is not necessarily to transform it. Little is to be gained by upending idealism into mechanical materialism, making thought a function of reality rather than vice versa. Ironically enough, this gesture mimes idealism in the act of upbraiding it, since a thought reduced to a 'reflex' or 'sublimate' is quite as immaterial as one sequestered from reality. The celebrated *camera obscura* image is telling here, suggesting as it does that the Hegelians have simply got the world the wrong way up. The image itself has a history stretching back to the father of empiricist philosophy John Locke, who like many others saw the *camera obscura* as a prototype of exact, scientific reflection. It is thus ironic, as W.J.T. Mitchell points out, that Marx should use this same device as the very model of illusion.[11] Yet the empiricist history behind the metaphor is retained in Marx's deployment of it: the human mind is like a camera, passively recording objects in the external world. Given the assumption that the camera cannot lie, the only way in which it *could* generate distortion would be by some kind of built-in interference with the image. For this camera has no operator, and we therefore cannot speak of ideology on this model as an *active* slanting, editing and misinterpreting of social reality, as we could, say, in the case of the hand-held camera of the news photographer. The implication of the metaphor, then, is that idealism is really a kind of inverted empiricism. Instead of deriving ideas from reality, it derives reality from ideas. But this is surely a caricature of philosophical idealism, one partly determined by the image in question. For the thinkers whom Marx and Engels are seeking to combat are not just topsy-turvy empiricists or capsized mechanical materialists: on the contrary, one of the most valuable aspects of their theory for Marxism itself is that human consciousness is an active, dynamic force. Marxist thinkers as diverse as Lenin and Lukács will later turn this notion to revolutionary ends; but the *camera obscura* model is really unable to accommodate it. This distinctly uninnocent figure forces idealism into its own empiricist mould, defining it as its mere opposite.

This blindspot has disabling effects on the text's overall theory of ideology. For it is hard to see on this account how ideology can be in any sense an active social force, organizing the experience of human subjects in accordance with the requirements of a specific social order. Its effects, instead, would seem almost entirely negative: it is merely a set of chimeras which perpetuate that order by *distracting* its citizens from otherwise palpable inequality and injustice. Ideology here is essentially *otherworldliness*: an imaginary resolution of real contradictions which blinds men and women to the harsh actuality of their social conditions. Its function is less to equip them with certain discourses of value and belief relevant to their daily tasks, than to denigrate that whole quotidian realm in contrast with a fantasized metaphysical world. It is as though ideology has no particular interest in, say, inculcating the virtues of thrift, honesty and industriousness in the working class by a range of disciplinary techniques, but simply denies that the sphere of work has much significance at all in contrast with the kingdom of heaven or the Absolute Idea. And whether any regime could reproduce itself by dint of an ideology as generalized and negative as this is surely questionable.

W.J.T. Mitchell has pointed out that one implication of the *camera obscura* figure is of a pure, unmediated relation between human subjects and their social environment, and that this emphasis is clearly at odds with what the text has to say elsewhere about consciousness as a social product.[12] Indeed, as Mitchell observes, the assumption that the sensuous world is given directly to consciousness is part of what the authors of *The German Ideology* criticize elsewhere in the work of Feuerbach. Marx and Engels, in other words, tend to counterpose a doctrine of the socially constructed nature of knowledge against a naive sensuous empiricism, and a naive sensuous empiricism against idealism's insistence on the discursively mediated nature of reality. At one level, they perpetuate in transformed mode the 'ideology' of the Enlightenment, reducing ideas to sensational life – though that life is now firmly defined as practical, social and productive. At another level, from a wholly opposed political perspective, they share in Napoleon's brisk pragmatic contempt for 'ideology', in the sense of a fantastical idealism.

For *The German Ideology*, ideological consciousness would seem to involve a double movement of *inversion* and *dislocation*. Ideas are assigned priority in social life, and simultaneously disconnected from it. One can follow the logic of this dual operation easily enough: to make ideas the source of history is to deny their social determinants, and so to uncouple them from history. But it is not clear that such an inversion need always entail such a dislocation. One could imagine someone holding that consciousness was autonomous of material life without necessarily believing that it was its foundation; and one can equally imagine someone asserting that mind was the essence of all reality without claiming that it was isolated from it. In fact the latter position is probably that of Hegel himself. Does ideology essentially consist in seeing ideas as socially determining, or in regarding them as autonomous? An ideologue like de Tracy might be said to hold to the former case, but not to the latter. Marx himself thought the French ideologues were idealists, in so far as they dehistoricized human consciousness and ascribed it a foundational social role; but they are plainly not idealists in the sense of believing that ideas drop from the sky. There is a problem, in other words, about how far this model of ideology can be generalized as a paradigm of all false consciousness. Marx and Engels are of course examining the *German* ideology, a particular current of neo-Hegelian idealism, but their formulations have often enough a universalizing flavour about them. In fact – in a deleted passage of the work – they remark that what is true of German thought is true of other nations too. The obvious riposte to this, as Marx and Engels in other moods well knew, is that not all ideology is idealist. Marx certainly regarded Hobbes, Condillac and Bentham as full-blooded ideologists, yet all three are in some sense materialists. Only in a broad sense of 'idealism', meaning in effect *dehistoricizing* or presuming some invariable human essence, can they be said to be guilty of the charge. But to dehistoricize is not synonymous with being an idealist, just as, conversely, an idealism such as Hegel's is profoundly historical.

Is it not possible that certain ideas may have a firm root in material reality, yet still be ideological? *Must* ideas be empty illusions to qualify for ideological status? Marx and Engels do not of course assume that any old abstract idea is ideological: mathematical concepts are not usually so. But the disconnectedness of thought from practical existence, in ways which serve objectionable political ends, would seem for them definitive of the notion. There is then a strong temptation to believe that we have only to put ideas and reality back together again for all to be well. This is not, of course, Marx and Engels's own case: to overcome false consciousness demands tackling the social contradictions which generate it, not simply reuniting abstruse ideas with their lost social origins. But in the hands of somewhat more 'vulgar' Marxists, there is sometimes a suggestion that ideas are in a healthy state when closely imbricated with social practice. The objection to this is that Edmund Burke would have found it entirely unobjectionable. A whole lineage of conservative thought has turned on the 'organic' interpenetration of conceptual thought and lived experience, as nervous as Marx and Engels themselves of purely speculative notions. It is then possible to imagine that ideology is not particular kinds of ideas with specific functions and effects, but just ideas which have somehow come unstuck from sensuous reality.

'The ideas of the ruling class', *The German Ideology* famously proclaims, 'are in every epoch the ruling ideas, i.e. the class which is the ruling *material* force of society, is at the same time its ruling *intellectual* force.'[13] He who dominates material production controls mental production too. But this *political* model of ideology does not entirely square with the more epistemological conception of it as thought oblivious to its social origin. What is it, then, that makes ideas ideological? That they are cut loose from their social moorings, or that they are weapons of a dominant class? And does the latter necessarily entail the former? 'The ruling ideas', the text goes on to comment, 'are nothing more than the ideal expression of the dominant material relationships, the dominant material relationships grasped as ideas.'[14] This would suggest a more 'internal' relation between ideology and material life than the 'illusion' model perhaps permits; but elsewhere the work runs both emphases together by speaking of these ruling ideas as 'merely the *illusory* forms in which the real struggles of the different classes are fought out.'[15] Yet if these forms encode real struggles, in what sense are they illusory? Perhaps in the sense that they are purely 'phenomenal' modes concealing ulterior motivations; yet *this* sense of 'illusory' need not be synonymous with 'false'. Appearances, as Lenin reminds us, are after all real enough; there may be a *discrepancy* between material conflicts and the ideological forms which express them, but this does not necessarily mean that those forms are either false (untrue to what is the case) or 'unreal'.

The text, in other words, hesitates significantly between a political and an epistemological definition of ideology. Ideas may be said to be ideological because they deny their roots in social life with politically oppressive effects; or they may be ideological for exactly the opposite reason – that they are the direct expressions of material interests, real instruments of class warfare. It so happens that Marx and Engels are confronting a ruling class whose consciousness is heavily 'metaphysical' in character; and since this metaphysic is put to politically dominative uses, the two opposed senses of ideology are at one in the historical situation *The German Ideology* examines. But there is no reason to suppose that *all* ruling classes need to inflect their interests in such a speculative style. Later on, in the *Preface* to the *Contribution to a Critique of Political Economy* (1859), Marx will write of 'the legal, political, religious, aesthetic, or philosophic – in short, ideological forms in which men become conscious of this (economic) conflict and fight it out.' The reference to *illusory* forms, significantly, has here been dropped; there is no particular suggestion that these 'superstructural' modes are in any sense chimerical or fantastic. The definition of ideology, we may note, has also been widened to encompass *all* 'men', rather than just the governing class; ideology has now the rather less pejorative sense of the class struggle at the level of ideas, with no necessary implication that these ideas are always false. In fact in *Theories of Surplus Value* Marx draws a distinction between what he calls 'the ideological component parts of the ruling class' and the 'free spiritual production of this particular social formation', one instance of the latter being art and poetry.

The *Preface* to *A Contribution to the Critique of Political Economy* lays out the famous (or notorious) Marxist formulation of 'base' and 'superstructure', and seems to locate ideology firmly within the latter:

> In the social production of their life, men enter into definite relations that are indispensable and independent of their will, relations of production that correspond to a definite stage of development of their material productive forces. The sum total of these relations of production constitutes the economic structure of society, the real foundation, on which rises a legal and political superstructure and to which correspond definite forms of social consciousness. The mode of production of material life conditions the social, political and intellectual life process in general. It is not the consciousness of men that determines their being but, on the contrary, their social being that determines their consciousness.[16]

We can take it, perhaps, that 'definite forms of social consciousness' is equivalent to ideology, though the equation is not unproblematic. There could be forms of social consciousness which were non-ideological, either in the sense of not helping to legitimate class-rule, or in the sense that they were not particularly central to any form of power-struggle. Marxism itself is a form of social consciousness, but whether it is an ideology depends on which meaning of the term one has in mind. Marx clearly has in mind here specific historical belief-systems and 'world views'; and, as I have argued in the case of *The German Ideology*, it is rather more plausible to see consciousness in *this* sense as determined by material practice, rather than consciousness in its wider sense of meanings, values, intentions and the rest. It is hard to see how *that* can be simply 'superstructural', if it is actually internal to material production.

But if Marx is speaking historically here, what are we to make of the final sentence of the quotation? 'It is not the consciousness of men that determines their being but, on the contrary, their social being that determines their consciousness'. This is an ontological, not just an historical, claim; it follows for Marx from the way the human animal is constituted, and would be true of all men and women in all historical epochs. One effect of this properly universalizing doctrine is to make the 'base–superstructure' thesis with which it sits cheek by jowl appear to be universal too. Not all Marxists, however, have taken this view; and whether Marx himself did elsewhere in his work is a matter of debate. For we can always raise the question: why does human productive activity *need* a superstructure? And one answer to that question would be: because in all history to date it has involved exploitative social relations, which must then be ratified and regulated in legal, political and ideological terms. A superstructure is necessary because the material base is self-divided. And were it to overcome those divisions, so some Marxists have contended, the superstructure would wither away. In a full communist society, so the argument goes, there would no longer be any need for a political state which set itself over against civil society, or for a legitimating ruling ideology, or even for the paraphernalia of an abstract 'legality'.

Implicit in the notion of a superstructure, in other words, is the idea of certain institutions which are *estranged* from material life, set over against it as a dominative force. Whether such institutions – law courts, the political state, ideological apparatuses – could in fact ever be abolished, or whether such a claim is idly utopian, is not the point to pursue here. What is rather at issue is the apparent contradiction between this *historical* version of the base-superstructure doctrine, which would see the superstructure as functional for the regulation of class struggle, and the more universal implications of Marx's comment about consciousness and social being. On the former model, ideology has a limited historical life-span: once the contradictions of class society had been surmounted, it would wither away along with the rest of the superstructure. On the latter version, ideology might be taken to mean something like the way the whole of our consciousness is conditioned by material factors. And *this* will presumably not change with the establishment of full communism, since it is just as much a part of our biological make-up as the need to eat. The twin emphases of the quoted passage, then, point respectively towards the narrower and the broader senses of ideology that we have examined already; but the relationship between them is not exactly clear. A political case is caught up, somewhat obscurely, with an ontological or epistemological one: is a superstructure (and ideology along with it) a historically functional phenomenon, or is it as natural to human societies as breathing?

The base-superstructure doctrine has been widely attacked for being static, hierarchical, dualistic and mechanistic, even in those more sophisticated accounts of it in which the superstructure reacts back dialectically to condition the material base. It might therefore be timely and suitably unfashionable to enter a word or two in its defence. Let us be clear first what it is *not* asserting. It is not out to argue that prisons and parliamentary democracy, school rooms and sexual fantasies, are any less *real* than steel mills or sterling. Churches and cinemas are quite as material as coal mines; it is just that, on this argument, they cannot be the ultimate catalysts of revolutionary social change. The point of the base-superstructure doctrine lies in the question of determinations – of what 'level' of social life most powerfully and crucially conditions the others, and therefore of what arena of activity would be most relevant to effecting a thoroughgoing social transformation.

To select material production as this crucial determinant is in one sense to do no more than state the obvious. For there is surely no doubt that this is what the vast majority of men and women throughout history have spent their time engaged on. A socialist is just someone who is unable to get over his or her astonishment that most people who have lived and died have spent lives of wretched, fruitless, unremitting toil. Arrest history at any point whatsoever, and this is what we will find. The sheer struggle for material survival and reproduction, in conditions of real or artificially induced scarcity, has tied up such enormous resources of human energy that we would surely expect to find its traces inscribed in the rest of what we do. Material production, then, is 'primary' in the sense that it forms the major narrative of history to date; but it is primary also in the sense that without *this* particular narrative, no other story would ever get off the ground. Such production is the precondition of the whole of our thought. The base-superstructure model, to be sure, claims more than just this: it asserts not only that material production is the precondition of our other activities, but that it is the most fundamental *determinant* of them. 'Food first, morals later' is only a statement of the doctrine if some causal efficacy of food upon morals is being suggested. It is not just a question of priorities. How then is this determinacy best to be grasped?

'Superstructure' is a *relational* term. It designates the way in which certain social institutions act as 'supports' of the dominant social relations. It invites us to contextualize such institutions in a certain way – to consider them in their functional relations to a ruling social power. What is misleading, in my view at least, is to leap from this 'adjectival' sense of the term to a substantive – to a fixed, given 'realm' of institutions which form 'the superstructure', and which includes, say, film. Are cinemas superstructural phenomena? The answer is sometimes yes and sometimes no. There may be aspects of a particular movie which underwrite the given power relations, and which are to that extent 'superstructural'. But there may be other aspects of it which do not. An institution may behave 'superstructurally' at one point in time, but not at another, or in some of its activities but not in others. You can examine a literary text in terms of its publishing history, in which case, as far as the Marxist model goes, you are treating it as part of the material base of social production. Or you can count up the number of semicolons, an activity which would seem to fit neatly into neither level of the model. But once you explore that text's relations to a dominant ideology, then you are treating it superstructurally. The doctrine, in other words, becomes rather more plausible when it is viewed less as an ontological carving of the world down the middle than as a question of different perspectives. If it is doubtful whether Marx and Engels themselves would have agreed with this reformulation of their thesis, it is also doubtful in my view whether it matters much.

So far, then, we seem to be landed by Marx with at least three contending senses of ideology, with no very clear idea of their interrelations. Ideology can denote illusory or socially disconnected beliefs which see themselves as the ground of history, and which by distracting men and women from their actual social conditions (including the social determinants of their ideas), serve to sustain an oppressive political power. The opposite of this would be an accurate, unbiased knowledge of practical social conditions. Alternatively, ideology can signify those ideas which directly express the material interests of the dominant social class, and which are useful in promoting its rule. The opposite of this might be either true scientific knowledge, or the conscious-ness of the non-dominant classes. Finally, ideology can be stretched to encompass all of the conceptual forms in which the class struggle as a whole is fought out, which would presumably include the valid consciousness of politically revolutionary forces. What the opposite of *this* might be is presumably any conceptual form not currently caught up in such struggle.

As if all this were not enough, Marx's later economic writing will come up with a quite different version of ideology, to which we can now turn.

In his chapter on 'The Fetishism of Commodities' in Volume One of *Capital* (1867), Marx argues that in capitalist society the actual social relations between human beings are governed by the apparently autonomous inter-actions of the commodities they produce:

A commodity, therefore, is a mysterious thing, simply because in it the social character of men's labour appears to them as an objective character stamped upon the product of that labour; because the relation of the producers to the sum total of their own labour is presented to them as a social relation, existing not between themselves, but between the products of their labour.... It is a definite social relation between men, that assumes, in their eyes, the fantastic form of a relation between things. In order ... to find an analogy, we must have recourse to the mist-enveloped regions of the religious world. In that world, the productions of the human brain appear as independent beings endowed with life, and entering into relations both with one another and with the human race. So it is in the world of commodities with the products of men's hands.[17]

The earlier theme of alienation is here extended: men and women fashion products which then come to escape their control and determine their conditions of existence. A fluctuation on the stock exchange can mean unemployment for thousands. By virtue of this 'commodity fetishism', real human relations appear, mystifyingly, as relations between things; and this has several consequences of an ideological kind. First, the real workings of society are thereby veiled and occluded: the social character of labour is concealed behind the circulation of commodities, which are no longer recognizable as social products. Secondly – though this is a point developed only by the later Marxist tradition – society is fragmented by this commodity logic: it is no longer easy to grasp it as a totality, given the atomizing operations of the commodity, which transmutes the collective activity of social labour into relations between dead, discrete things. And by ceasing to appear as a totality, the capitalist order renders itself less vulnerable to political critique. Finally, the fact that social life is dominated by *inanimate* entities lends it a spurious air of naturalness and inevitability: society is no longer perceptible as a human construct, and therefore as humanly alterable.

It is clear, then, that the motif of inversion passes over from Marx's early comments on ideology to his 'mature' work. Several things, however, have decisively altered in transit. To begin with, this curious inversion between human subjects and their conditions of existence is now inherent in social reality itself. It is not simply a question of the distorted perception of human beings, who invert the real world in their consciousness and thus *imagine* that commodities control their lives. Marx is not claiming that under capitalism commodities *appear* to exercise a tyrannical sway over social relations; he is arguing that they actually do. Ideology is now less a matter of reality becoming inverted in the mind, than of the mind reflecting a real inversion. In fact it is no longer primarily a question of *consciousness* at all, but is anchored in the day-to-day economic operations of the capitalist system. And if this is so then ideology has been, so to speak, transferred from the superstructure to the base, or at least signals some peculiarly close relation between them. It is a function of the capitalist economy itself, which as Alex Callinicos observes 'produces its own misperception',[18] rather than in the first place a matter of discourses, beliefs and 'superstructural' institutions. We need, then, as Etienne Balibar puts it, 'to think both the real and the imaginary within ideology',[19] rather than conceiving of these realms as simply external to one another.

Elsewhere in *Capital*, Marx argues that there is a disjunction in capitalism between how things actually are and how they present themselves –

between, in Hegelian terms, 'essences' and 'phenomena'. The wage relation, for example, is in reality an unequal, exploitative affair; but it 'naturally' presents itself as an equal, reciprocal exchange of so much money for so much labour. As Jorge Larrain usefully summarizes these dislocations:

> Circulation, for instance, appears as that which is immediately present on the surface of bourgeois society, but its immediate being is pure semblance.... Profit is a phenomenal form of surplus-value which has the virtue of obscuring the real basis of its existence. Competition is a phenomenon which conceals the determination of value by labour-time. The value-relation between commodities disguises a definite social relation between men. The wage-form extinguishes every trace of the division of the working-day into necessary labour and surplus labour, and so on.[20]

Once again, all this is not in the first place a question of some misperceiving consciousness: it is rather that there is a kind of dissembling or duplicity built into the very economic structures of capitalism, such that it cannot help presenting itself to consciousness in ways askew to what it actually is. Mystification, so to speak, is an 'objective' fact, embedded in the very character of the system: there is an unavoidable structural contradiction between that system's real contents, and the phenomenal forms in which those contents proffer themselves spontaneously to the mind. As Norman Geras has written: 'There exists, at the interior of capitalism, a kind of internal rupture between the social relations which obtain and the manner in which they are experienced.'[21] And if this is so, then ideology cannot spring in the first instance from the consciousness of a dominant class, still less from some sort of conspiracy. As John Mepham puts the point: ideology is now not a matter of the *bourgeoisie*, but of *bourgeois society*.[24]

In the case of commodity fetishism, the mind reflects an inversion in reality itself; and there are thorny theoretical problems about what an 'inversion in reality' could possibly mean. In the case of some other capitalist economic processes, however, the mind reflects a phenomenal form which is itself an inversion of the real. For the sake of explication, we can break this operation down into three distinct moments. First, some kind of inversion takes place in the real world: instead of living labour employing inanimate capital, for example, dead capital controls live labour. Secondly, there is a disjunction or contradiction between this real state of affairs, and the way it 'phenomenally' appears: in the wage contract, the outward form rectifies the inversion, to make the relations between labour and capital seem equal and symmetrical. In a third moment, this phenomenal form is obediently reflected by the mind, and this is how ideological consciousness is bred. Note that whereas in *The German Ideology* ideology was a matter of not seeing things as they really were, it is a question in *Capital* of reality itself being duplicitous and deceitful. Ideology can thus no longer be unmasked simply by a clear-eyed attention to the 'real life-process', since that process, rather like the Freudian unconscious, puts out a set of semblances which are somehow structural to it, includes its falsity within its truth. What is needed instead is 'science' – for science, as Marx comments, becomes necessary once essences and appearances fail to coincide. We would not require scientific labour if the law of physics were spontaneously apparent to us, inscribed on the bodies of the objects around us.

The advantage of this new theory of ideology over the case pressed in *The German Ideology* is surely clear. Whereas ideology in the earlier work appeared as idealist speculation, it is now given a secure grounding in the material practices of bourgeois society. It is no longer wholly reducible to false consciousness: the idea of falsity lingers on in the notion of deceptive appearances, but these are less fictions of the mind than structural effects of capitalism. If capitalist reality folds its own falsehood within itself, then this falsehood must be somehow real. And there are ideological effects such as commodity fetishism which are by no means unreal, however much they may involve mystification. One might feel, however, that if *The German Ideology* risks relegating ideological forms to a realm of unreality, the later work of Marx pulls them a little too close to reality for comfort. Have we not merely replaced a potential *idealism* of ideology with an incipient *economism* of it? Is all that we dub ideology really reducible to the economic operations of capitalism? Georg Lukács will claim later that 'there is no problem that does not ultimately lead back to [the] question [of commodity production]; and that this structure 'permeat[es] every expression of life';[23] but one might find the claim a trifle overweening. In what important sense, for instance, can the doctrine that men are superior to women, or whites to blacks, be traced back to some secret source in commodity production? And what are we to say of the ideological formations of societies to which commodity production is as yet unknown, or not yet central? A certain essentialism of ideology would seem at play here, reducing the variety of ideological mechanisms and effects to a homogeneous cause. Moreover, if the capitalist economy has its own built-in devices of deception – if, as Theodor Adorno somewhere remarks, 'the commodity is its own ideology' – what need is there for specifically ideological institutions at the level of the 'super-structure'? Perhaps just to reinforce effects already endemic in the economy; but the answer is surely a little lame. Marx may well have discovered one potent source of false consciousness in bourgeois society; but whether this can be generalized to account for ideology as a whole is surely questionable. In what sense, for example, is this view of ideology tied up with class struggle? The theory of commodity fetishism forges a dramatically immediate link between capitalist productive activity and human conscious-ness, between the economic and the experiential; but it does so, one might claim, only by short-circuiting the level of the specifically political. Are all social classes indifferently in the grip of commodity fetishism? Do workers, peasants and capitalists all share the same ideological universe, universally imprinted as they are by the material structures of capitalism?

Marx's case in the 'Fetishism of Commodities' chapter would seem to retain two dubious features from his earlier version of ideology: its empiricism, and its negativism. *Capital* appears to argue that our perception (or misperception) of reality is somehow already immanent in reality itself; and this belief, that the real already contains the knowledge or mis-knowledge of itself, is arguably an empiricist doctrine. What it suppresses is precisely the business of what human agents *make*, variably and conflictively, of these material mechanisms – of how they discursively construct and interpret them in accordance with particular interests and beliefs. Human subjects figure here as the mere passive recipients of certain objective effects, the dupes of a social structure given spontaneously to their consciousness. The philosopher Ludwig Wittgenstein is said to have enquired of a colleague why people considered it more natural to hold that the sun moved round the earth rather than vice versa. On being told that it simply *looked* that way, he enquired what it would look like if the earth moved round the sun. The point, of course, is that one does not here simply derive an error from the nature of the appearances, for the appearances are in both cases the same.

If the later theory also reproduces the negativism of *The German Ideology*, it is because ideology would once more seem to have no other purpose than to *conceal* the truth of class society. It is less an active force in the constitution of human subjectivity than a mask or screen which prevents an already constituted subject from grasping what lies in front of it. And this, whatever partial truth it may contain, surely fails to account for the real power and complexity of ideological formations.

Marx himself never used the phrase 'false consciousness', a distinction which must be accorded instead to his collaborator Frederick Engels. In a letter to Franz Mehring of 1893, Engels speaks of ideology as a process of false consciousness because 'the real motives impelling [the agent] remain unknown to him, otherwise it would not be an ideological process at all. Hence he imagines false or apparent motives.' Ideology is here in effect rationalization – a kind of double motivation, in which the surface meaning serves to block from consciousness the subject's true purpose. It is perhaps not surprising that this definition of ideology should have arisen in the age of Freud. As Joe McCarney has argued, the falsehood at stake here is a matter of self-deception, not of getting the world wrong.[24] There is no reason to suppose that the surface belief necessarily involves empirical falsity, or is in any sense 'unreal'. Someone really may love animals, while being unaware that his benign authority over them compensates for a lack of power within the labour process. Engels goes on in his letter to add the familiar rider from *The German Ideology* about 'autonomous' thought; but it is not evident why all those who are deceived about their own motives should be victims of a gullible trust in 'pure thought'. What Engels means is that in the process of rationalization the true motive stands to the apparent one as the 'real life-process' stands to the illusory idea in the earlier model. But in that model, the ideas in question were also often false 'in themselves', metaphysical delusions with no root in reality, whereas the apparent motive in rationalization may be authentic enough.

Towards the end of the nineteenth century, in the period of the Second International, ideology continues to retain the sense of false consciousness, in contrast to a 'scientific socialism' which has discerned the true laws of historical development. Ideology, according to Engels in *Anti-Dühring*, can then be seen as the 'deduction of reality not from itself but from a concept'[25] – a formulation which it is hard to make much sense of. Lurking on the edges of this particular definition, however, is a broader sense of ideology as any kind of socially determined thought, which is really too elastic to be of much use. For the Marx of *The German Ideology*, all thought is socially determined, but ideology is thought which *denies* this determination, or rather thought so socially determined as to deny its own determinants. But a new current is also stirring in this period, which picks up on the later Marx's sense of ideology as the mental forms within which men and women fight out their social conflicts, and which thus begins to speak boldly of 'socialist ideology', a phrase which for *The German Ideology* would have been oxymoronic. The revisionist Marxist Eduard Bernstein was the first to dub Marxism itself an ideology, and in *What Is To Be Done?* we find Lenin declaring that 'the *only* choice is – either bourgeois or socialist ideology'. Socialism, Lenin writes, is 'the ideology of struggle of the proletarian class'; but he does not mean by this that socialism is the spontaneous expression of proletarian consciousness. On the contrary, 'in the class struggle of the proletariat which develops spontaneously, as an elemental force, on the basis of capitalist relations, socialism is *introduced* by the ideologues.'[26] Ideology, in short, has now become identical with the scientific theory of historical materialism, and we have returned full circle to the Enlightenment *philosophes*. The 'ideologist' is no longer one floundering in false consciousness but the exact reverse, the scientific analyst of the fundamental laws of society and its thought formations.

The situation, in short, is now thoroughly confused. Ideology would now seem to denote simultaneously false consciousness (Engels), all socially conditioned thought (Plekhanov), the political crusade of socialism (Bernstein and sometimes Lenin), and the scientific theory of socialism (Lenin). It is not hard to see how these confusions have come about. They stem in effect from the equivocation we noted in the work of Marx between ideology as illusion, and ideology as the intellectual armoury of a social class. Or, to put it another way, they reflect a conflict between the epistemological and political meanings of the term. In the second sense of the word, what matters is not the character of the beliefs in question, but their function and perhaps their origin; and there is thus no reason why these beliefs should necessarily be false in themselves. True conceptions can be put to the service of a dominant power. The falsity of ideology in this context, then, is the 'falsity' of class rule itself; but here, crucially, the term 'false' has shifted ground from its epistemological to its ethical sense. Once one has adopted this definition, however, the path is then open to extending the term ideology to proletarian class consciousness too, since that is also a matter of deploying ideas for political purposes. And if ideology thus comes to mean any system of doctrines expressive of class interests and serviceable in their realization, there is no reason why it should not, *à la* Lenin, be used of Marxism itself.

As the meaning of ideology mutates in this way, so, inevitably, does whatever is held to be its opposite. For *The German Ideology*, the opposite of ideology would seem to be seeing reality as it actually is; for *Capital* things are not so simple, since that reality, as we have seen, is now intrinsically treacherous, and there is thus the need for a special discourse known as science to penetrate its phenomenal forms and lay bare its essences. Once ideology shifts from its epistemological to its more political sense, there are now two candidates available as its antithesis, and the relations between them are deeply fraught. What can counter the dominant ideology is either the science of historical materialism, or proletarian class consciousness. For 'historicist' Marxism, as we shall see in the next chapter, the former is essentially an 'expression' of the latter: Marxist theory is the fullest self-consciousness of the revolutionary working class. For Leninism, ideology in the sense of 'scientific theory' must maintain a certain enabling distance from ideology in the sense of proletarian class consciousness, in order to intervene creatively within it.

But the wider meaning of ideology as any form of socially determined thought intervenes to interrogate this distinction. If all thought is socially determined, then so too must be Marxism, in which case what becomes of its claims to scientific objectivity? Yet if these claims are simply dropped, how are we to adjudicate between the truth of Marxism and the truth of the belief systems it opposes? Would not the opposite of the ruling ideology then be simply an alternative ideology, and on what rational grounds would we choose between them? We are sliding, in short, into the mire of historical relativism; but the only alternative to that would appear to be some form of positivism or scientific rationalism which repressed its own enabling historical conditions, and so was ideological in all the worst ways outlined by *The German Ideology*. What if, in the most striking irony of all, Marxism itself has ended up as a prime example of the very forms of metaphysical or transcendental thought it set out to discredit, trusting to a scientific rationalism which floated disinterestedly above history?

4

FROM LUKÁCS TO GRAMSCI

TO THINK of Marxism as the scientific analysis of social formations, and to think of it as ideas in active struggle, will tend to yield two quite different epistemologies. In the former case, consciousness is essentially contemplative, seeking to 'match' or 'correspond to' its object in the greatest possible accuracy of cognition. In the latter case, consciousness is much more obviously *part* of social reality, a dynamic force in its potential transformation. And if this is so, then to a thinker like Georg Lukács it would not seem entirely appropriate to speak of whether such thought 'reflects' or 'fits' the history with which it is inseparably bound up.

If consciousness is grasped in this way as a transformative force at one with the reality it seeks to change, then there would seem to be no 'space' between it and that reality in which false consciousness might germinate. Ideas cannot be 'untrue' to their object if they are actually part of it. In the terms of the philosopher J.L. Austin, we can speak of a 'constative' utterance, one which aims to describe the world, as either true or false; but it would not make sense to speak of a 'performative' statement as either correctly or incorrectly 'reflecting' reality. I am not *describing* anything when I promise to take you to the theatre, or curse you for spilling ink on my shirt. If I ceremonially name a ship, or stand with you before a clergyman and say 'I do', these are material events in reality, acts as efficacious as ironing my socks, not 'pictures' of some state of affairs which could be said to be accurate or mistaken.

Does this mean, then, that the model of consciousness as *cognitive* (or miscognitive) should be ousted by an image of consciousness as *performative*? Not exactly: for it is clear that this opposition can be to some degree deconstructed. There is no point in my promising to take you to the theatre if the theatre in question was closed down for gross obscenity last week and I am unaware of the fact. My act of cursing is empty if what I thought was an ink stain on my shirt is just part of the floral design. All 'performative' acts involve cognition of some kind, implicate some sense of how the world actually is; it is futile for a political group to hone its ideas in the struggle with some oppressive power if the power in question collapsed three years ago and they simply have not noticed.

In his great work *History and Class Consciousness* (1922), the Hungarian Marxist Georg Lukács takes full account of this point. 'It is true', Lukács writes there, 'that reality is the criterion for the correctness of thought. But reality is not, it becomes – and to become the participation of thought is needed.'[1] Thought, we might say, is at once cognitive and creative: in the act of understanding its real conditions, an oppressed group or class has begun in that very moment to fashion the forms of consciousness which will contribute to changing them. And this is why no simple 'reflection' model of consciousness will really do. 'Thought and existence', Lukács writes, 'are not identical in the sense that they "correspond" to each other, or "reflect" each other, that they "run parallel" to each other or "coincide" with each other (all expressions that conceal a rigid duality). Their identity is that they are aspects of one and the same real historical and dialectical process.'[2] The cognition of the revolutionary proletariat, for Lukács, is part of the situation it cognizes, and alters that situation at a stroke. If this logic is pressed to an extreme, then it would seem that we never simply know some 'thing', since our act of knowing it has already transformed it into something else. The model tacitly underlying this doctrine is that of *self*-knowledge; for to know myself is no longer to be the self that I was a moment before I knew it. It would seem, in any case, that this whole conception of consciousness as essentially active, practical and dynamic, which Lukács owes to the work of Hegel, will force us to revise any too simplistic notion of false consciousness as some lag, gap or disjunction between the way things are and the way we know them.

Lukács takes over from aspects of the Second International the positive, non-pejorative sense of the word ideology, writing unembarrassedly for Marxism as 'the ideological expression of the proletariat'; and this is at least one reason why the widespread view that ideology for him is synonymous with false consciousness is simply mistaken. But he retains at the same time the whole conceptual apparatus of Marx's critique of commodity fetishism, and thus keeps alive a more critical sense of the term. The 'other' or opposite of ideology in this negative sense, however, is no longer primarily 'Marxist science' but the concept of *totality*; and one of the functions of this concept in his work is to allow him to ditch the idea of some disinterested social science without thereby falling prey to historical relativism. All forms of class consciousness are ideological; but some, so to speak, are more ideological than others. What is specifically ideological about the bourgeoisie is its inability to grasp the structure of the social formation as a whole, on account of the dire effects of reification. Reification fragments and dislocates our social experience, so that under its influence we forget that society is a collective process and come see it instead merely as this or that isolated object or institution. As Lukács's contemporary Karl Korsch argues, ideology is essentially a form of synecdoche, the figure of speech in which we take the part for the whole. What is peculiar to proletarian consciousness, in its fullest political development, is its capacity to 'totalize' the social order, for without such knowledge the working class will never be able to understand and transform its own conditions. A true recognition of its situation will be, inseparably, an insight into the social whole within which it is oppressively positioned; so that the moments in which the proletariat comes to self-consciousness, and knows the capitalist system for what it is, are in effect identical.

Science, truth or theory, in other words, are no longer to be strictly counterposed to ideology; on the contrary, they are just 'expressions' of a *particular* class ideology, the revolutionary world view of the working class. Truth is just bourgeois society coming to consciousness of itself as a whole, and the 'place' where this momentous event occurs is in the self-awareness of the proletariat. Since the proletariat is the prototypical commodity, forced to sell its labour power in order to survive, it can be seen as the 'essence' of a social order based on commodity fetishism; and the self-consciousness of the proletariat is therefore, as it were, the commodity form coming to an awareness of itself, and in that act transcending itself.

In coming to write *History and Class Consciousness*, Lukács found himself faced with a kind of Hobson's choice or impossible opposition. On the one hand, there was the positivist fantasy (inherited from the Second International) of a Marxist science which appeared to repress its own historical roots; on the other hand, there was the spectre of historical relativism. Either knowledge was sublimely external to the history it sought to know, or it was just a matter of this or that specific brand of historical consciousness, with no more firm grounding than that. Lukács's way of circumventing this dilemma is by introducing the category of *self-reflection*. There are certain forms of knowledge – notably, the *self*-knowledge of an exploited class – which while thoroughly historical are nevertheless able to lay bare the limits of other ideologies, and so to figure as an emancipatory force. Truth, in Lukács's 'historicist' perspective,[3] is always relative to a particular historical situation, never a metaphysical affair beyond history altogether; but the proletariat, uniquely, is so historically positioned as to be able in principle to unlock the secret of capitalism as a whole. There is thus no longer any need to remain trapped within the sterile antithesis of ideology as false or partial consciousness on the one hand, and science as some absolute, unhistorical mode of knowledge on the other. For not all class consciousness is false consciousness, and science is simply an expression or encodement of 'true' class consciousness.

Lukács's own way of phrasing this argument is unlikely to win much unqualified allegiance today. The proletariat, he claims, is a potentially 'universal' class, since it bears with it the potential emancipation of all humanity. Its consciousness is thus in principle universal; but a universal subjectivity is in effect identical with objectivity. So what the working class knows, from its own partial historical perspective, must be objectively true. One does not need to be persuaded by this rather grandly Hegelian language to rescue the important insight buried within it. Lukács sees quite rightly that the contrast between merely partial ideological standpoints on the one hand, and some dispassionate views of the social totality on the other, is radically misleading. For what this opposition fails to take into account is the situation of oppressed groups and classes, who need to get some view of the social system as a whole, and of their own place within it, simply to be able to realize their own partial, particular interests. If women are to emancipate themselves, they need to have an interest in understanding something of the general structures of patriarchy. Such understanding is by no means innocent or disinterested; on the contrary, it is in the service of pressing political interests. But without, as it were, passing over at some point from the particular to the general, those interests are likely to founder. A colonial people, simply to survive, may find itself 'forced' to enquire into the global structures of imperialism, as their imperialist rulers need not do. Those who today fashionably disown the need for a 'global' or 'total' perspective may be privileged enough to dispense with it. It is where such a totality bears urgently in on one's own immediate social conditions that the intersection between part and whole is most significantly established. Lukács's point is that certain groups and classes need to inscribe their own condition within a wider context if they are to change that condition; and in doing so they will find themselves challenging the consciousness of those who have an interest in blocking this emancipatory knowledge. It is in this sense that the bugbear of relativism is irrelevant: for to claim that all knowledge springs from a specific social standpoint is not to imply that any old social standpoint is as valuable for these purposes as any other. If what one is looking for is some understanding of the workings of imperialism as a whole, then one would be singularly ill-advised to consult the Governor General or the *Daily Telegraph*'s Africa correspondent, who will almost certainly deny its existence.

There is, however, a logical problem with Lukács's notion of some 'true' class consciousness. For if the working class is the potential bearer of such consciousness, from what viewpoint is *this* judgement made? It cannot be made from the viewpoint of the (ideal) proletariat itself, since this simply begs the question; but if only that viewpoint is true, then it cannot be made from some standpoint external to it either. As Bhikhu Parekh points out, to claim that only the proletarian perspective allows one to grasp the truth of society as a whole already assumes that one knows what that truth is.[4] It would seem that truth is either wholly internal to the consciousness of the working class, in which case it cannot be assessed *as* truth and the claim becomes simply dogmatic; or one is caught in the impossible paradox of judging the truth from outside the truth itself, in which case the claim that this form of consciousness is true simply undercuts itself.

If the proletariat for Lukács is in principle the bearer of a knowledge of the social whole, it figures as the direct antithesis of a bourgeois class sunk in the mire of immediacy, unable to totalize its own situation. It is a traditional Marxist case that what forestalls such knowledge in the case of the middle class is its atomized social and economic conditions: each individual capitalist pursues his own interest, with little or no sense of how all of these isolated interests combine into a total system. Lukács, however, places emphasis rather on the phenomenon of reification – a concept he derives from Marx's doctrine of commodity fetishism, but to which he lends a greatly extended meaning. Splicing together Marx's economic analysis and

Max Weber's theory of rationalization, he argues in *History and Class Consciousness* that in capitalist society the commodity form permeates every aspect of social life, taking the shape of a pervasive mechanization, quantification and dehumanization of human experience. The 'wholeness' of society is broken up into so many discrete, specialized, technical operations, each of which comes to assume a semi-autonomous life of its own and to dominate human existence as a quasi-natural force. Purely formal techniques of calculability suffuse every region of society, from factory work to political bureaucracy, journalism to the judiciary; and the natural sciences themselves are simply one more instance of reified thought. Overwhelmed by an opaque world of autonomous objects and institutions, the human subject is rapidly reduced to an inert, contemplative being, incapable of recognizing any longer in these petrified products its own creative practice. The moment of revolutionary recognition arrives when the working class acknowledges this alienated world as its own confiscated creation, reclaiming it through political praxis. In the terms of the Hegelian philosophy which underlies Lukács's thought, this would signal the reunification of subject and object, torn grievously asunder by the effects of reification. In knowing itself for what it is, the proletariat becomes both subject and object of history. Indeed Lukács occasionally seems to imply that this act of self-consciousness is a revolutionary practice all in itself.

What Lukács has in effect done here is to replace Hegel's Absolute Idea – itself the identical subject–object of history – with the proletariat.[5] Or at least, to qualify the point, with the kind of politically desirable consciousness which the proletariat *could* in principle achieve – what he calls 'ascribed' or 'imputed' consciousness. And if Lukács is Hegelian enough in this, he is equally so in his trust that the truth lies in the whole. For the Hegel of *The Phenomenology of Spirit*, immediate experience is itself a kind of false or partial consciousness; it will yield up its truth only when it is dialectically mediated, when its latent manifold relations with the whole have been patiently uncovered. One might say, then, that on this view our routine consciousness is itself inherently 'ideological', simply by virtue of its partiality. It is not that the statements we make in this situation are necessarily false; it is rather that they are true only in some superficial, empirical way, for they are judgements about isolated objects which have not yet been incorporated into their full context. We can think back here to the assertion: 'Prince Charles is a thoughtful, conscientious fellow', which may be true enough as far as it goes, but which isolates the object known as

Prince Charles from the whole context of the institution of royalty. For Hegel, it is only by the operations of dialectical reason that such static, discrete phenomena can be reconstituted as a dynamic, developing whole. As to this extent one might say that a certain kind of false consciousness is for Hegel our 'natural' condition, endemic to our immediate experience.

For Lukács, by contrast, such partial seeing springs from specific historical causes – the process of capitalist reification – but is to be overcome in much the same way, by the workings of a 'totalizing' or dialectical reason. Bourgeois science, logic and philosophy are his equivalent of Hegel's routine, unredeemed mode of knowledge, breaking down what is in fact a complex, evolving totality into artificially autonomous parts. Ideology for Lukács is thus not exactly a discourse untrue to the way things are, but one true to them only in a limited, superficial way, ignorant of their deeper tendencies and connections. And this is another sense in which, contrary to widespread opinion, ideology is not in his view false consciousness in the sense of simple error or illusion.

To seize history as totality is to grasp it in its dynamic, contradictory development, of which the potential realization of human powers is a vital part. To this extent, a particular kind of *cognition* – knowing the whole – is for both Hegel and Lukács a certain kind of moral and political *norm*. The dialectical method thus reunites not only subject and object, but also 'fact' and 'value', which bourgeois thought has ripped asunder. To understand the world in a particular way becomes inseparable from acting to promote the free, full unfolding of human creative powers. We are not left high and dry, as we are in positivist or empiricist thought, with a dispassionate, value-free knowledge on the one hand, and an arbitrary set of subjective values on the other. On the contrary, the act of knowledge is itself both 'fact' and 'value', an accurate cognition indispensable for political emancipation. As Leszek Kolakowski puts the point: 'In this particular case [i.e. that of emancipatory knowledge] the understanding and transformation of reality are not two separate processes, but one and the same phenomenon.'[6]

Lukács's writings on class consciousness rank among the richest, most original documents of twentieth-century Marxism. They are, nevertheless, subject to a number of damaging criticisms. It could be argued, for example, that his theory of ideology tends towards an unholy mixture of economism and idealism. Economism, because he uncritically adopts the later Marx's implication that the commodity form is somehow the secret essence of all ideological consciousness in bourgeois society. Reification figures for Lukács not only as a central feature of the capitalist economy, but as 'the central structural problem of capitalist society in all aspects'.[7] A kind of essentialism of ideology is consequently at work here, homogenizing what are in fact very different discourses, structures and effects. At its worst, this model tends to reduce bourgeois society to a set of neatly layered 'expressions' of reification, each of its levels (economic, political, juridical, philosophical) obediently miming and reflecting the others. Moreover, as Theodor Adorno was later to suggest, this single-minded insistence upon reification as the clue to all crimes is itself covertly idealist: in Lukács's texts, it tends to displace such more fundamental concepts as economic exploitation. Much the same might be said of his use of the Hegelian category of totality, which sometimes pushes to one side an attention to modes of production, contradictions between the forces and relations of production and the like. Is Marxism, like Matthew Arnold's ideal poetic vision, just a matter of seeing reality steadily and seeing it whole? To parody Lukács's case a little: is revolution simply a question of making *connections*? And is not the social totality, for Marxism if not for Hegel, 'skewed' and asymmetrical, twisted out of true by the preponderance within it of economic determinants? Properly cautious of 'vulgar' Marxist versions of 'base' and 'superstructure', Lukács wishes to displace attention from this brand of mechanistic determinism to the idea of the social whole; but this social whole then risks becoming a purely 'circular' one, in which each 'level' is granted equal effectivity with each of the others.

Commodity fetishism, for Lukács as much as for Marx, is an objective material structure of capitalism, not just a state of mind. But in *History and Class Consciousness* another, residually idealist model of ideology is also confusingly at work, which would seem to locate the 'essence' of bourgeois society in the collective subjectivity of the bourgeois class itself. 'For a class to be ripe for hegemony', Lukács writes, 'means that its interests and consciousness enable it to organise the whole of society in accordance with those interests.'[8] What is it, then, which provides the ideological lynchpin of the bourgeois order? Is it the 'objective' system of commodity fetishism, which presumably imprints itself on all classes alike, or the 'subjective' strength of the dominant class's consciousness? Gareth Stedman Jones has argued that, as far as the latter view is concerned, it is as though ideology for Lukács takes grip through 'the saturation of the social totality by the ideological essence of a pure class subject.'[9] What this overlooks, as Stedman Jones goes on to point out, is that ideologies, far from being the 'subjective product of the "will to power" of different classes', are '*objective* systems determined by the *whole field* of social struggle between contending classes'. For Lukács, as for 'historicist' Marxism in general, it would sometimes appear as though each social class has its own peculiar, corporate 'world view', one directly expressive of its material conditions of existence; and ideological dominance then consists in one of these world views imposing its stamp on the social formation as a whole. It is not only that this version of ideological power is hard to square with the more structural and objective doctrine of commodity fetishism; it is also that it drastically simplifies the true unevenness and complexity of the ideological 'field'. For as Nicos Poulantzas has argued, ideology, like social class itself, is an inherently *relational* phenomenon: it expresses less the way a class lives its conditions of existence, than the way it lives them *in relation to the lived experience of other classes.*[10] Just as there can be no bourgeois class without a proletariat, or vice versa, so the typical ideology of each of these classes is constituted to the root by the ideology of its antagonist. Ruling ideologies, as we have argued earlier, must engage effectively with the lived experience of subordinate classes; and the way in which those subaltern classes live their world will be typically shaped and influenced by the dominant ideologies. Historicist Marxism, in short, presumes too organic and internal a relation between a 'class subject' and its 'world view'. There are social classes such as the petty bourgeoisie – 'contradiction incarnate', as Marx dubbed them – whose ideology is typically compounded of elements drawn from the classes both above and below them; and there are vital ideological themes such as nationalism which do not 'belong' to any particular social class, but which rather provide a bone of contention between them.[11] Social classes do not manifest ideologies in the way that individuals display a particular style of walking: ideology is, rather, a complex, conflictive field of meaning, in which some themes will be closely tied to the experience of particular classes, while others will be more 'free floating', tugged now this way and now that in the struggle between contending powers. Ideology is a realm of contestation and negotiation, in which there is a constant busy traffic: meanings and values are stolen, transformed, appropriated across the frontiers of different classes and groups, surrendered, repossessed, reinflected. A dominant class may 'live its experience' in part through the ideology of a previous dominant one: think of the aristocratic colouring of the English *haute bourgeosie*. Or it may fashion its ideology partly in terms of the beliefs of a subordinated class – as in the case of fascism, where a ruling sector of finance capitalism takes over for its own purposes the prejudices and anxieties of the lower middle class. There is no neat, one-to-one correspondence between classes and ideologies, as is evident in the case of revolutionary socialism. Any revolutionary ideology, to be politically effective, would have to be a good deal more than Lukács's 'pure' proletarian consciousness: unless it lent some provisional coherence to a rich array of oppositional forces, it would have scant chance of success.

The idea of social classes as 'subjects', central to Lukács's work, has also been contested. A class is not just some kind of collectivized individual, equipped with the sorts of attributes ascribed by humanist thought to the individual person: consciousness, unity, autonomy, self-determination and so on. Classes are certainly for Marxism historical *agents*; but they are structural, material formations as well as 'intersubjective' entities, and the problem is how to think these two aspects of them together. We have seen already that ruling classes are generally complex, internally conflictive 'blocs', rather than homogeneous bodies; and the same applies to their political antagonists. A 'class-ideology', then, is likely to display much the same kind of unevenness and contradictoriness.

The harshest criticism of Lukács's theory of ideology would be that, in a series of progressive conflations, he collapses Marxist theory into proletarian ideology; ideology into the expression of some 'pure' class subject; and this class subject to the essence of the social formation. But this case demands significant qualification. Lukács is not at all blind to the ways in which the consciousness of the working class is 'contaminated' by that of its rulers, and would seem to ascribe no organic 'world view' to it in non-revolutionary conditions. Indeed if the proletariat in its 'normal' state is little more than the commodity incarnate, it is hard to see how it can be a *subject* at all – and therefore hard to see how exactly it can make the transition to becoming a 'class for itself'. But this process of 'contamination' does not appear to work the other way round, in the sense that the *dominant* ideology seems in no way significantly shaped by a dialogue with its subordinates.

We have seen already that there are really two discrepant theories of ideology at work in *History and Class Consciousness* – the one deriving from commodity fetishism, the other from a historicist view of ideology as the world view of a class subject. As far as the proletariat is concerned, these two conceptions would seem to correspond respectively to its 'normal' and revolutionary states of being. In non-revolutionary conditions, working-class consciousness is passively subject to the effects of reification; we are given no clue as to how this situation is actively *constituted* by proletarian ideology, or of how it interacts with less obediently submissive aspects of that experience. How does the worker constitute herself as a subject on the basis of her objectification? But when the class shifts – mysteriously – to becoming a revolutionary subject, a historicist problematic takes over, and what was true of their rulers – that they 'saturated' the whole social formation with their own ideological conceptions – can now become true of them too. What is said of these rulers, however, is inconsistent: for this *active* notion of ideology in their case is at odds with the view that they, too, are simply victims of the structure of commodity fetishism. How can the middle class govern by virtue of its unique, unified world view when it is simply subjected along with other classes to the structure of reification? Is the dominant ideology a matter of the bourgeoisie, or of bourgeois society?

It can be claimed that *History and Class Consciousness* is marred by a typically idealist overestimation of 'consciousness' itself. 'Only the consciousness of the proletariat', Lukács writes, 'can point to the way that leads out of the impasse of capitalism';[12] and while this is orthodox enough in one sense, since an *un*conscious proletariat is hardly likely to do the trick, its emphasis is nonetheless revealing. For it is not in the first place the *consciousness* of the working class, actual or potential, which leads Marxism to select it as the prime agency of revolutionary change. If the working class figures as such an agent, it is for structural, material reasons – the fact that it is the only body so located within the productive process of capitalism, so trained and organized by that process and utterly indispensable to it, as to be capable of taking it over. In this sense it is capitalism, not Marxism, which 'selects' the instruments of revolutionary overthrow, patiently nurturing its own potential gravedigger. When Lukács observes that the strength of a social formation is always in the last resort a 'spiritual' one, or when he writes that 'the fate of the revolution ... will depend on the ideological maturity of the proletariat, i.e. on its class consciousness',[13] he is arguably in danger of displacing these material issues into questions of pure consciousness – and a consciousness which, as Gareth Stedman Jones has pointed out, remains curiously disembodied and ethereal, a matter of 'ideas' rather than practices or institutions.

If Lukács is residually idealist in the high priority he assigns to consciousness, so is he also in his Romantic hostility to science, logic and technology.[14] Formal and analytic discourses are simply modes of bourgeois reification, just as all forms of mechanization and rationalization would seem inherently alienating. The progressive, emancipatory side of these processes in the history of capitalism is merely ignored, in an elegaic nostalgia typical of Romantic conservative thought. Lukács does not wish to deny that Marxism is a science; but this science is the 'ideological expression of the proletariat', not some set of timeless analytic propositions. This certainly offers a powerful challenge to the 'scientism' of the Second International – the belief that historical materialism is a purely objective knowledge of the immanent laws of historical development. But to react against such metaphysical fantasies by *reducing* Marxist theory to revolutionary ideology is hardly more adequate. Are the complex equations of *Capital* no more than a theoretical 'expression' of socialist consciousness? Is not that consciousness partly *constituted* by such theoretical labour? And if only proletarian self-consciousness will deliver us the truth, how do we come to accept this truth as true in the first place, if not by a certain theoretical understanding which must be relatively independent of it?

I have already argued that it is mistaken to see Lukács as equating ideology with false consciousness *tout court*. Working-class socialist ideology is not of course in his view false; and even bourgeois ideology is illusory only in a complex sense of the term. Indeed we might claim that whereas for the early Marx and Engels, ideology is thought false to the true situation, for Lukács it is thought true to a false situation. Bourgeois ideas do indeed accurately mirror the state of things in bourgeois society; but it is this very state of affairs which is somehow twisted out of true. Such consciousness is faithful to the reified nature of the capitalist social order, and often enough makes true claims about this condition; it is 'false' in so far as it cannot penetrate this world of frozen appearances to lay bare the totality of tendencies and connections which underlies it. In the breathtaking central section of *History and Class Consciousness*, 'Reification and the Consciousness of the Proletariat', Lukács boldly rewrites the whole of post-Kantian philosophy as a secret history of the commodity form, of the schism between empty subjects and petrified objects; and in this sense such thought is accurate to the dominant social categories of capitalist society, structured by them to its roots. Bourgeois ideology is false less because it distorts, inverts or denies the material world, than because it is unable to press beyond certain limits structural to bourgeois society as such. As Lukács writes: 'Thus the barrier which converts the class consciousness of the bourgeoisie into "false" consciousness is objective; it is the class situation itself. It is the objective result of the economic set-up, and is neither arbitrary, subjective nor psychological.'[15] We have here, then, yet another definition of ideology, as 'structurally constrained thought', which runs back at least as far as Marx's *The Eighteenth Brumaire of Louis Bonaparte*. In a discussion in that text of what makes certain French politicians representatives of the petty bourgeoisie, Marx comments that it is 'the fact that in their minds they do not get beyond the limits which the [petty bourgeoisie] does not get beyond in life'. False consciousness is thus a kind of thought which finds itself baffled and thwarted by certain barriers in society rather than in the mind; and only by transforming society itself could it therefore be dissolved.

One can put this point in another way. There are certain kinds of error which result simply from lapses of intelligence or information, and which can be resolved by a further refinement of thought. But when we keep running up against a limit to our conceptions which stubbornly refuses to give way, then this obstruction may be symptomatic of some 'limit' built into our social life. In this situation, no amount of intelligence or ingenuity, no mere 'evolution of ideas', will serve to get us further forward, for what is awry here is the whole cast and frame of our consciousness, conditioned as it is by certain material constraints. Our social practices pose the obstacle to the very ideas which seek to explain them; and if we want to advance those ideas, we will have to change our forms of life. It is precisely this which Marx argues of the bourgeois political economists, whose searching theoretical enquiries find themselves continually rebuffed by problems which mark the inscription on the interior of their discourse of the social conditions surrounding it.

It is thus that Lukács can write of bourgeois ideology as 'something which is *subjectively* justified in the social and historical situation, as some-thing which can and should be understood, i.e. as "right". At the same time, *objectively*, it by-passes the essence of the evolution of society and fails to pinpoint and express it adequately.'[16] Ideology is now a long way from being some mere illusion; and the same is true if one reverses these terms 'objec-tive' and 'subjective'. For one might equally claim, so Lukács remarks, that bourgeois ideology fails 'subjectively' to achieve its self-appointed goals (freedom, justice and so on), but exactly in so failing helps to further certain objective aims of which it is ignorant. By which he means, presumably, helping to promote the historical conditions which will finally bring socialism to power. Such class consciousness involves an *un*consciousness of one's true social conditions and is thus a kind of self-deception; but whereas Engels, as we have seen, tended to dismiss the conscious motivation involved here as sheer illusion, Lukács is prepared to accord it a certain limited truth. 'Despite all its objective falseness', he writes, 'the self-deceiving "false" consciousness that we find in the bourgeoisie is at least in accord with its class situation.'[17] Bourgeois ideology may be false from the standpoint of some putative social totality, but this does not mean that it is false to the situation as it currently is.

This way of putting the point may perhaps help to make some sense of the otherwise puzzling notion of ideology as thought true to a false situation. For what seems spurious about this formulation is the very idea that a *situation* might be said to be false. Statements about deep-sea diving may be true or false, but not deep-sea diving itself. As a Marxist humanist, however, Lukács himself has a kind of answer to this problem. A 'false' situation for him is one in which the human 'essence' – the full potential of those powers which humanity has historically developed – is being unnecessarily blocked and estranged; and such judgements are thus always made from the standpoint of some possible and desirable future. A false situation can be identified only subjunctively or retrospectively, from the vantage-point of what *might* be possible were these thwarting, alienating forces to be abolished. But this does not mean taking one's stand in the empty space of some speculative future, in the manner of 'bad' utopianism; for in Lukács's view, and indeed in the view of Marxism in general, the outline of that desirable future can already be detected in certain potentialities stirring within the present. The present is thus not identical with itself: there is that within it which points beyond it, as indeed the shape of every historical present is structured by its anticipation of a possible future.

If the critique of ideology sets out to examine the social foundations of thought, then it must logically be able to give some account of its own historical origins. What was the material history which gave rise to the notion of ideology itself? Can the study of ideology round upon its own conditions of possibility?

The concept of ideology, it can be argued, arose at the historical point where systems of ideas first became aware of their own partiality; and this came about when those ideas were forced to encounter alien or alternative forms of discourse. It was with the rise of bourgeois society, above all, that the scene was set for this occurrence. For it is characteristic of that society, as Marx noted, that everything about it, including its forms of consciousness, is in a state of ceaseless flux, in contrast to some more tradition-bound social order. Capitalism survives only by a restless development of the productive forces; and in this agitated social condition new ideas tumble upon one another's heels as dizzyingly as do fashions in commodities. The entrenched authority of any single world view is accordingly undermined by the very nature of capitalism itself. Moreover, such a social order breeds plurality and fragmentation as surely as it generates social deprivation, transgressing time-hallowed boundaries between diverse forms of life and pitching them together in a *mêlée* of idioms, ethnic origins, life-styles, national cultures. It is exactly this which the Soviet critic Mikhail Bakhtin means by 'polyphony'. Within this atomized space, marked by a proliferating division of intellectual labour, a variety of creeds, doctrines and modes of perception jostle for authority; and this thought should give pause to those postmodern theorists for whom difference, plurality and heterogeneity are unequivocally 'progressive'. Within this turmoil of competing creeds, any particular belief system will find itself wedged cheek by jowl with unwelcome competitors; and its own frontiers will thus be thrown into sharp relief. The stage is then set for the growth of philosophical scepticism and relativism – for the conviction that, within the unseemly hubbub of the intellectual market-place, no single way of thinking can claim more validity than any other. If all thought is partial and partisan, then all thought is 'ideological'.

In a striking paradox, then, the very dynamism and mutability of the capitalist system threaten to cut the authoritative ground from under its own feet; and this is perhaps most obvious in the phenomenon of imperialism. Imperialism needs to assert the absolute truth of its own values at exactly the point where those values are confronting alien cultures; and this can prove a notably disorientating experience. It is hard to remain convinced that your own way of doing things is the only possible one when you are busy trying to subjugate another society which conducts its affairs in a radically different but apparently effective way. The fiction of Joseph Conrad turns on this disabling contradiction. In this as in other ways, then, the historical emergence of the concept of ideology testifies to a corrosive anxiety – to the embarrassed awareness that your own truths only strike you as plausible because of where you happen to be standing at the time.

The modern bourgeoisie is accordingly caught in something of a cleft stick. Unable to retreat to old-style metaphysical certainties, it is equally loath to embrace a full-blooded scepticism which would simply subvert the legitimacy of its power. One early twentieth-century attempt to negotiate this dilemma is Karl Mannheim's *Ideology and Utopia* (1929), written under the influence of Lukács's historicism in the political tumult of the Weimar republic. Mannheim sees well enough that with the rise of middle-class society the old monological world view of the traditional order has disappeared forever. An authoritarian priestly and political caste, which once confidently monopolised knowledge, has now yielded ground to a 'free' intelligentsia, caught on the hop between conflicting theoretical perspectives. The aim of a 'sociology of knowledge' will thus be to spurn all transcendental truths and examine the social determinants of particular belief systems, while guarding at the same time against the disabling relativism which would level all these beliefs to one. The problem, as Mannheim is uneasily aware, is that any criticism of another's views as ideological is always susceptible to a swift *tu quoque*. In pulling the rug out from beneath one's intellectual antagonist, one is always in danger of pulling it out from beneath oneself.

Against such relativism, Mannheim speaks up for what he calls 'relationism', meaning the location of ideas within the social system which gives birth to them. Such an enquiry into the social basis of thought, he considers, need not run counter to the goal of objectivity; for though ideas are internally shaped by their social origins, their truth value is not reducible to them. The inevitable one-sidedness of any particular standpoint can be corrected by synthesizing it with its rivals, thus building up a provisional, dynamic totality of thought. At the same time, by a process of self-monitoring, we can come to appreciate the limits of our own perspective, and so attain a restricted sort of objectivity. Mannheim thus emerges as the Matthew Arnold of Weimar Germany, concerned to see life steadily and see it whole. Blinkered ideological viewpoints will be patiently subsumed into some greater totality by those dispassionate enough to do so – which is to say, by 'free' intellectuals with a remarkable resemblance to Karl Mannheim. The only problem with this approach is that it merely pushes the question of relativism back a stage; for we can always ask about the tendentious standpoint from which this synthesis is actually launched. Isn't the interest in totality just another interest?

Such a sociology of knowledge is for Mannheim a welcome alternative to the older style of ideology critique. Such critique, in his view, is essentially a matter of *unmasking* one's antagonist's notions, exposing them as lies, deceptions or illusions fuelled by conscious or unconscious social motivations. Ideology critique, in short, is here reduced to what Paul Ricoeur would call a 'hermeneutic of suspicion', and is plainly inadequate for the subtler, more ambitious task of eliciting the whole 'mental structure' which underlies a group's prejudices and beliefs. Ideology pertains only to specific deceptive assertions, whose roots, so Mannheim at one point argues, may be traced to the psychology of particular individuals. That this is something of a straw target of ideology is surely clear: Mannheim pays scant regard to such theories as the fetishism of commodities, where deception, far from springing from psychologistic sources, is seen as generated by an entire social structure.

The ideological function of the 'sociology of knowledge' is in fact to defuse the whole Marxist conception of ideology, replacing it with the less embattled, contentious conception of a 'world view'. Mannheim, to be sure, does not believe that such world views can ever be non-evaluatively analysed; but the drift of his work is to downplay concepts of mystification, rationalization and the power-function of ideas in the name of some synoptic survey of the evolution of forms of historical consciousness. In a sense, then, this post-Marxist approach to ideology returns to a *pre*-Marxist view of it, as simply 'socially determined thought'. And since this applies to any thought whatsoever, there is a danger of the concept of ideology cancelling all the way through.

In so far as Mannheim *does* retain the concept of ideology, he does so in a singularly unilluminating way. As a historicist, truth for Mannheim means ideas adequate to a particular stage of historical development; and ideology then signifies a body of beliefs incongruous with its epoch, out of sync with what the age demands. Conversely, 'utopia' denotes ideas ahead of their time and so similarly discrepant with social reality, but capable nonetheless of shattering the structures of the present and transgressing its frontiers. Ideology, in short, is antiquated belief, a set of obsolescent myths, norms and ideals unhinged from the real; utopia is premature and unreal, but should be reserved as a term for those conceptual prefigurations which really do succeed in realizing a new social order. Ideology emerges in this light as a kind of failed utopia, unable to enter upon material existence; and this definition of it then simply throws us back to the patently insufficient early Marxian notion of ideology as ineffectual otherworldiness. Mannheim would appear to lack all sense of ideologies as forms of consciousness often all too well adapted to current social requirements, productively entwined with historical reality, able to organize practical social activity in highly effective ways. In his denigration of utopia, which is similarly a 'distortion of reality', he is simply blinded to the ways in which what 'the age demands' may be precisely a thought which moves beyond it. 'Thought', he remarks, 'should contain neither less nor more than the reality in whose medium it operates'[18] – an identification of the concept with its object which Theodor Adorno, ironically enough, will denounce as the very essence of ideological thought.

In the end, Mannheim either stretches the term ideology beyond all serviceable use, equating it with the social determination of any belief whatsoever, or unduly narrows it to specific acts of deception. He fails to grasp that ideology cannot be synonymous with partial or perspectival thinking – for of what thinking is this not true? If the concept is not to be entirely vacuous it must have rather more specific connotations of power-struggle and legitimation, structural dissemblance and mystification. What he does usefully suggest, however, is a third way between those who would hold that the truth or falsity of statements is sublimely untainted by their social genesis, and those who would abruptly reduce the former to the latter. For Michel Foucault, it would seem that the truth value of a proposition is entirely a matter of its social function, a reflex of the power interests it promotes. As the linguists might say, what is enunciated is wholly collapsible to the conditions of the enunciation; what matters is not so much *what* is said, but who says it to whom for what purposes. What this overlooks is that, while enunciations are certainly not independent of their social conditions, a statement such as 'Eskimos are generally speaking just as good as anyone else' is true no matter who says it for what end; and one of the important features of a claim such as 'Men are superior to women' is that, whatever power interests it may be promoting, it is also, as a matter of fact, false.

Another thinker on whom the Lukácsian mantle descends is the Romanian-born sociologist Lucien Goldmann. Goldmann's method of 'genetic structuralism' seeks to identify the 'mental structures' of a particular social group or class, especially as these are revealed in literature and philosophy. Everyday consciousness is a haphazard, amorphous affair; but certain exceptionally gifted members of a class – artists, for example – can rise above this mixed, uneven experience and express the class's interests in purer, more diagrammatic form. This 'ideal' structure Goldmann names a 'world view' – a specific organization of mental categories which silently informs the art and thought of a social group, and which is the product of its collective consciousness. The Goldmannian world view is thus a version of Lukács's 'imputed' consciousness: that style of thought at which a social class would ideally arrive were it to grasp its real situation and articulate its true aspirations.

Goldmann enforces a distinction between this world view and mere ideology. The former is global in reach, and typifies a social class at the height of its powers, whereas the latter is a partial, distorting perspective characteristic of a class in decline. There is some warrant for this opposition, as we have seen, in a certain reading of Marx, who contrasts the genuine universality of an emergent revolutionary class with the deceptive rationalizations of its subsequent career. All the same, the distinction would seem somewhat shaky: is a world view non-ideological in the sense of being innocent of power? Is there no sense in which it strives to legitimate particular social interests? It is as though Goldmann wishes to safeguard the 'purity' of the world view from the shame of the sheerly ideological; and one reason he needs to do so is because the totality of the world view, for him as for Lukács, offers a vantage-point other than the now discredited 'science' from which specific ideologies may be assessed. This is not to claim that every world view is 'true'; for Goldmann, the Kantian vision is tragically constrained by the categories of bourgeois society. But it is true to actual historical conditions, and so to be contrasted with the mere speciousness of an ideology. World view is ideology purified, elevated, and largely purged of its negative elements.

In his major work *The Hidden God* (1955), Goldmann examines the tragic world view of a sector of the seventeenth-century French bourgeoisie, demonstrating how the works of writers as apparently disparate as Racine and Pascal display an invariable 'deep' structure of categories expressive of the vain search for absolute value in a world now stripped of numinous meaning by scientific rationalism and empiricism. All of the elements of 'historicist' Marxism are clearly in evidence here. Social classes are viewed not primarily as objective material structures but as 'collective subjects', furnished with what – ideally, at least – is a highly homogeneous consciousness. This conciousness stands in directly expressive relation to the class's social conditions; and works of art and philosophy are in turn expressive of this world view. There is no particular room in this model for 'non-class' forms of consciousness, and little room either for any serious complications, dislocations or contradictions between its various levels. The social formation presents itself as an 'expressive totality', within which social conditions, class, world view and literary artefacts unproblematically reflect one another.

In his later work *Towards a Sociology of the Novel* (1964), Goldmann turns from the concept of world view to the theory of reification. This methodological shift, he considers, reflects a real mutation from classical to advanced capitalism; for the later stages of the system, with their pervasive rationalizing and dehumanizing of existence, have now definitively blocked off the possibility of global totality at the level of consciousness. What this suggests is that the notion of world view, and the theory of commodity fetishism, cannot really coexist as accounts of ideology. If, as we have seen, they stand in uneasy interrelation in the work of Lukács, they divide into chronologically successive phases of the history of capitalism in the writings of Goldmann. So the question which we raised in the case of Lukács returns in the instance of his disciple: is the dominant ideology a matter of the ruling class somehow imposing its coherently organized consciousness upon society as a whole, or is it a matter of the material structures of the capitalist economy itself?

The key category in the writing of Lukács's Western Marxist colleague Antonio Gramsci is not ideology but *hegemony*; and it is worth pondering the distinction between these two terms. Gramsci normally uses the word hegemony to mean the ways in which a governing power wins consent to its rule from those it subjugates – though it is true that he occasionally uses the term to cover both consent and coercion together. There is thus an immediate difference from the concept of ideology, since it is clear that ideologies may be forcibly imposed. Think, for example, of the workings of racist ideology in South Africa. But hegemony is also a broader category than ideology: it *includes* ideology, but is not reducible to it. A ruling group or class may secure consent to its power by ideological means; but it may also do so by, say, altering the tax system in ways favourable to groups whose support it needs, or creating a layer of relatively affluent, and thus somewhat politically quiescent, workers. Or hegemony may take political rather than economic forms: the parliamentary system in Western democracies is a crucial aspect of such power, since it fosters the illusion of self-government on the part of the populace. What uniquely distinguishes the political form of such societies is that the people are supposed to believe that they govern themselves, a belief which no slave of antiquity or medieval serf was expected to entertain. Indeed Perry Anderson goes so far as to describe the parliamentary system as 'the hub of the ideological apparatus of capitalism', to which such institutions as the media, churches and political parties play a critical but complementary role. It is for this reason, as Anderson points out, that Gramsci is mistaken when he locates hegemony in 'civil society' alone, rather than in the state, for the political form of the capitalist state is itself a vital organ of such power.[19]

Another powerful source of political hegemony is the supposed neutrality of the bourgeois state. This is not, in fact, simply an ideological illusion. In capitalist society, political power is indeed relatively autonomous of social and economic life, as opposed to the political set-up in pre-capitalist formations. In feudal regimes, for example, the nobility who economically exploit the peasantry also exercise certain political, cultural and juridical functions in their lives, so that the relation between economic and political power is here more visible. Under capitalism, economic life is not subject to such continuous political supervision: as Marx comments, it is the 'dull compulsion of the economic', the need simply to survive, which keeps men and women at work, divorced from any framework of political obligations, religious sanctions or customary responsibilities. It is as though in this form of life the economy comes to operate 'all by itself', and the political state can thus take something of a back seat, sustaining the general structures within which this economic activity is conducted. This is the real material basis of the belief that the bourgeois state is supremely dis-interested, holding the ring between contending social forces; and in this sense, once again, hegemony is built into its very nature.

Hegemony, then, is not just some successful kind of ideology, but may be discriminated into its various ideological, cultural, political and economic aspects. Ideology refers specifically to the way power-struggles are fought out at the level of signification; and though such signification is involved in all hegemonic processes, it is not in all cases the *dominant* level by which rule is sustained. Singing the National Anthem comes as close to a 'purely' ideological activity as one could imagine; it would certainly seem to fulfil no other purpose, aside perhaps from annoying the neighbours. Religion, similarly, is probably the most purely ideological of the various institutions of civil society. But hegemony is also carried in cultural, political and economic forms – in non-discursive practices as well as in rhetorical utterances.

With certain notable inconsistencies, Gramsci associates hegemony with the arena of 'civil society', by which he means the whole range of institutions intermediate between state and economy. Privately owned television stations, the family, the boy scout movement, the Methodist church, infant schools, the British Legion, the *Sun* newspaper: all of these would count as hegemonic apparatuses, which bind individuals to the ruling power by consent rather than by coercion. Coercion, by contrast, is reserved to the state, which has a monopoly on 'legitimate' violence. (We should note, however, that the coercive institutions of a society – armies, law courts and the rest – must themselves win a general consent from the people if they are to operate effectively, so that the opposition between coercion and consent can be to some extent deconstructed.) In modern capitalist regimes, civil society has come to assume a formidable power, in contrast to the days when the Bolsheviks, living in a society poor in such institutions, could seize the reins of government by a frontal attack on the state itself. The concept of hegemony thus belongs with the question: How is the working class to take power in a social formation where the dominant power is subtly, pervasively diffused throughout habitual daily practices, intimately interwoven with 'culture' itself, inscribed in the very texture of our experience from nursery school to funeral parlour? How do we combat a power which has become the 'common sense' of a whole social order, rather than one which is widely perceived as alien and oppressive?

In modern society, then, it is not enough to occupy factories or confront the state. What must also be contested is the whole area of 'culture', defined in its broadest, most everyday sense. The power of the ruling class is spiritual as well as material; and any 'counterhegemony' must carry its political campaign into this hitherto neglected realm of values and customs, speech habits and ritual practices. Perhaps the shrewdest comment ever passed on this topic was Lenin's, in a speech to the Moscow conference of trade unions in 1918:

> The whole difficulty of the Russian revolution is that it was much easier for the Russian revolutionary working class to start than it is for the West European classes, but it is much more difficult for us to continue. It is more difficult to start a revolution in West European countries because there the revolutionary proletariat is opposed by the higher thinking that comes with culture, while the working class is in a state of cultural slavery.[20]

What Lenin means is that the relative lack of 'culture' in Tsarist Russia, in the sense of a dense network of 'civil' institutions, was a key factor in making the revolution possible, since the ruling class could not secure its hegemony by these means. But the very same absence of culture, in the sense of a literate, well-educated population, developed technological forces and so on, also plunged the revolution into grave problems as soon as it occurred. Conversely, it is the preponderance of culture in the West, in the sense of a complex array of hegemonic institutions in civil society, which makes political revolution difficult to inaugurate; but this same culture, in the sense of a society rich in technical, material and 'spiritual' resources, would make political revolution easier to sustain once it came about. This is perhaps the place to remark that for Lenin, as indeed for all Marxist thinkers up to Stalin, socialism was inconceivable without a high level of development of the productive forces, and more generally of 'culture'. Marxism was never intended to be a theory and practice of how desperately backward societies could leap, isolated and unaided, into the twentieth century; and the material consequence of such an attempt is generally known as Stalinism.

If the concept of hegemony extends and enriches the notion of ideology, it also lends this otherwise somewhat abstract term a material body and political cutting edge. It is with Gramsci that the crucial transition is effected from ideology as 'systems of ideas' to ideology as lived, habitual social practice – which must then presumably encompass the unconscious, inarticulate dimensions of social experience as well as the workings of formal institutions. Louis Althusser, for whom ideology is largely unconscious and always institutional, will inherit both of these emphases; and hegemony as a 'lived' process of political domination comes close in some of its aspects to what Raymond Williams calls a 'structure of feeling'. In his own discussion of Gramsci, Williams acknowledges the *dynamic* character of hegemony, as against the potentially static connotations of 'ideology': hegemony is never a once-and-for-all achievement, but 'has continually to be renewed, recreated, defended, and modified'.[21] As a concept, then, hegemony is inseparable from overtones of struggle, as ideology perhaps is not. No single mode of hegemony, so Williams argues, can exhaust the meanings and values of any society; and any governing power is thus forced to engage with counter-hegemonic forces in ways which prove partly constitutive of its own rule. Hegemony is thus an inherently relational, as well as practical and dynamic, notion; and it offers in this sense a signal advance on some of the more ossified, scholastic definitions of ideology to be found in certain 'vulgar' currents of Marxism.

Very roughly, then, we might define hegemony as a whole range of practical strategies by which a dominant power elicits consent to its rule from those its subjugates. To win hegemony, in Gramsci's view, is to establish moral, political and intellectual leadership in social life by diffusing one's own 'world view' throughout the fabric of society as a whole, thus equating one's own interests with the interests of society at large. Such consensual rule is not, of course, peculiar to capitalism; indeed one might claim that *any* form of political power, to be durable and well-grounded, must evoke at least a degree of consent from its underlings. But there are good reasons to believe that in capitalist society in particular, the ratio between consent and coercion shifts decisively towards the former. In such conditions, the power of the state to discipline and punish – what Gramsci terms 'domination' – remains firmly in place, and indeed in modern societies grows more formidable as the various technologies of oppression begin to proliferate. But the institutions of 'civil society' – schools, families, churches, media and the rest – now play a more central role in the processes of social control. The bourgeois state will resort to direct violence if it is forced to it; but in doing so it risks suffering a drastic loss of ideological credibility. It is preferable on the whole for power to remain conveniently invisible, disseminated throughout the texture of social life and thus 'naturalized' as custom, habit, spontaneous practice. Once power nakedly reveals its hand, it can become an object of political contestation.[22]

A shift from coercion to consent is implicit in the very material conditions of middle-class society. Since that society is composed of 'free', apparently autonomous individuals, each pursuing their own private interests, any centralized political supervision of these atomized subjects becomes considerably harder to sustain. Each of them must consequently become his or her own seat of self-government; each must 'internalize' power, make it spontaneously their own and bear it around with them as a principle inseparable from their identities. A social order must be constructed, Gramsci writes, 'in which the individual can govern himself without his self-government thereby entering into conflict with political society – but rather becoming its normal continuation, its organic complement'.[23] 'State life', he adds, must become 'spontaneous', at one with the individual subject's 'free' identity; and if this is the 'psychological' dimension of hegemony, it is one with a solid material basis in middle-class life.

In his *Prison Notebooks*, Gramsci rejects out of hand any purely negative use of the term ideology. This 'bad' sense of the term has become widespread, he remarks, 'with the effect that the theoretical analysis of the concept of ideology has been modified and denatured'.[24] Ideology has been too often seen as pure appearance or mere obtuseness, whereas a distinction must in fact be drawn between 'historically organic' ideologies – meaning those necessary to a given social structure – and ideology in the sense of the arbitrary speculations of individuals. This parallels to some extent the opposition we have observed elsewhere between 'ideology' and 'world view', though we should note that for Marx himself the negative sense of ideology was by no means confined to arbitrary subjective speculation. Gramsci also dismisses any economistic reduction of ideology to the mere bad dream of the infrastructure: on the contrary, ideologies must be viewed as actively organizing forces which are psychologically 'valid', fashioning the terrain on which men and women act, struggle and acquire consciousness of their social positions. In any 'historical bloc', Gramsci comments, material forces are the 'content', and ideologies the 'form'.

The German Ideology's equation of ideology with speculative illusion is for Gramsci simply one historically determinate phase through which such ideologies pass: every conception of the world, he observes, might at some point come to assume a speculative form which represents at once its historical highpoint and the beginnings of its dissolution.

> One could say, that is, that every culture has its speculative and religious moment, which coincides with the period of complete hegemony of the social group of which it is the expression and perhaps coincides exactly with the moment in which the real hegemony disintegrates at the base, molecularly: but precisely because of this disintegration, and to react against it, the system of thought perfects itself as a dogma and becomes a transcendental 'faith'.[25]

What the early Marx and Engels are tempted to see as the eternal form of all ideology is for Gramsci a specific historical phenomenon.

Gramsci's theory of ideology, then, is cast like Lukács's in what is known as the 'historicist' mould. He is as suspicious as Lukács of any appeal to a 'scientific' Marxism which ignores the practical, political, historically relative nature of Marxist theory, and grasps that theory as the expression of revolutionary working-class consciousness. An 'organic' ideology is not simply false consciousness, but one adequate to a specific stage of historical development and a particular political moment. To judge the whole of past philosophy as mere 'delirium and folly', in the manner of 'vulgar' Marxism, is an anachronistic error which assumes that men and women in the past should have thought as we do today. But it is also, ironically, a hangover from the metaphysical dogma of that past, presupposing as it does an eternally valid form of thought by which all ages can be judged. The fact that theoretical systems have been superseded does not mean that they were not once historically valid. Marxism is simply the form of historical consciousness adequate to the present moment, and will wither away when that moment is in its turn surpassed. If it seizes hold of historical contradictions, it also grasps itself as one element of those contradictions, and indeed is their most complete, because most conscious, expression. For Marxism to assert that every supposedly eternal truth has practical historical origins is inevitably for it to turn this perspective upon itself. When this fails to happen, Marxism itself rapidly petrifies into a metaphysical ideology.

For Gramsci, the consciousness of subordinated groups in society is typically fissured and uneven. Two conflicting conceptions of the world usually exist in such ideologies, the one drawn from the 'official' notions of the rulers, the other derived from an oppressed people's practical experience of social reality. Such conflicts might take the form of what we have seen earlier as a 'performative contradiction' between what a group or class says, and what it tacitly reveals in its behaviour. But this is not to be seen as mere self-deception: such an explanation, Gramsci thinks, might be adequate in the case of particular individuals, but not in the case of great masses of men and women. These contradictions in thought must have an historical base; and Gramsci locates this in the contrast between the emergent concept of the world which a class displays when it acts as an 'organic totality', and its submission in more 'normal' times to the ideas of those who govern it. One aim of revolutionary practice, then, must be to elaborate and make explicit the potentially creative principles implicit in the practical understanding of the oppressed – to raise these otherwise inchoate, ambiguous elements of its experience to the status of a coherent philosophy or 'world view'.

What is at stake here, to put the matter in Lukács's terms, is a transition from the 'empirical' consciousness of the working class to its 'possible' consciousness – to the world view it could attain in propitious conditions, and which is even now implicit in its experience. But whereas Lukács is disturbingly vague about how such a transition is to come about, Gramsci offers a highly precise answer to this question: the activity of the 'organic' intellectuals. 'Organic' intellectuals, of whom Gramsci himself was one, are the product of an emergent social class; and their role is to lend that class some homogeneous self-consciousness in the cultural, political and economic fields. The category of organic intellectual thus spans not only ideologues and philosophers but political activists, industrial technicians, political economists, legal specialists and so on. Such a figure is less a contemplative thinker, in the old idealist style of the intelligentsia, than an organizer, constructor, 'permanent persuader', who actively participates in social life and helps bring to theoretical articulation those positive political currents already contained within it. Philosophical activity, Gramsci remarks, must be seen 'as above all a cultural battle to transform the popular "mentality" and to diffuse the philosophical innovations which will prove themselves to be "historically true" to the extent that they become concretely - i.e. historically and socially - universal'.[26] The organic in- tellectual thus provides the link or pivot between philosophy and the people, adept at the former but actively identified with the latter. His or her goal is to construct out of the common consciousness a 'cultural-social' unity in which otherwise heterogeneous individual wills are welded together on the basis of a common conception of the world.

The organic intellectual thus neither sentimentally acquiesces in the current state of awareness of the masses, nor brings to them some alien truth from 'above', as in the usual banal caricature of Leninism widespread today even on the political left. (It is worth nothing here that Gramsci himself, far from being the precursor of a 'liberal' Marxism which regards political leadership as 'elitist', was a revolutionary Marxist-Leninist.) All men and women, he asserts, are in some sense intellectuals, in that their practical activity involves an implicit 'philosophy' or conception of the world. The role of the organic intellectual, as we have seen, is to give shape and cohesion to this practical understanding, thus unifying theory and practice. 'One can construct', Gramsci argues, 'on a specific practice, a theory which, by coinciding and identifying itself with the decisive elements of the practice itself, can accelerate the historical process that is going on, rendering practice more homogeneous, more coherent, more efficient in all its elements, and thus, in other words, developing its potential to the maxi- mum ...'[27]

To do this, however, means combatting much that is negative in the empirical consciousness of the people, to which Gramsci gives the title of 'common sense'. Such common sense is a 'chaotic aggregate of disparate conceptions' - an ambiguous, contradictory zone of experience which is on the whole politically backward. How could we expect it to be otherwise, if a ruling bloc has had centuries in which to perfect its hegemony? In Gramsci's view there is a certain continuum between 'spontaneous' and 'scientific' consciousness, such that the difficulties of the latter should not be intimidatingly overestimated; but there is also a permanent war between revolutionary theory and the mythological or folkloric conceptions of the masses, and the latter is not to be patronizingly romanticized at the expense of the former. Certain 'folk' conceptions, Gramsci holds, do indeed spontaneously reflect important aspects of social life; 'popular consciousness' is not to be dismissed as purely negative, but its more progressive and more reactionary features must instead be carefully distinguished.[28] Popular morality, for example, is partly the fossilized residue of an earlier history, partly 'a range of often creative and progressive innovations ... which go against, or merely differ from, the morality of the ruling strata of society'.[29] What is needed is not just some paternalist endorsement of existing popular consciousness, but the construction of 'a new common sense and with it a new culture and a new philosophy which will be rooted in the popular consciousness with the same solidity and imperative quality as traditional beliefs'.[30] The function of the organic intellectuals, in other words, is to forge the links between 'theory' and 'ideology', creating a two-way passage between political analysis and popular experience. And the term ideology here 'is used in its highest sense of a conception of the world that is implicitly manifest in art, in law, in economic activity and in all manifestations of individual and collective life'.[31] Such a 'world view' cements together a social and political bloc, as a unifying, organizing, inspirational principle rather than a system of abstract ideas.

The opposite of the organic intellectual is the 'traditional' one, who believes himself quite independent of social life. Such figures (clerics, idealist philosophers, Oxford dons and the rest) are in Gramsci's view hangovers from some previous historical epoch, and in this sense the distinction between 'organic' and 'traditional' can be to some extent deconstructed. A traditional intellectual was perhaps once organic, but is now no longer so; idealist philosophers served the middle class well in its revolutionary heyday, but are now a marginal embarrassment. The distinction between traditional and organic intellectual corresponds roughly to one we have traced between the negative and the positive senses of ideology: ideology as thought which has come unstuck from reality, as opposed to ideology as ideas in the active service of a class's interests. The traditional intellectual's trust in his or her independence of the ruling class is for Gramsci the material basis of philosophical idealism – of the gullible faith, denounced by *The German Ideology*, that the source of ideas is other ideas. For Marx and Engels, by contrast, ideas have no *independent* history at all: they are the products of specific historical conditions. But this belief in the autonomy of thought may serve a particular ruling class exceedingly well; and to this extent the now traditional intellectual may once have fulfilled an 'organic' function precisely in his social disconnectedness. Indeed Gramsci himself suggests as much when he claims that the speculative view of the world belongs to a class at the acme of its power. We should remember in any case that the traditional intellectual's trust in the autonomy of ideas is not sheer illusion: given the material conditions of middle-class society, such members of the intelligentsia really do occupy a highly 'mediated' position in relation to social life.

Like Lukács and Goldmann, Gramsci is an historicist Marxist who believes that truth is historically variable, relative to the consciousness of the most progressive social class of a particular epoch. Objectivity, he writes, always means 'humanly objective', which can in turn be decoded as 'historically or universally subjective'. Ideas are true in so far as they serve to cohere and promote those forms of consciousness which are in tune with the most significant tendencies of an era. The alternative case to this is to claim that the assertion that Julius Caesar was assassinated, or that the wage-relation under capitalism is exploitative, is either true or it is not. A universal consensus might always prove retrospectively to have been false. Moreover, by what criteria do we judge that a specific historical development *is* progressive? How do we decide what counts as the 'possible' consciousness or most richly elaborated world view of the working class? How do we determine what a class's true interests are? If there are no criteria for such judgements outside that class's own consciousness, then it would seem that we are trapped here in just the same kind of vicious epistemological circle we noted in the case of Georg Lukács. If those ideas are true which serve to realize certain social interests, does this not open the door to a cynical pragmatism which, as with Stalinism, defines objectivity as whatever happens politically to suit you? And if the *test* of the truth of ideas is that they do in fact promote such desirable interests, how can we ever be sure that it was the ideas in question which did the promoting, rather than some other historical factor?

Gramsci has been criticized by 'structuralist' Marxists such as Nicos Poulantzas for committing the historicist error of reducing ideology to the expression of a social class, and reducing a dominant class to the 'essence' of the social formation.[32] For Poulantzas, it is not the hegemonic class which binds society together; on the contrary, the unity of a social formation is a structural affair, an effect of the interlocking of several 'levels' or 'regions' of social life under the finally determining constraints of a mode of production. The political reality of a ruling class is one level within this formation, not the principle which gives unity and direction to the whole. In a similar way, ideology is a complex material structure, not just a kind of collective subjectivity. A dominant ideology reflects not just the world view of the rulers, but the relations between governing and dominated classes in society *as a whole*. Its task is to recreate, at an 'imaginary' level, the unity of the entire social formation, not just to lend coherence to the consciousness of its rulers. The relation between a hegemonic class and a dominant ideology is thus indirect: it passes, so to speak, through the mediation of the total social structure. Such an ideology cannot be deciphered from the consciousness of the governing bloc taken in isolation, but must be grasped from the standpoint of the whole field of class struggle. In Poulantzas's eyes, historicist Marxism is guilty of the idealist mistake of believing that it is a dominant ideology or world view which secures the unity of society. For him, by contrast, the dominant ideology *reflects* that unity, rather than *constituting* it.

Gramsci's work is certainly vulnerable at points to Poulantzas's critique of historicism; but he is by no means enamoured of any 'pure' class subject. An oppositional world view is not for him just the expression of proletarian consciousness, but an irreducibly composite affair. Any effective revolutionary movement must be a complex alliance of forces; and its world view will result from a transformative synthesis of its various ideological components into a 'collective will'. Revolutionary hegemony, in other words, involves a complex practice *upon* given radical ideologies, rearticulating their motifs into a differentiated whole.[33] Nor does Gramsci overlook the *relational* nature of such world views, as Lukács is occasionally tempted to do. We have seen already that he by no means underestimates the extent to which the consciousness of the oppressed is 'tainted' by the beliefs of its superiors; but this relation also works the other way round. Any hegemonic class, he writes in *The Prison Notebooks*, must take account of the interests and tendencies of those over whom it exerts power, and must be prepared to compromise in this respect. Nor does he always posit a direct relation between a dominant class and a dominant ideology: 'A class some of whose strata still have a Ptolemaic conception of the world can none the less be the representative of a very advanced historical situation.'[34] 'Structuralist' Marxism has customarily accused its historicist counterpart of failing to distinguish between a *dominant* and a *determinant* social class – of overlooking the fact that one class can exercise political dominance on the basis of the economic determinacy of another. Indeed something of the kind could be said of nineteenth-century Britain, where the economically determinant middle class largely 'delegated' its political power to the aristocracy. This is not a situation which any theory assuming a one-to-one relation between classes and ideologies can easily decipher, since the resultant ruling ideology will be typically a hybrid of elements drawn from the experience of *both* classes. It is a sign of Gramsci's subtle historical insight, however, that his brief comments on British social history in *The Prison Notebooks* run very much along these lines:

> [In nineteenth-century England] there is a very extensive category of organic intellectuals – those, that is, who come into existence on the same industrial terrain as the economic group – but in the higher sphere we find that the old land-owning class preserves its position of virtual monopoly. It loses its economic supremacy but maintains for a long time a politico-intellectual supremacy and is assimilated as 'traditional intellectuals' and as a directive group by the new group in power. The old land-owning aristocracy is joined to the industrialists by a kind of suture which is precisely that which in other countries unites the traditional intellectuals with the new dominant classes.[35]

A whole vital aspect of British class history is here summarized with brilliant succinctness, as enduring testimony to the creative originality of its author.

5

FROM ADORNO TO BOURDIEU

WE SAW in chapter 3 how a theory of ideology can be generated from the commodity form. But at the heart of Marx's economic analysis lies another category also of relevance to ideology, and this is the concept of exchange value. In the first volume of *Capital*, Marx explains how two commodities with quite different 'use-values' can be equally exchanged, on the principle that both contain the same amount of abstract labour. If it takes the same quantity of labour-power to produce a Christmas pudding and a toy squirrel, then these products will have the same exchange-value, which is to say that the same amount of money can buy them both. But the specific differences between these objects are thereby suppressed, as their use-value becomes subordinate to their abstract equivalence.

If this principle reigns in the capitalist economy, it can also be observed at work in the higher reaches of the 'superstructure'. In the political arena of bourgeois society, all men and women are abstractly equal as voters and citizens; but this theoretical equivalence serves to mask their concrete inequalities within 'civil society'. Landlord and tenant, businessman and prostitute, may end up in adjacent polling booths. Much the same is true of the juridical institutions: all individuals are equal before the law, but this merely obscures the way in which the law itself is ultimately on the side of the propertied. Is there, then, some way of tracking this principle of false equivalence even further up the so-called superstructure, into the heady realms of ideology?

For the Frankfurt School Marxist Theodor Adorno, this mechanism of abstract exchange is the very secret of ideology itself. Commodity exchange effects an equation between things which are in fact incommensurable, and so, in Adorno's view, does ideological thought. Such thought is revolted by the sight of 'otherness', of that which threatens to escape its own closed system, and violently reduces it to its own image and likeness. 'If the lion had a consciousness', Adorno writes in *Negative Dialectics*, 'his rage at the antelope he wants to eat would be ideology'. Indeed Fredric Jameson has suggested that the fundamental gesture of all ideology is exactly such a rigid binary opposition between the self or familiar, which is positively valorized, and the non-self or alien, which is thrust beyond the boundaries of intelligibility.[1] The ethical code of good versus evil, so Jameson considers, is then the most exemplary model of this principle. Ideology for Adorno is thus a form of 'identity thinking' – a covertly paranoid style of rationality which inexorably transmutes the uniqueness and plurality of things into a mere simulacrum of itself, or expels them beyond its own borders in a panic-stricken act of exclusion.

On this account, the opposite of ideology would be not truth or theory, but difference or heterogeneity. And in this as in other ways, Adorno's thought strikingly prefigures that of the post-structuralists of our own day. In the face of this conceptual straitjacketing, he affirms the essential *non*-identity of thought and reality, the concept and its object. To suppose that the idea of freedom is identical with the poor travesty of it available in the capitalist market place is to fail to see that this object does not live up to its concept. Conversely, to imagine that the being of any object can be exhausted by the concept of it is to erase its unique materiality, since concepts are ineluctably general and objects stubbornly particular. Ideology *homogenizes* the world, spuriously equating distinct phenomena; and to undo it thus demands a 'negative dialectics', which strives, perhaps impossibly, to include within thought that which is heterogeneous to it. For Adorno, the highest paradigm of such negative reason is art, which speaks up for the differential and non-identical, promoting the claims of the sensuous particular against the tyranny of some seamless totality.[2]

Identity, then, is in Adorno's eyes the 'primal form' of all ideology. Our reified consciousness reflects a world of objects frozen in their monotonously self-same being, and in thus binding us to what *is*, to the purely 'given', blinds us to the truth that 'what is, is more than it is'.[3] In contrast with much post-structuralist thinking, however, Adorno neither uncritically celebrates the notion of difference nor unequivocally denounces the principle of identity. For all its paranoid anxiety, the identity principle carries with it a frail hope that one day true reconciliation will come about; and a world of pure differences would be indistinguishable from one of pure identities. The idea of utopia travels beyond both conceptions: it would be, instead, a 'togetherness in diversity'.⁴ The aim of socialism is to liberate the rich diversity of sensuous use-value from the metaphysical prison-house of exchange-value – to emancipate history from the specious equivalences imposed upon it by ideology and commodity production. 'Reconciliation', Adorno writes, 'would release the non-identical, would rid it of coercion, including spiritualized coercion; it would open the road to the multiplicity of different things and strip dialectics of its power over them.'⁵

How this is to come about, however, is not easy to see. For the critique of capitalist society demands the use of analytic reason; and such reason would seem for Adorno, at least in some of his moods, intrinsically oppressive and reificatory. Indeed logic itself, which Marx once described as a 'currency of the mind', is a kind of generalized barter or false equalization of concepts analogous to the exchanges of the market place. A dominative rationality, then, can be unlocked only with concepts already irredeemably contaminated by it; and this proposition itself, since it obeys the rules of analytic reason, must already be on the side of dominion. In *Dialectic of Enlightenment* (1947), co-authored by Adorno and his colleague Max Horkheimer, reason has become inherently violent and manipulative, riding roughshod over the sensuous particularities of Nature and the body. Simply to think is to be guiltily complicit with ideological domination; yet to surrender instrumental thought altogether would be to lapse into barbarous irrationalism.

The identity principle strives to suppress all contradiction, and for Adorno this process has been brought to perfection in the reified, bureaucratized, administered world of advanced capitalism. Much the same bleak vision is projected by Adorno's Frankfurt School colleague Herbert Marcuse, in his *One-Dimensional Man* (1964). Ideology, in short, is a 'totalitarian' system which has managed and processed all social conflict out of existence. It is not only that this thesis would come as something of a surprise to those who actually run the Western system; it is also that it parodies the whole notion of ideology itself. The Frankfurt School of Marxism, several of whose members were refugees from Nazism, simply projects the 'extreme' ideological universe of fascism onto the quite different structures of liberal capitalist regimes. Does *all* ideology work by the identity principle, ruthlessly expunging whatever is heterogeneous to it? What, for example, of the ideology of liberal humanism, which in however specious and restricted a fashion is able to make room for variousness, plurality, cultural relativity, concrete particularity? Adorno and his fellow workers deliver us something of a straw target of ideology, in the manner of those post-structuralist theorists for whom all ideology without exception would appear to turn upon metaphysical absolutes and transcendental foundations. The real ideological conditions of Western capitalist societies are surely a good deal more mixed and self-contradictory, blending 'metaphysical' and pluralistic discourses in various measures. An opposition to monotonous self-identity ('It takes all kinds to make a world'); a suspicion of absolute truth claims ('Everyone's entitled to their point of view'); a rejection of reductive stereotypes ('I take people as I find them'); a celebration of difference ('It'd be a strange world if we all thought the same'): these are part of the stock-in-trade of popular Western wisdom, and nothing is to be politically gained by caricaturing one's antagonist. Simply to counterpose difference to identity, plurality to unity, the marginal to the central, is to lapse back into binary opposition, as the more subtle deconstructors are perfectly aware. It is pure formalism to imagine that otherness, heterogeneity and marginality are unqualified political benefits regardless of their concrete social content. Adorno, as we have seen, is not out simply to replace identity with difference; but his suggestive critique of the tyranny of equivalence leads him too often to 'demonize' modern capitalism as a seamless, pacified, self-regulating system. This, no doubt, is what the system would *like* to be told; but it would probably be greeted with a certain scepticism in the corridors of Whitehall and Wall Street.

The later Frankfurt School philosopher Jürgen Habermas follows Adorno in dismissing the concept of a Marxist science, and in refusing to assign any particular privilege to the consciousness of the revolutionary proletariat. But whereas Adorno is then left with little to pit against the system but art and negative dialectics, Habermas turns instead to the resources of communicative language. Ideology for him is a form of communication systematically distorted by power – a discourse which has become a medium of domination, and which serves to legitimate relations of organized force. For hermeneutical philosophers like Hans-Georg Gadamer, misunderstandings and lapses of communication are textual blockages to be rectified by sensitive interpretation. Habermas, by contrast, draws attention to the possibility of an entire discursive system which is somehow deformed. What warps such discourse out of true is the impact upon it of extra-discursive forces: ideology marks the point at which language is bent out of communicative shape by the power interests which impinge upon it. But this besieging of language by power is not just an external matter: on the contrary, such dominion inscribes itself on the inside of our speech, so that ideology becomes a set of effects internal to particular discourses themselves.

If a communicative structure is *systematically* distorted, then it will tend to present the appearance of normativity and justness. A distortion which is so pervasive tends to cancel all the way through and disappear from sight – just as we would not describe as a deviation or disability a condition in which everybody limped or dropped their aitches all the time. A systematically deformed network of communication thus tends to conceal or eradicate the very norms by which it might be judged to *be* deformed, and so becomes peculiarly invulnerable to critique. In this situation, it becomes impossible to raise *within* the network the question of its own workings or conditions of possibility, since it has, so to speak, confiscated these enquiries from the outset. The system's historical conditions of possibility are redefined by the system itself, thus evaporating into it. In the case of a 'successful' ideology, it is not as though one body of ideas is perceived to be more powerful, legitimate or persuasive than another, but that the very grounds for choosing rationally between them have been deftly removed, so that it becomes impossible to think or desire outside the terms of the system itself. Such an ideological formation curves back upon itself like cosmic space, denying the possibility of any 'outside', forestalling the generation of new desires as well as frustrating those we already have. If a 'universe of discourse' is truly a *universe* then there is no standpoint beyond it where we might find a point of leverage for critique. Or if other universes are acknowledged to exist, then they are simply defined as incommensurable with one's own.

Habermas, to his credit, subscribes to no such fantastic dystopian vision of an all-powerful, all-absorbent ideology. If ideology is language wrenched out of true, then we must presumably have some idea of what an 'authentic' communicative act would look like. There is, as we have noted, no appeal open for him to some scientific metalanguage which would adjudicate in this respect among competing idioms; so he must seek instead to extract from our linguistic practices the structure of some underlying 'communicative rationality' – some 'ideal speech situation' which glimmers faintly through our actual debased discourses, and which may therefore furnish a norm or regulative model for the critical assessment of them.[6]

The ideal speech situation would be one entirely free of domination, in which all participants would have symmetrically equal chances to select and deploy speech acts. Persuasion would depend on the force of the better argument alone, not on rhetoric, authority, coercive sanctions and so on. This model is no more than a heuristic device or necessary fiction, but it is in some sense implicit even so in our ordinary, unregenerate verbal dealings. All language, even of a dominative kind, is in Habermas's view inherently oriented to communication, and thus tacitly towards human consensus: even when I curse you I expect to be understood, otherwise why should I waste my breath? Our most despotic speech acts betray, despite themselves, the frail outlines of a communicative *rationality*: in making an utterance a speaker implicitly claims that what she says is intelligible, true, sincere and appropriate to the discursive situation. (Quite how this applies to such speech acts as jokes, poems and shouts of glee is not so apparent.) There is, in other words, a kind of 'deep' rationality built into the very structures of our language, regardless of what we actually say; and it is this which provides Habermas with the basis for a critique of our actual verbal practices. In a curious sense, the very *act* of enunciation can become a normative judgement on what is enunciated.

Habermas holds to a 'consensus' rather than 'correspondence' theory of truth, which is to say that he thinks truth less some adequation between mind and world than a question of the kind of assertion which everyone who could enter into unconstrained dialogue with the speaker would come to accept. But social and ideological domination currently prohibit such unconstrained communication; and until we can transform this situation (which for Habermas would mean fashioning a participatory socialist democracy), truth is bound to be, as it were, deferred. If we want to know the truth, we have to change our political form of life. Truth is thus deeply bound up with social justice: my truth claims refer themselves forward to some altered social condition where they might be 'redeemed'. It is thus that Habermas is able to observe that 'the truth of statements is linked in the last analysis to the intention of the good and the true life.'[7]

There is an important difference between this style of thought and that of the more senior members of the Frankfurt school. For them, as we have seen, society as it exists seems wholly reified and degraded, sinisterly successful in its capacity to 'administer' contradictions out of existence. This gloomy vision does not prevent them from discerning some ideal alternative to it, of the kind that Adorno discovers in modernist art; but it is an alternative with scant foundation in the given social order. It is less a dialectical function of that order, than a 'solution' parachuted in from some ontological outer space. It thus figures as a form of 'bad' utopianism, as opposed to that 'good' utopianism which seeks somehow to anchor what is desirable in what is actual. A degraded present must be patiently scanned for those tendencies which are at once indissolubly bound up with it, yet which – interpreted in a certain way – may be seen to point beyond it. So it is that Marxism, for example, is not just some kind of wishful thinking, but an attempt to discover an alternative to capitalism latent in the very dynamic of that form of life. In order to resolve its structural contradictions, the capitalist order would *have* to transcend itself into socialism; it is not simply a matter of believing that it would be pleasant for it to do so. The idea of a communicative rationality is another way of securing an internal bond between present and future, and so, like Marxism itself, is a form of 'immanent' critique. Rather than passing judgement on the present from the Olympian height of some absolute truth, it installs itself *within* the present in order to decipher those fault lines where the ruling social logic presses up against its own structural limits, and so could potentially surpass itself. There is a clear parallel between such immanent critique and what is nowadays known as deconstruction, which seeks similarly to occupy a system from the inside in order to expose those points of impasse or indeterminacy where its governing conventions begin to unravel.

Habermas has often enough been accused of being a rationalist, and there is no doubt some justice in the charge. How far is it really possible, for example, to disentangle the 'force of the better argument' from the rhetorical devices by which it is conveyed, the subject-positions at stake, the play of power and desire which will mould such utterances from within? But if a rationalist is one who opposes some sublimely disinterested truth to mere sectoral interests, then Habermas is certainly not of this company. On the contrary, truth and knowledge are for him 'interested' to their roots. We need types of instrumental knowledge because we need to control our environment in the interests of survival. Similarly, we need the sort of moral or political knowledge attainable in practical communication because without it there could be no collective social life at all. 'I believe that I can show', Habermas remarks, 'that a species that depends for its survival on the structures of linguistic communication and cooperative, purposive-rational action must *of necessity* rely on reason.'[8] Reasoning, in short, is in our interests, grounded in the kind of biological species we are. Otherwise why would we bother to find out anything at all? Such 'species-specific' interests move, naturally, at a highly abstract level, and will tell us little about whether we should vote Tory to keep the rates down. But as with communicative rationality, they can serve even so as a political norm: ideological interests which damage the structures of practical communication can be judged inimical to our interests as a whole. As Thomas McCarthy puts it, we have a practical interest in 'securing and expanding possibilities of mutual and self-understanding in the conduct of life',[9] so that a kind of politics is derivable from the sort of animals we are. Interests are *constitutive* of our knowledge, not just (as the Enlightenment believed) obstacles in its path. But this is not to deny that there are kinds of interest which threaten our fundamental requirements as a species, and these are what Habermas terms 'ideological'.

The opposite of ideology for Habermas is not exactly truth or knowledge, but that particular form of 'interested' rationality we call *emancipatory critique*. It is in our interests to rid ourselves of unnecessary constraints on our common dialogue, for unless we do the kinds of truths we need to establish will be beyond our reach. An emancipatory critique is one which brings these institutional constraints to our awareness, and this can be achieved only by the practice of collective self-reflection. There are certain forms of knowledge that we need at all costs in order to be free; and an emancipatory critique such as Marxism or Freudianism is simply whatever form of knowledge this currently happens to be. In this kind of discourse, 'fact' (cognition) and 'value' (or interest) are not really separable: the patient in psychoanalysis, for example, has an interest in embarking on a process of self-reflection because without this style of cognition he will remain imprisoned in neurosis or psychosis. In a parallel way, an oppressed group or class, as we have seen in the thought of Lukács, has an interest in getting to understand its social situation, since without this self-knowledge it will remain a victim of it.

This analogy may be pursued a little further. Dominative social institutions are for Habermas somewhat akin to neurotic patterns of behaviour, since they rigidify human life into a compulsive set of norms and thus block the path to critical self-reflection. In both cases we become dependent on hypostasized powers, subject to constraints which are in fact cultural but which bear in upon us with all the inexorability of natural forces. The gratificatory instincts which such institutions thwart are then either driven underground, in the phenomenon Freud dubs 'repression', or sublimated into metaphysical world views, ideal value systems of one kind or another, which help to console and compensate individuals for the real-life restrictions they must endure. These value systems thus serve to legitimate the social order, channelling potential dissidence into illusory forms; and this, in a nutshell, is the Freudian theory of ideology. Habermas, like Freud himself, is at pains to emphasize that these idealized world views are not *just* illusions: however distortedly, they lend voice to genuine human desires, and thus conceal a utopian core. What we can now only dream of might always be realized in some emancipated future, as technological development liberates individuals from the compulsion of labour.

Habermas regards psychoanalysis as a discourse which seeks to emancipate us from systematically distorted communication, and so as sharing common ground with the critique of ideology. Pathological behaviour, in which our words belie our actions, is thus roughly equivalent to ideology's 'performative contradictions'. Just as the neurotic may vehemently deny a wish which nevertheless manifests itself in symbolic form on the body, so a ruling class may proclaim its belief in liberty while obstructing it in practice. To interpret these deformed discourses means not just translating them into other terms, but reconstructing their conditions of possibility and accounting for what Habermas calls 'the genetic conditions of the unmeaning'.[10] It is not enough, in other words, to unscramble a distorted text: we need rather to explain the causes of the textual distortion itself. As Habermas puts the point with unwonted pithiness: 'The mutilations [of the text] have meaning as such.'[11] It is not just a question of deciphering a language accidentally afflicted with slippages, ambiguities and non-meanings; it is rather a matter of explaining the forces at work of which these textual obscurities are a necessary effect. 'The breaks in the text', Habermas writes, 'are places where an interpretation has forcibly prevailed that is ego-alien even though it is produced by the self ... The result is that the ego necessarily deceives itself about its identity in the symbolic structures that it consciously produces.'[12]

To analyse a form of systematically distorted communication, whether dream or ideology, is thus to reveal how its lacunae, repetitions, elisions and equivocations are themselves significant. As Marx puts the point in *Theories of Surplus Value*: 'Adam Smith's contradictions are of significance because they contain problems which it is true he does not resolve, but which he reveals by contradicting himself.'[13] If we can lay bare the social conditions which 'force' a particular discourse into certain deceptions and disguises, we can equally examine the repressed desires which introduce distortions into the behaviour of a neurotic patient, or into the text of a dream. Both psycho-analysis and 'ideology critique', in other words, focus upon the points where *meaning* and *force* intersect. In social life, a mere attention to meaning, as in hermeneutics, will fail to show up the concealed power interests by which these meanings are internally moulded. In psychical life, a mere concentration on what Freud calls the 'manifest content' of the dream will blind us to the 'dream work' itself, where the forces of the unconscious are most stealthily operative. Both dream and ideology are in this sense 'doubled' texts, conjunctures of signs and power; so that to accept an ideology at face value would be like falling for what Freud terms 'secondary revision', the more or less coherent version of the dream text that the dreamer delivers when she wakes. In both cases, *what* is produced must be grasped in terms of its conditions of production; and to this extent Freud's own argument has much in common with *The German Ideology*. If dreams cloak unconscious motivations in symbolic guise, then so do ideological texts.

This suggests a further analogy between psychoanalysis and the study of ideology, which Habermas himself does not adequately explore. Freud describes the neurotic symptom as a 'compromise formation', since within its structure two antagonistic forces uneasily coexist. On the one hand there is the unconscious wish which seeks expression; on the other hand there is the censorious power of the ego, which strives to thrust this wish back into the unconscious. The neurotic symptom, like the dream text, thus reveals and conceals at once. But so also, one might claim, do dominant ideologies, which are not to be reduced to mere 'disguises'. The middle-class ideology of liberty and individual autonomy is no mere fiction: on the contrary, it signified in its time a real political victory over a brutally repressive feudalism. At the same time, however, it serves to mask the genuine oppressiveness of bourgeois society. The 'truth' of such ideology, as with the neurotic symptom, lies neither in the revelation nor the concealment alone, but in the contradictory unity they compose. It is not just a matter of stripping off some outer disguise to expose the truth, any more than an individual's self-deception is just a 'guise' he assumes. It is rather that what is revealed takes place in terms of what is concealed, and *vice versa*.

Marxists often speak of 'ideological contradictions', as well as of 'contrad-ictions in reality' (though whether this latter way of talking makes much sense is a bone of contention amongst them). It might then be thought that ideological contradictions somehow 'reflect' or 'correspond to' contradictions in society itself. But the situation is in fact more complex than this suggests. Let us assume that there is a 'real' contradiction in capitalist society between bourgeois freedom and its oppressive effects. The ideological discourse of bourgeois liberty might also be said to be contradictory; but this is not exactly because it reproduces the 'real' contradiction in question. Rather, the ideology will tend to represent what is positive about such liberty, while masking, repressing or displacing its odious corollaries; and this masking or repressing work, as with the neurotic symptom, is likely to interfere from the inside with what gets genuinely articulated. One might claim, then, that the ambiguous, self-contradictory nature of the ideology springs precisely from its *not* authentically reproducing the real contradiction; indeed were it really to do so, we might hesitate about whether to term this discourse 'ideological' at all.

There is a final parallel between ideology and psychical disturbance which we may briefly examine. A neurotic pattern of behaviour, in Freud's view, is not simply *expressive* of some underlying problem, but is actually a way of trying to cope with it. It is thus that Freud can speak of neurosis as the confused glimmerings of a kind of solution to whatever is awry. Neurotic behaviour is a *strategy* for tackling, encompassing and 'resolving' genuine conflicts, even if it resolves them in an imaginary way. The behaviour is not just a passive reflex of this conflict, but an active, if mystified, form of engagement with it. Just the same can be said of ideologies, which are no mere inert by-products of social contradictions but resourceful strategies for containing, managing and imaginarily resolving them. Etienne Balibar and Pierre Macherey have argued that works of literature do not simply 'take' ideological contradictions, in the raw, as it were, and set about lending them some factitious symbolic resolution. If such resolutions are possible, it is because the contradictions in question have already been surreptitiously processed and transformed, so as to appear in the literary work *in the form of* their potential dissolution.[14] The point may be applied to ideological discourse as such, which *works* upon the conflicts it seeks to negotiate, 'softening', masking and displacing them as the dream work modifies and transmutes the 'latent contents' of the dream itself. One might therefore attribute to the language of ideology something of the devices employed by the unconscious, in their respective labour upon their 'raw materials': condensation, displacement, elision, transfer of affect, considerations of symbolic representability and so on. And the aim of this labour in both cases is to recast a problem in the form of its potential solution.

Any parallel between psychoanalysis and the critique of ideology must necessarily be imperfect. For one thing, Habermas himself tends in rationalist style to downplay the extent to which the psychoanalytic cure comes about less through self-reflection than through the drama of transference between patient and analyst. And it is not easy to think up an exact political analogy to this. For another thing, as Russell Keat has pointed out, the emancipation wrought by psychoanalysis is a matter of remembering or 'working through' repressed materials, whereas ideology is less a question of something we have *forgotten* than of something we never knew in the first place.[15] We may note finally that in Habermas's view the discourse of the neurotic is a kind of privatized symbolic idiom which has become split off from public communication, whereas the 'pathology' of ideological language belongs fully to the public domain. Ideology, as Freud might have said, is a kind of psychopathology of everyday life – a system of distortion so pervasive that it cancels all the way through and presents every appearance of normality.

Unlike Lukács, Theodor Adorno has little time for the notion of reified consciousness, which he suspects as residually idealist. Ideology, for him as for the later Marx, is not first of all a matter of consciousness, but of the material structures of commodity exchange. Habermas, too, regards a primary emphasis on consciousness as belonging to an outmoded 'philosophy of the subject', and turns instead to what he sees as the more fertile ground of social discourse.

The French Marxist philosopher Louis Althusser is equally wary of the doctrine of reification, though for rather different reasons from Adorno's.[16] In Althusser's eyes, reification, like its companion category of alienation, presupposes some 'human essence' which then undergoes estrangement; and since Althusser is a rigorously 'anti-humanist' Marxist, renouncing all idea of an 'essential humanity', he can hardly found his theory of ideology upon such 'ideological' concepts. Neither, however, can he base it on the alternative notion of a 'world view'; for if Althusser is anti-humanist he is equally anti-historicist, sceptical of the whole conception of a 'class subject' and firm in his belief that the science of historical materialism is quite independent of class consciousness. What he does, then, is to derive a theory of ideology, of impressive power and originality, from a combination of Lacanian psycho-analysis and the less obviously historicist features of Gramsci's work; and it is this theory that can be found in his celebrated essay 'Ideology and Ideological State Apparatuses', as well as in scattered fragments of his volume *For Marx*.[17]

Althusser holds that all thought is conducted within the terms of an unconscious 'problematic' which silently underpins it. A problematic, rather like Michel Foucault's 'episteme', is a particular organization of categories which at any given historical moment constitutes the limits of what we are able to utter and conceive. A problematic is not in itself 'ideological': it includes, for example, the discourses of true science, which for Althusser is free of all ideological taint. But we can speak of the problematic *of* a specific ideology or set of ideologies; and to do so is to refer to an underlying struc-ture of categories so organized as to exclude the possibility of certain conceptions. An ideological problematic turns around certain eloquent silences and elisions; and it is so constructed that the questions which are posable within it already presuppose certain kinds of answer. Its funda-mental structure is thus closed, circular and self-confirming: wherever one moves within it, one will always be ultimately returned to what is securely known, of which what is unknown is merely an extension or repetition. Ideologies can never be taken by surprise, since like a counsel leading a witness in a law court they signal what would count as an acceptable answer in the very form of their questions. A scientific problematic, by contrast, is characterized by its open-endedness: it can be 'revolutionized' as new scientific objects emerge and a new horizon of questions opens up. Science is an authentically exploratory pursuit, whereas ideologies give the appearance of moving forward while marching stubbornly on the spot.

In a controversial move within Western Marxism,[18] Althusser insists on a rigorous distinction between 'science' (meaning among other things Marxist theory) and 'ideology'. The former is not just to be grasped in historicist style as the 'expression' of the latter; on the contrary, science or theory is a specific kind of labour with its own protocols and procedures, one demarcated from ideology by what Althusser calls an 'epistemological break'. Whereas histor-icist Marxism holds that theory is validated or invalidated by historical practice, Althusser holds that social theories, rather like mathematics, are verified by methods which are purely internal to them. Theoretical proposi-tions are true or false regardless of who happens to hold them for what historical reasons, and regardless of the historical conditions which give birth to them.

Such an absolute opposition between science and ideology finds few defenders nowadays, and is clearly open to a range of cogent criticisms. To carve the world down the middle between science and ideology is to squeeze out the whole area we call 'practical' consciousness – statements such as 'it's raining' or 'do you need a lift?', which are neither scientific nor (in any especially useful sense of the term) ideological. In a regression to Enlightenment rationalism, Althusser in effect equates the opposition between science and ideology with one between truth and error – though in his *Essays in Self-Criticism* he acknowledges the 'theoreticist' nature of this move.[19] There are several reasons why this homology will not work. For one thing, ideology, as we have seen, is not just erroneous; and as Barry Barnes points out, ideological interests of a dubious kind can themselves further the advance of scientific knowledge. (Barnes cites the case of Karl Pearson's school of statistics, which involved some rather sinister eugenic theory but led to valuable scientific work.)[20] For another thing, science itself is a ceaseless process of trial and error. Not all ideology is error, and not all error is ideological. A science may serve ideological functions, as Marx considered the work of the early political economists to do, and as Lenin considered Marxist science to be the ideology of the revolutionary proletariat. Marx certainly judged the work of the bourgeois political economists to be scientific, able to some degree to penetrate the appearances of capitalist society; but he also thought it was inhibited at key points by ideological interests, and so was scientific and ideological at one and the same time. Science, to be sure, is not *reducible* to ideology: it is hard to see how research on the pancreas is no more than an expression of bourgeois interests, or how algebraic topology helps to legitimate the capitalist state. But it is, for all that, deeply inscribed by and embedded within ideology – either in the more neutral sense of the term as a whole socially determined way of seeing, or sometimes in the more pejorative sense of mystification. In modern capitalist society, what is ideological about science is not just this or that particular hypothesis, but the whole social phenomenon of science itself. Science as such – the triumph of technological, instrumental ways of seeing the world – acts as an important part of the ideological legitimation of the bourgeoisie, which is able to translate moral and political questions into technical ones resolvable by the calculations of experts. One does not need to deny the genuine cognitive content of much scientific discourse to claim that science is a potent modern myth. Althusser is thus mistaken to view all ideology, as he occasionally does, as 'pre-scientific', a body of prejudices and superstitions with which science effects a preternaturally clean break.

It is important, even so, to combat certain common travesties of his case. In his central essay on ideology, Althusser is not arguing that ideology is somehow inferior to theoretical knowledge; it is not a lesser, more confused sort of knowledge, but strictly speaking no kind of knowledge at all. Ideology, as we saw in chapter 1, denotes for Althusser the realm of 'lived relations' rather than theoretical cognition; and it makes no more sense to suggest that such lived relations are inferior to scientific knowledge than it does to claim that feeling one's blood boil is somehow inferior to measuring someone's blood pressure. Ideology is not a matter of truth or falsehood, any more than grinning or whistling are. Science and ideology are simply different registers of being, radically incommensurable with one another. There is no hint in *this* formulation that ideology is a negative phenomenon, any more than 'experience' itself is. To write a Marxist treatise on the politics of the Middle East would be for Althusser a scientific project; but it is not necessarily more important than the ideological act of shouting 'Down with the imperialists!', and in some circumstances might be a good deal less so.

The Althusserian distinction between science and ideology is an epistemological, not a sociological one. Althusser is not asserting that a cloistered elite of intellectuals have the monopoly of absolute truth, while the masses flounder about in some ideological quagmire. On the contrary, a middle-class intellectual may well live more or less entirely within the sphere of ideology, while a class-conscious worker may be an excellent theoretician. We cross back and forth all the time over the frontier between theory and ideology: a woman may chant feminist slogans on a demonstration in the morning (for Althusser an ideological practice), and pen an essay on the nature of patriarchy in the afternoon (a theoretical activity). Nor is Althusser's position theoreticist, holding that theory exists for its own sake. For him as for any Marxist, theory exists primarily for the sake of political practice; it is just that in his view its truth or falsity is not *determined* by that practice, and that, as a form of labour with its own material conditions of existence, it must be viewed as distinct from it.

Moreover, if the methods of theoretical inquiry are peculiar to it, its materials are not. Theory goes to work, among other things, on ideology; and in the case of historical materialism this means the actual political experience of the working class, from which – for Althusser as much as for Lenin – the theorist must ceaselessly learn. Finally, though theory is the guarantee of its own truth, it is not some metaphysical dogmatism. What distinguishes a scientific from an ideological proposition is that the former can always be *wrong*. A scientific hypothesis is one that could always in principle be falsified; whereas it is hard to see how one could falsify a cry like 'Reclaim the night!', or 'Long live the Fatherland!'

Althusser, then, is not quite the austere high priest of theoretical terrorism lampooned by an enraged E.P. Thompson in *The Poverty of Theory*.[21] In his later work, Althusser comes to modify the absoluteness of the science/ideology antithesis, arguing that Marx himself was able to launch his scientific labours only after he had first taken up a 'proletarian position' in politics.[22] But he does not thereby surrender his scientistic prejudice that, strictly speaking, only scientific discourse counts as real knowledge; and he does not abandon his claim that knowledge itself is in no sense historical. Althusser refuses to recognize that the very categories within which we think are historical products. It is one thing to reject the historicist case that theory is simply an 'expression' of historical conditions – a case which tends to suppress the specificity of theoretical procedures. It is quite another thing to hold that theory is entirely independent of history, or to argue that it is wholly self-validating. Magical thought and scholastic theology are both rigorous, internally consistent bodies of doctrine, but Althusser would presumably not wish to rank them on a level with historical materialism.

There is a difference between holding that historical circumstances thoroughly condition our knowledge, and believing that the validity of our truth claims is simply *reducible* to our historical interests. The latter case, as we shall see in the next chapter, is really that of Friedrich Nietzsche; and though Althusser's own case about knowledge and history is about as far from Nietzsche's as could be imagined, there is an ironic sense in which his major theses about ideology owe something to his influence. For Nietzsche, all human action is a kind of fiction: it presumes some coherent, autonomous human agent (which Nietzsche regards as an illusion); implies that the beliefs and assumptions by which we act are firmly grounded (which for Nietzsche is not the case); and assumes that the effects of our actions can be rationally calculated (in Nietzsche's eyes yet another sad delusion). Action for Nietzsche is an enormous, if necessary, oversimplification of the un-fathomable complexity of the world, which thus cannot coexist with reflection. To act at all means to repress or suspend such reflectiveness, to suffer a certain self-induced amnesia or oblivion. The 'true' conditions of our existence, then, must necessarily be absent from consciousness at the moment of action. This absence is, so to speak, structural and determined, rather than a mere matter of oversight – rather as for Freud the concept of the unconscious means that the forces which determine our being cannot by definition figure within our consciousness. We become conscious agents only by virtue of a certain determinate lack, repression or omission, which no amount of critical self-reflection could repair. The paradox of the human animal is that it comes into being as a subject only on the basis of a shattering repression of the forces which went into its making.

The Althusserian antithesis of theory and ideology proceeds roughly along these lines. One might venture, in a first, crudely approximate formulation, that theory and practice are at odds for Nietzsche because he entertains an irrationalist suspicion of the former, whereas they are eternally discrepant for Althusser because he harbours a rationalist prejudice against the latter. All action for Althusser, including socialist insurrection, is carried on within the sphere of ideology; as we shall see in a moment, it is ideology alone which lends the human subject enough illusory, provisional coherence for it to become a practical social agent. From the bleak standpoint of theory, the subject has no such autonomy or consistency at all: it is merely the 'overdetermined' product of this or that social structure. But since we would be loath to get out of bed if this truth was held steadily in mind, it must disappear from our 'practical' consciousness. And it is in this sense that the subject, for Althusser as for Freud, is the product of a structure which must necessarily be repressed in the very moment of 'subjectivation'.

One can appreciate, then, why for Althusser theory and practice must always be somewhat at odds, in a way scandalous to the classical Marxism which insists on a dialectical relation between the two. But it is harder to see exactly what this discrepancy *means*. To claim that one cannot act and theorize simultaneously may be like saying that you cannot play the *Moonlight Sonata* and analyse its musical structure at one and the same time; or that you cannot be conscious of the grammatical rules governing your speech in the very heat of utterance. But this is hardly more significant than saying that you cannot chew a banana and play the bagpipes simultaneously; it has no *philosophical* import at all. It is certainly a far cry from maintaining *à la* Nietzsche that all action entails a necessary ignorance of its own enabling conditions. The trouble with *this* case, at least for a Marxist, is that it seems to rule out the possibility of theoretically informed practice, which Althusser, as an orthodox Leninist, would be hard put to it to abandon. To claim that your practice is theoretically informed is not of course the same as imagining that you could engage in intensive theoretical activity at the very moment you are closing the factory gates to lock out the police. What must happen, then, is that a theoretical understanding does indeed realize itself in practice, but only, as it were, through the 'relay' of ideology – of the 'lived fictions' of the actors concerned. And this will be a radically different form of understanding from that of the theorist in his study, involving as it does for Althusser an inescapable element of misrecognition.

What is misrecognized in ideology is not primarily the world, since ideology for Althusser is not a matter of knowing or failing to know reality at all. The misrecognition in question is essentially a *self*-misrecognition, which is an effect of the 'imaginary' dimension of human existence. 'Imaginary' here means not 'unreal' but 'pertaining to an image': the allusion is to Jacques Lacan's essay 'The mirror stage as formative of the function of the I', in which he argues that the small infant, confronted with its own image in a mirror, has a moment of jubilant misrecognition of its own actual, physically uncoordinated state, imagining its body to be more unified than it really is.[23] In this imaginary condition, no real distinction between subject and object has yet set in; the infant identifies with its own image, feeling itself at once within and in front of the mirror, so that subject and object glide ceaselessly in and out of each other in a sealed circuit. In the ideological sphere, similarly, the human subject transcends its true state of diffuseness or decentrement and finds a consolingly coherent image of itself reflected back in the 'mirror' of a dominant ideological discourse. Armed with this imaginary self, which for Lacan involves an 'alienation' of the subject, it is then able to act in socially appropriate ways.

Ideology can thus be summarized as 'a representation of the imaginary relationships of individuals to their real conditions of existence'. In ideology, Althusser writes, 'men do indeed express, not the relation between them and their conditions of existence, but *the way* they live the relation between them and their conditions of existence: this presupposes both a real relation and an '*imaginary*', '*lived*' relation ... In ideology, the real relation is inevitably invested in the imaginary relation.'[24] Ideology exists only in and through the human subject; and to say that the subject inhabits the imaginary is to claim that it compulsively refers the world back to itself. Ideology is subject-centred or 'anthropomorphic': it causes us to view the world as somehow naturally oriented to ourselves, spontaneously 'given' to the subject; and the subject, conversely, feels itself a natural part of that reality, claimed and required by it. Through ideology, Althusser remarks, society 'interpellates' or 'hails' us, appears to single us out as uniquely valuable and address us by name. It fosters the illusion that it could not get on without us, as we can imagine the small infant believing that if *it* disappeared then the world would vanish along with it. In thus 'identifying' us, beckoning us personally from the ruck of individuals and turning its face benignly towards us, ideology brings us into being as individual subjects.

All of this, from the standpoint of a Marxist science, is in fact an illusion, since the dismal truth of the matter is that society has no need of me at all. It may need *someone* to fulfil my role within the process of production, but there is no reason why this particular person should be me. Theory is conscious of the secret that society has no 'centre' at all, being no more than an assemblage of 'structures' and 'regions'; and it is equally aware that the human subject is just as centreless, the mere 'bearer' of these various structures. But for purposive social life to get under way, these unpalatable truths must be masked in the register of the imaginary. The imaginary is thus in one sense clearly false: it veils from our eyes the way subjects and societies actually work. But it is not false in the sense of being mere arbitrary deception, since it is a wholly indispensable dimension of social existence, quite as essential as politics or economics. And it is also not false in so far as the *real* ways we live our relations to our social conditions are invested in it.

There are a number of logical problems connected with this theory. To begin with, how does the individual human being recognize and respond to the 'hailing' which makes it a subject if it is not a subject already? Are not response, recognition, understanding, subjective faculties, so that one would need to be a subject already in order to become one? To this extent, absurdly, the subject would have to pre-date its own existence. Conscious of this conundrum, Althusser argues that we are indeed 'always-already' subjects, even in the womb: our coming, so to speak, has always been prepared for. But if this is true then it is hard to know what to make of his insistence on the 'moment' of interpellation, unless this is simply a convenient fiction. And it seems odd to suggest that we are 'centred' subjects even as embryos. For another thing, the theory runs headlong into all the dilemmas of any notion of identity based upon self-reflection. How can the subject recognize its image in the mirror as itself, if it does not somehow recognize itself already? There is nothing obvious or natural about looking in a mirror and concluding that the image one sees is oneself. Would there not seem a need here for a third, higher subject, who could compare the real subject with its reflection and establish that the one was truly identical with the other? And how did this higher subject come to identify itself?

Althusser's theory of ideology involves at least two crucial misreadings of the psychoanalytic writings of Jacques Lacan – not surprisingly, given the sybilline obscurantism of the latter. To begin with, Althusser's imaginary subject really corresponds to the Lacanian *ego*, which for psychoanalytic theory is merely the tip of the iceberg of the self. It is the ego, for Lacan, which is constituted in the imaginary as a unified entity; the subject 'as a whole' is the split, lacking, desiring effect of the unconscious, which for Lacan belongs to the 'symbolic' as well as the imaginary order. The upshot of this misreading, then, is to render Althusser's subject a good deal more stable and coherent than Lacan's, since the buttoned-down ego is standing in here for the dishevelled unconscious. For Lacan, the imaginary dimension of our being is punctured and traversed by insatiable desire, which suggests a subject rather more volatile and turbulent than Althusser's serenely centred entities. The political implications of this misreading are clear: to expel desire from the subject is to mute its potentially rebellious clamour, ignoring the ways in which it may attain its allotted place in the social order only ambiguously and precariously. Althusser, in effect, has produced an ideology of the ego, rather than one of the human subject; and a certain political pessimism is endemic in this misrepresentation. Corresponding to this ideological misperception of his on the side of the 'little' or individual subject is a tendentious interpretation of the 'big' Subject, the governing ideological signifiers with which the individual identifies. In Althusser's reading, this Subject would seem more or less equivalent to the Freudian superego, the censorious power which keeps us obediently in our places; in Lacan's work, however, this role is played by the 'Other', which means something like the whole field of language and the unconscious. Since this, in Lacan's view, is a notoriously elusive, treacherous terrain in which nothing quite stays in place, the relations between it and the individual subject are a good deal more fraught and fragile than Althusser's model would imply.[25] Once again, the political implications of this misunderstanding are pessimistic: if the power which subjects us is singular and authoritarian, more like the Freudian superego than the shifting, self-divided Lacanian Other, the chances of opposing it effectively would seem remote.

If Althusser's subject were as split, desirous and unstable as Lacan's, then the process of interpellation might figure as a more chancy, contradictory affair than it actually does. 'Experience shows', Althusser writes with solemn banality, 'that the practical telecommunication of hailings is such that they hardly ever miss their man: verbal call or whistle, the one hailed always recognises that it is really him who is being hailed.'[26] The fact that Louis Althusser's friends apparently never mistook his cheery shout of greeting in the street is offered here as irrefutable evidence that the business of ideological interpellation is invariably successful. But is it? What if we fail to recognize and respond to the call of the Subject? What if we return the reply: 'Sorry, you've got the wrong person?' That we have to be interpellated as *some* kind of subject is clear: the alternative, for Lacan, would be to fall outside the symbolic order altogether into psychosis. But there is no reason why we should always accept society's identification of us as this *particular* sort of subject. Althusser simply runs together the necessity of some 'general' identification with our submission to specific social roles. There are, after all, many different ways in which we can be 'hailed', and some cheery cries, whoops and whistles may strike us as more appealing than some others. Someone may be a mother, Methodist, house-worker and trade unionist all at the same time, and there is no reason to assume that these various forms of insertion into ideology will be mutually harmonious. Althusser's model is a good deal too monistic, passing over the discrepant, contradictory ways in which subjects may be ideologically accosted – partially, wholly, or hardly at all – by discourses which themselves form no obvious cohesive unity.

As Peter Dews has argued, the cry with which the Subject greets us must always be *interpreted*; and there is no guarantee that we will do this in the 'proper' fashion.[27] How can I know for sure what is being demanded of me, that it is *I* who am being hailed, whether the Subject has identified me aright? And since, for Lacan, I can never be fully present as a 'whole subject' in any of my responses, how can my accession to being interpellated be taken as 'authentic'? Moreover, if the response of the Other to me is bound up with my response to it, as Lacan would argue, then the situation becomes even more precarious. In seeking the recognition of the Other, I am led by this very desire to misrecognize it, grasping it in the imaginary mode; so the fact that there is desire at work here – a fact which Althusser overlooks – means that I can never quite grasp the Subject and its call as they really are, just as it can never quite know whether I have 'truly' responded to its invocation. In Lacan's own work, the Other just signifies this ultimately inscrutable nature of all individual subjects. No *particular* other can ever furnish me with the confirmation of my identity I seek, since my desire for such confirmation will always 'go beyond' this figure; and to write the other as Other is Lacan's way of signalling this truth.

The political bleakness of Althusser's theory is apparent in his very conception of how the subject emerges into being. The word 'subject' literally means 'that which lies beneath', in the sense of some ultimate foundation; and throughout the history of philosophy there have been a number of candidates for this function. It is only in the modern period that the individual subject becomes in this sense foundational. But it is possible by a play on words to make 'what lies beneath' mean 'what is kept down', and part of the Althusserian theory of ideology turns on this convenient verbal slide. To be 'subjectified' is to be 'subjected': we become 'free', 'autonomous' human subjects precisely by submitting ourselves obediently to the Subject, or Law. Once we have 'internalized' this Law, made it thoroughly our own, we begin to act it out spontaneously and unquestioningly. We come to work, as Althusser comments, 'all by ourselves', without need of constant coercive supervision; and it is this lamentable condition that we misrecognize as our freedom. In the words of the philosopher who stands behind all of Althusser's work – Baruch Spinoza – men and women 'fight for their slavery as if they were fighting for their liberation' (Preface to *Tractatus Theologico-Politicus*). The model behind this argument is the subjection of the Freudian ego to the superego, source of all conscience and authority. Freedom and autonomy, then, would seem to be sheer illusions: they signify simply that the Law is so deeply inscribed in us, so intimately at one with our desire, that we mistake it for our own free initiative. But this is only one side of the Freudian narrative. For Freud, as we shall see later, the ego will rebel against its imperious master if his demands grow too insupportable; and the political equivalent of this moment would be insurrection or revolution. Freedom, in short, can transgress the very Law of which it is an effect; but Althusser maintains a symptomatic silence about this more hopeful corollary of his case. For him, as even more glaringly for Michel Foucault, subjectivity itself would seem just a form of self-incarceration; and the question of where political resistance springs from must thus remain obscure. It is this stoicism in the face of an apparently all-pervasive power or inescapable metaphysical closure which will flow into the current of post-structuralism.

There is, then, a distinctly pessimistic note in the whole Althusserian conception of ideology, a pessimism which Perry Anderson has identified as an abiding feature of Western Marxism as such.[28] It is as though the subjection to ideology which makes of us individual subjects is secured even before it has properly taken place. It works, so Althusser comments, 'in the vast majority of cases, with the exception of the "bad subjects" who on occasion provoke the intervention of one of the detachments of the (repressive) State apparatuses'.[29] One year before Althusser published these words, those 'bad subjects' – a mere aside in his text – came close to toppling the French state, in the political turmoil of 1968. Throughout his essay on 'Ideology and Ideological State Apparatuses', there is a notable tension between two quite different versions of the topic.[30] On the one hand, he acknowledges from time to time that any enquiry into ideology must begin from the realities of class struggle. What he calls the ideological state apparatuses – school, family, church, media and the rest – are sites of such conflict, theatres of confrontation between the social classes. Having underlined this point, however, the essay appears to forget about it, veering off into what is really a functionalist account of ideology as that which helps to 'cement' together the social formation and adapt individuals to its requirements. This case owes something to Gramsci; but it is also only a short step from the commonplace doctrines of bourgeois sociology. After passing over the inherently conflictive nature of ideology for some thirty pages, the essay then abruptly reinstates this perspective in a belatedly added postscript. There is, in other words, a hiatus between what Althusser asserts of the *political* nature of the ideological apparatuses – that they are fields of class struggle – and a 'sociologistic' notion of ideology which is much more politically neutral.

A functionalist approach to social institutions reduces their material complexity to the status of mere supports for other institutions, placing their significance outside themselves; and such a view is strongly evident in Althusser's argument. For it is difficult to see that schools, churches, families and media are *sheerly* ideological structures, with no other purpose than to buttress the dominant power. Schools may teach civic responsibility and saluting the flag; but they also teach children to read and write, and sometimes how to fasten their shoelaces, which would presumably be necessary in a socialist order too. It would come as a pleasant surprise to His Holiness the Pope to learn that the church in Latin America was nothing more than a support of imperial power. Television disseminates bourgeois values; but it also tells us how to cook a curry or whether it might snow tomorrow, and occasionally broadcasts programmes highly embarrassing to the government. The family is an arena of oppression, not least for women and children; but it occasionally offers kinds of value and relationship at odds with the brutally uncaring world of monopoly capitalism. All of these institutions, in short, are internally contradictory, serving different social ends; and though Althusser sometimes recalls this, he just as quickly represses it again. Not all aspects of such apparatuses are ideological all of the time: it is misleading to think of the ideological 'superstructure' as a fixed realm of institutions which operate in an invariable way.[31]

What these institutions are functional *for* is in Althusser's view the economic 'base' of society. Their main role is to equip subjects with the forms of consciousness necessary for them to assume their 'posts' or functions within material production. But this is surely too economistic and 'technicist' a model of ideology, as Althusser, in his appended postscript to the essay, has clearly become aware. It leaves no room for non-class ideologies such as racism and sexism; and even in class terms it is drastically reductive. The political, religious and other ideologies of a society are not exhausted by their functions within economic life. Althusser's theory of ideology would appear to lurch from the economic to the psychological with a minimum of mediation. It also suffers from a certain 'structuralist' bias: it is as though the social division of labour is a structure of locations to which particular forms of consciousness are automatically assigned, so that to occupy such a location is spontaneously to assume the kind of subjectivity appropriate to it. That this flattens out the real complexity of class consciousness, quite apart from ignoring its entwinement with non-class ideologies, is surely clear. And as if all this were not enough, Althusser has even been accused, ironically enough, of committing the humanist error of equating all subjects with human ones; for legally speaking companies and local authorities can be subjects too.

Whatever its flaws and limits, Althusser's account of ideology represents one of the major breakthroughs in the subject in modern Marxist thought. Ideology is now not just a distortion or false reflection, a screen which intervenes between ourselves and reality or an automatic effect of commodity production. It is an indispensable medium for the production of human subjects. Among the various modes of production in any society, there is one whose task is the production of forms of subjectivity themselves; and this is quite as material and historically variable as the production of chocolate bars or automobiles. Ideology is not primarily a matter of 'ideas': it is a structure which imposes itself upon us without necessarily having to pass through consciousness at all. Viewed psychologically, it is less a system of articulated doctrines than a set of images, symbols and occasionally concepts which we 'live' at an unconscious level. Viewed sociologically, it consists in a range of material practices or rituals (voting, saluting, genuflecting and so on) which are always embedded in material institutions. Althusser inherits this notion of ideology as habitual behaviour rather than conscious thought from Gramsci; but he presses the case to a quasi-behaviourist extreme in his claim that the subject's ideas '*are* his material actions inserted into material practices governed by material rituals which are themselves defined by the material ideological apparatus …'.[32] One does not abolish consciousness simply by an hypnotic repetition of the word 'material'. Indeed in the wake of Althusser's work this term rapidly dwindled to the merest gesture, grossly inflated in meaning. If *everything* is 'material', even thought itself, then the word loses all discriminatory force. Althusser's insistence on the materiality of ideology – the fact that it is always a matter of concrete practices and institutions – is a valuable corrective to Georg Lukács's largely disembodied 'class consciousness'; but it also stems from a structuralist hostility to consciousness as such. It forgets that ideology is a matter of meaning, and that meaning is not material in the sense that bleeding or bellowing are. It is true that ideology is less a question of ideas than of feelings, images, gut reactions; but ideas often figure importantly within it, as is obvious enough in the 'theoretical ideologies' of Aquinas and Adam Smith.

If the term 'material' suffers undue inflation at Althusser's hands, so also does the concept of ideology itself. It becomes, in effect, identical with lived experience; but whether all lived experience can usefully be described as ideological is surely dubious. Expanded in this way, the concept threatens to lose all precise political reference. If loving God is ideological, then so, presumably, is loving Gorgonzola. One of Althusser's most controversial claims – that ideology is 'eternal', and will exist even in communist society – then follows logically from this stretched sense of the word. For since there will be human subjects and lived experience under communism, there is bound to be ideology as well. Ideology, Althusser declares, has no history – a formulation adapted from *The German Ideology,* but harnessed to quite different ends. Though its contents are of course historically variable, its structural mechanisms remain constant. In this sense, it is analogous to the Freudian unconscious: everyone dreams differently, but the operations of the 'dream work' remain constant from one time or place to another. It is hard to see how we could ever know that ideology is unchanging in its basic devices; but one telling piece of evidence against this claim is the fact that Althusser offers as a *general* theory of ideology what is arguably specific to the bourgeois epoch. The idea that our freedom and autonomy lie in a submission to the Law has its sources in Enlightenment Europe. In what sense an Athenian slave regarded himself as free, autonomous and uniquely individuated is a question Althusser leaves unanswered. If ideological subjects work 'all by themselves', then some would seem to do so rather more than others.

Like the poor, then, ideology is always with us; indeed the scandal of Althusser's thesis for orthodox Marxism is that it will actually outlast them. Ideology is a structure essential to the life of all historical societies, which 'secrete' it organically; and post-revolutionary societies would be no different in this respect. But there is a sliding in Althusser's thought here between three quite different views of why ideology is in business in the first place. The first of these, as we have seen, is essentially political: ideology exists to keep men and women in their appointed places in class society. So ideology in *this* sense would not linger on once classes had been abolished; but ideology in its more functionalist or sociological meaning clearly would. In a classless social order, ideology would carry on its task of adapting men and women to the exigencies of social life: it is 'indispensable in any society if men are to be formed, transformed and equipped to respond to the demands of their conditions of existence'.[33] Such a case, as we have seen, follows logically from this somewhat dubiously stretched sense of the term; but there is also another reason why ideology will persist in post-class society, which is not quite at one with this. Ideology will be necessary in such a future, as it is necessary now, because of the inevitable complexity and opaqueness of social processes. The hope that in communism such processes might become transparent to human consciousness is denounced by Althusser as a humanist error. The workings of the social order as a whole can be known only to theory; as far as the practical lives of individuals go, ideology is needed to provide them with a kind of imaginary 'map' of the social totality, so that they can find their way around it. These individuals may also of course have access to a scientific knowledge of the social forma-tion; but they cannot exercise this knowledge in the dust and heat of everyday life.

This case, we may note, introduces a hitherto unexamined element into the debate over ideology. Ideology, so the argument goes, springs from a situation in which social life has become too complex to be grasped as a whole by everyday consciousness. There is thus the need for an imaginary model of it, which will bear something of the oversimplifying relation to social reality that a map does to an actual terrain. It is a case which goes back at least as far as Hegel, for whom ancient Greece was a society immediately transparent as a whole to all its members. In the modern period, however, the division of labour, the fragmentation of social life and the proliferation of specialized discourses have expelled us from that happy garden, so that the concealed connections of society can be known only to the dialectical reason of the philosopher. Society, in the terminology of the eighteenth century, has become 'sublime': it is an object which cannot be *represented*. For the people as a whole to get their bearings within it, it is essential to construct a myth which will translate theoretical knowledge into more graphic, immediate terms. 'We must have a new mythology', Hegel writes,

> but this mythology must be in the service of Ideas; it must be a mythology of *Reason*. Until we express the Ideas aesthetically, that is, mythologically, they have no interest for *the people*; and conversely, until mythology is rational the philosopher must be ashamed of it. Thus in the end enlightened and unenlightened must clasp hands: mythology must become philosophical in order to make people rational, and philosophy must become mythological in order to make the philosophers sensible.[34]

A somewhat parallel view of ideology can be found in the work of the anthropologist Clifford Geertz. In his essay 'Ideology as a Cultural System', Geertz argues that ideologies arise only when the traditional, pre-reflective rationales for a way have life have broken down, perhaps under the pressure of political dislocation. No longer able to rely on a spontaneous feel for social reality, individuals in these new conditions need a 'symbolic map' or set of 'suasive images' to help them plot their way around society and orient them to purposive action. Ideology emerges, in other words, when political life becomes autonomous of mythic, religious or metaphysical sanctions, and must be charted in more explicit, systematic ways.[35]

Hegel's myth, then, is Althusser's ideology, at least in one of its versions. Ideology adapts individuals to their social functions by providing them with an imaginary model of the whole, suitably schematized and fictionalized for their purposes. Since this model is symbolic and affective rather than austerely cognitive, it can furnish motivations for action as some mere theoretical comprehension might not. Communist men and women of the future will require such an enabling fiction just like anyone else; but meanwhile, in class-society, it serves the additional function of helping to thwart true insight into the social system, thus reconciling individuals to their locations within it. The 'imaginary map' function of ideology, in other words, fulfils both a political and a sociological role in the present; once exploitation has been overcome, ideology will live on in its purely 'sociological' function, and mystification will yield to the *mythical*. Ideology will still be in a certain sense false; but its falsity will no longer be in the service of dominant interests.

I have suggested that ideology is not for Althusser a pejorative term; but this claim now requires some qualification. It would be more accurate to say that his texts are simply inconsistent on this score. There are times in his work when he speaks explicitly of ideology as false and illusory, *pace* those commentators who take him to have broken entirely with such epistemological notions.[36] The imaginary mappings of ideological fictions are false from the standpoint of theoretical knowledge, in the sense that they actually get society wrong. So it is not here simply a question of *self*-misrecognition, as we saw in the case of the imaginary subject. On the other hand, this falsity is absolutely indispensable and performs a vital social function. So although ideology is false, it is not *pejoratively* so. We need only protest when such falsehood is harnessed to the purpose of reproducing exploitative social relations. There need be no implication that in post-revolutionary society ordinary men and women will not be equipped with a theoretical understanding of the social totality; it is just that this understanding cannot be 'lived', so that ideology is essential here too. At other times, however, Althusser writes as though terms like 'true' and 'false' are quite inapplicable to ideology, since it is no kind of knowledge at all. Ideology implicates subjects; but for Althusser knowledge is a 'subjectless' process, so ideology must by definition be non-cognitive. It is a matter of experience rather than insight; and in Althusser's eyes it would be an empiricist error to believe that experience could ever give birth to knowledge. Ideology is a subject-centred view of reality; and as far as theory is concerned, the whole perspective of subjectivity is bound to get things wrong, viewing what is in truth a centreless world from some deceptively 'centred' standpoint. But though ideology is thus false when viewed from the external vantage-point of theory, it is not false 'in itself' – for this subjective slant on the world is a matter of lived relations rather than controvertible propositions.

Another way of putting this point is to say that Althusser oscillates between a *rationalist* and a *positivist* view of ideology. For the rationalist mind, ideology signifies error, as opposed to the truth of science or reason; for the positivist, only certain sorts of statements (scientific, empirical) are verifiable, and others – moral prescriptions, for instance – are not even candidates for such truth/falsity judgements. Ideology is sometimes seen as wrong, and sometimes as not even propositional enough to be wrong. When Althusser relegates ideology to the false 'other' of true knowledge, he speaks like a rationalist; when he dismisses the idea that (say) moral utterances are in any sense cognitive, he writes like a positivist. A somewhat similar tension can be observed in the work of Emile Durkheim, for whose *The Rules of Sociological Method* ideology is simply an irrational obstruction to scientific knowledge, but whose *The Elementary Forms of Religious Life* views religion as an essential set of collective representations of social solidarity.

Ideology for Althusser is one of three 'regions' or 'instances' – the other two are the economic and the political – which together make up a social formation. Each of these regions is relatively autonomous of the others; and in the case of ideology this allows Althusser to steer between an economism of ideology, which would reduce it to a reflex of material production, and an idealism of ideology, which would regard it as quite disconnected from social life.

This insistence on a non-reductive account of ideology is characteristic of Western Marxism as a whole, in its sharp reaction to the economism of its late-nineteenth-century forebears; but it is also a position forced upon Marxist theory by the political history of the twentieth century. For it is impossible to understand a phenomenon like fascism without noting the extraordinarily high priority it assigns to ideological questions – a priority which could at times be at loggerheads with the political and economic requirements of the fascist system. At the height of the Nazi war effort, women were prohibited from factory work on ideological grounds; and the so-called 'final solution' disposed of many individuals whose skills might have been useful to the Nazis, as well as tying up manpower and resources which could have been deployed elsewhere. Later in the century, a similarly high priority is ascribed to ideology by a quite different political movement: feminism. There seems no way in which the oppression of women can be merely deduced from the imperatives of material production, interwoven with such matters though it doubtless is. Throughout the 1970s, then, the appeal of Althusserianism had much to do with the space it appeared to open up for emergent political movements of a non-class kind. We shall see later that this valuable shift away from a reductive Marxism sometimes ended up in a dismissal of social class altogether.

In his *Political Power and Social Classes*, the Althusserian theorist Nicos Poulantzas carries Althusser's distinction between social 'regions' into the field of ideology itself. Ideology can itself be discriminated into various 'instances' – moral, political, juridical, religious, aesthetic, economic and so on; and in any given ideological formation one of these instances will typically be dominant, thus securing that formation's unity. In feudalism, for example, it is religious ideology which predominates, whereas in capitalism the juridico-political instance comes to the fore. What 'level' of ideology is dominant will be determined primarily by which of them masks the realities of economic exploitation most effectively.

A distinguishing feature of bourgeois ideology, Poulantzas argues, is the absence from its discourse of all trace of class domination. Feudal ideology, by contrast, is much more explicit about such class relations, but justifies them as naturally or religiously grounded. Bourgeois ideology, in other words, is that form of dominative discourse which would present itself as entirely innocent of power – just as the bourgeois state tends to offer itself as representing the general interests of society at large, rather than as an oppressive apparatus. In bourgeois ideology, Poulantzas holds, this dissembling of power takes a specific form: the concealment of political interests behind the mask of *science*. The end-of-ideology thinkers, who applauded the supposed transition from a 'metaphysical' to a 'technological' rationality, are thus simply endorsing what was endemic in bourgeois ideology all along. Such ideologies, so Poulantzas argues, are notable for their lack of appeal to the sacred or transcendental; instead they ask to be accepted as a body of scientific techniques.

Among contemporary theorists, this view of bourgeois ideology as a radically 'this-worldly' discourse has gained considerable ground. For Raymond Boudon, ideologies are doctrines based on spurious scientific theories; they are, in a word, bad science.[37] Dick Howard argues that ideology is a matter of the 'immanent value-logic of capitalism': capitalism requires no transcendental legitimation, but is in some sense its own ideology.[38] Alvin Gouldner defines ideology as 'the mobilisation of the masses of public projects via the rhetoric of rational discourse', and sees it as striving to close the gap between private interests and the public good. 'Ideology', Gouldner writes, 'thus entailed the emergence of a new mode of political discourse; discourse that sought action but did not merely seek it by invoking authority or tradition, or by emotive rhetoric alone. It was discourse predicted on the idea of grounding political action in secular and rational theory ...'[39] Ideology in Gouldner's view thus involves a break with religious or mythological conceptions; and a similar case is urged by Claude Lefort, for whom ideology renounces all appeal to otherworldly values and seeks to conceal social divisions in secular terms alone.[40] Jürgen Habermas claims that ideologies 'replace traditional legitimations of power by appearing in the mantle of modern science and by deriving their justification from the critique of ideology (in the sense of metaphysical systems)'.[41] To this extent, there can be no pre-bourgeois ideology: ideology as a phenomenon is born with the bourgeois epoch, as an organic part of its secularizing, rationalizing tendencies.

Suggestive though this case is, it is surely too one-sided. The dominant ideology in Britain today, for example, encompasses both 'rational' and traditionalist elements: appeals to technical efficiency on the one hand, the adulation of monarchy on the other. The most pragmatist, technocratic society in the world – the United States – is also one of the most full-bloodedly 'metaphysical' in its ideological values, solemnly invoking God, Freedom and Nation. The businessman justifies his activity at the office by 'rational' criteria before returning to the sacred rituals of the family hearth. Indeed the more drearily utilitarian a dominant ideology is, the more refuge will be sought in compensatory rhetorics of a 'transcendental' kind. It is not uncommon for the best-selling author of pulp fiction to believe in the unfathomable mysteries of artistic creation. To see ideology simply as an alternative to myth and metaphysics is to miss an important contradiction in modern capitalist societies. For such societies still feel the need to legitimate their activities at the altar of transcendental values, not least religious ones, while steadily undermining the credibility of those doctrines by their own ruthlessly rationalizing practices. The 'base' of modern capitalism is thus to some extent at odds with its 'superstructure'. A social order for which truth means pragmatic calculation continues to cling to eternal verities; a form of life which in dominating Nature expels all mystery from the world still ritually invokes the sacred.

It is hard to know what bourgeois society can do about this dissonance. If it were to renounce all metaphysical gestures, drawing its legitimation instead from its actual social behaviour, it would risk discrediting itself; but as long as it clings to transcendental meanings, the discrepancy between them and its everyday practice will be painfully evident. The dilemma is usually resolved by a sort of double think: when we hear talk of freedom, justice and the sacredness of the individual, we both believe and do not believe that such talk should make a difference to what we actually do. We hold fervently that such values are precious; we also believe that, as the man said, it is when religion starts to interfere with your everyday life that it is time to give it up.

Althusser's thinking about ideology is on a fairly grand scale, revolving on such 'global' concepts as the Subject and ideological state apparatuses, whereas the French sociologist Pierre Bourdieu is more concerned to examine the mechanisms by which ideology takes hold in everyday life. To tackle this problem, Bourdieu develops in his *Outline of a Theory of Practice* (1977) the concept of *habitus*, by which he means the inculcation in men and women of a set of durable dispositions which generate particular practices. It is because individuals in society act in accordance with such internalized systems – what Bourdieu calls the 'cultural unconscious' – that we can explain how their actions can be objectively regulated and harmonized without being in any sense the result of conscious obedience to rules. Through these structured dispositions, human actions may be lent a unity and consistency without any reference to some conscious intention. In the very 'spontaneity' of our habitual behaviour, then, we reproduce certain deeply tacit norms and values; and habitus is thus the relay or transmission mechanism by which mental and social structures become incarnate in daily social activity. The habitus, rather like human language itself, is an open-ended system which enables individuals to cope with unforeseen, ever-changing situations; it is thus a 'strategy-generating principle' which permits ceaseless innovation, rather than a rigid blueprint.

The term ideology is not particularly central to Bourdieu's work; but if habitus is relevant to the concept, it is because it tends to induce in social agents such aspirations and actions as are compatible with the objective requirements of their social circumstances. At its strongest, it rules out all other modes of desiring and behaving as simply unthinkable. Habitus is thus 'history turned into nature', and for Bourdieu it is through this matching of the subjective and the objective, what we feel spontaneously disposed to do and what our social conditions demand of us, that power secures itself. A social order strives to naturalize its own arbitrariness through this dialectic of subjective aspirations and objective structures, defining each in terms of the other; so that the 'ideal' condition would be one in which the agents' consciousness would have the same limits as the objective system which gives rise to it. The recognition of legitimacy, Bourdieu states, 'is the misrecognition of arbitrariness'.

What Bourdieu calls *doxa* belongs to the kind of stable, tradition-bound social order in which power is fully naturalized and unquestionable, so that no social arrangement different from the present could even be imagined. Here, as it were, subject and object merge indistinguishably into each other. What matters in such societies is what 'goes without saying', which is determined by tradition; and tradition is always 'silent', not least about itself as tradition. Any challenge to such *doxa* is then *heterodoxy*, against which the given order must assert its claims in a new *orthodoxy*. Such orthodoxy differs from *doxa* in that the guardians of tradition, of what goes without saying, are now compelled to speak in their own defence, and thus implicitly to present themselves as simply one possible position, among others.

Social life contains a number of different habitus, each system appropriate to what Bourdieu terms a 'field'. A field, he argues in *Questions de sociologie* (1980), is a competitive system of social relations which functions according to its own internal logic, composed of institutions or individuals who are competing for the same stake. What is generally at stake in such fields is the attainment of maximum dominance within them – a dominance which allows those who achieve it to confer legitimacy on other participants, or to withdraw it from them. To achieve such dominance involves amassing the maximum amount of the particular kind of 'symbolic capital' appropriate to the field; and for such power to become 'legitimate' it must cease to be recognized for what it is. A power which is tacitly rather than explicitly endorsed is one which has succeeded in legitimating itself.

Any such social field is necessarily structured by a set of unspoken rules for what can be validly uttered or perceived within it; and these rules thus operate as a mode of what Bourdieu terms 'symbolic violence'. Since symbolic violence is legitimate, it generally goes unrecognized *as* violence. It is, Bourdieu remarks in *Outline of a Theory of Practice*, 'the gentle, invisible form of violence, which is never recognised as such, and is not so much undergone as chosen, the violence of credit, confidence, obligation, personal loyalty, hospitality, gifts, gratitude, piety....'[42] In the field of education, for example, symbolic violence operates not so much by the teacher speaking 'ideologically' to the students, but by the teacher being perceived as in possession of an amount of 'cultural capital' which the student needs to acquire. The educational system thus contributes to reproducing the dominant social order not so much by the viewpoints it fosters, but by this regulated distribution of cultural capital. As Bourdieu argues in *Distinction* (1979), a similar form of symbolic violence is at work in the whole field of culture, where those who lack the 'correct' taste are unobtrusively excluded, relegated to shame and silence. 'Symbolic violence' is thus Bourdieu's way of rethinking and elaborating the Gramscian concept of hegemony; and his work as a whole represents an original contribution to what one might call the 'microstructures' of ideology, complementing the more general notions of the Marxist tradition with empirically detailed accounts of ideology as 'everyday life'.

6

FROM SCHOPENHAUER TO SOREL

FOR THE Enlightenment, as we saw earlier, the enemy of ideology was, paradoxically, ideology. Ideology in the sense of a science of ideas would combat ideology in the sense of dogma, prejudice and mindless tradition-alism. Behind this belief lay a supreme confidence in reason typical of the middle class in its 'progressive' phase: nature, society and even the human mind itself were now raw materials in its hands, to be analysed, mastered and reconstructed.

As this confidence gradually wanes throughout the nineteenth century, with the emergence of a fully fledged industrial capitalist order about which there seemed little rational, a new current of thought comes to the fore. In a society where 'reason' has more to do with the calculation of self-interest than with some noble dream of emancipation, a scepticism about its lofty powers steadily gathers force. The harsh reality of this new social order would seem not reason, but appetite and interest; if reason has a role at all, it is the purely secondary one of estimating how the appetites can be most effectively gratified. Reason can help to promote our interests, but it is powerless to pass critical judgement on them. If it can 'ventriloquize' the passions, it remains itself entirely mute.

Such a standpoint had already been part of the familiar stock-in-trade of English empiricist philosophy, from Thomas Hobbes to David Hume. For Hume, reason can only ever be the slave of passion; and for this trend of thought in general the task of reason is to ascertain the nature of things as exactly as possible, so that we may the better realize our appetitive ends. But there is a latent tension between the two parts of this statement. For if 'man' is essentially a self-interested animal, will not these interests tend to distort his rational judgement? How can he be at once an impartial analyst of the world, and a partisan creature who views objects only in relation to his own needs and desires? To know what is rationally the case, I must so to speak remove myself and my prejudices from the scene of inquiry, behave as though I were not there; but such a project can clearly never get off the ground.

There is, in fact, a distinction between passions and interests, which Albert Hirschman has usefully examined.[1] For seventeenth- and eighteenth-century thought, to follow one's interests was on the whole positive, whereas to follow one's passions was not. 'Interests' suggested a degree of rational calculation, as opposed to being driven on by blind desire; it acts as a kind of intermediary category between the passions, which are generally base, and the reason, which is generally ineffectual. In the idea of 'interests', so Hirschman argues, the passions are upgraded by reason, while reason is lent force and direction by passion. Once the sordid passion of greed can be transmuted to the social interest of making money, it can suddenly be acclaimed as a noble goal. There was always of course the risk that this opposition could be deconstructed – that 'promoting one's interests' just meant counterposing one set of passions to another; but 'interest' had the sense of a *rational* self-love about it, and was seen as conveniently predictable, whereas desire was not. 'As the physical world is ruled by the laws of movement', proclaimed Helvetius, 'so is the moral universe ruled by laws of interest';[2] and we shall see that it is only a short step from this classic bourgeois doctrine to the assumptions of postmodernism.

It is an easy step from holding that reason is simply a neutral instrument of the passions, to claiming that it is a mere reflex of them. What if the supposed antithesis between reason and interests could be deconstructed, and reason be grasped simply as a modality of desire? What if this most elevated of the human faculties, which traditionally brings us within the orbit of divinity, were in reality just a disguised form of malice, longing, loathing, aggression? If this is so, then reason ceases to be the opposite of ideology, and becomes itself ideological through and through. It is ideological, moreover, in two senses of the word: first, because it is no more than an expression of interests; secondly, because it dissembles these interests behind a mask of impartiality.

A logical consequence of this view of things is that we can no longer speak of false consciousness. For now *all* consciousness is inherently false; whoever says 'consciousness' says distortion, delusion, estrangement. It is not that our perception of the world is sometimes clouded by passing prejudices, false social interests, pragmatic constraints or the mystifying effects of an opaque social structure. To be conscious just *is* to be deceived. The mind itself is chronically distorting: it is simply a fact about it that it travesties and disfigures reality, squints at the world sideways, grasps it from the falsifying perspective of some egoistic desire. The Fall is a fall up into consciousness, not one down to the beasts. Consciousness is just an accidental by-product of the evolutionary process, and its coming was never prepared for. The human animal is alienated from the world just because it can think, which puts it at a disabling distance from a mindless nature and opens up an unspannable abyss between subject and object. Reality is inhospitable to the mind, and is ultimately opaque to it. If we can speak any longer of 'ideology' at all, it must be in the manner of Francis Bacon's *Novum Organum*, which argues that some of the 'idols' or false notions which mystify humanity have their roots deep in the mind itself.

In the transition from Hegel to Arthur Schopenhauer, we can observe this dramatic shift of perspective taking place. Hegel's philosophy represents a last-ditch, eleventh-hour attempt to redeem the world for Reason, setting its face sternly against all mere intuitionism; but what in Hegel is the principle or Idea of Reason, unfurling its stately progress through history, has become in Schopenhauer the blind, voracious Will – the empty, insatiable hankering which lies at the core of all phenomena. The intellect for Schopenhauer is just a crude, blundering servant of this implacable force, twisted out of true by it, an inherently misrepresenting faculty which believes itself pathetically to present things as they really are. What for Marx and Engels is a specific social condition, in which ideas obscure the true nature of things, is in Schopenhauer generalized to the structure of the mind as such. And from a Marxist standpoint, nothing could be more ideological than this view that all thought is ideological. It is as though Schopenhauer in *The World as Will and Representation* (1819) does just what he describes the intellect as doing: offering as an objective truth about reality what is in fact the partisan perspective of a society governed increasingly by interest and appetite. The greed, malice and aggressiveness of the bourgeois market place are now simply the way it is with humanity, mystified to a metaphysical Will.

Schopenhauer stands at the fountainhead of a long tradition of irrationalist thought for which concepts are always ineffectual and approximate, incapable of capturing the ineffable quality of lived experience. The intellect carves up the complexity of that experience into arbitrary chunks, freezing its fluidity into static categories. Such speculations are rife in Romanticism, pass into the 'vitalist' thought of Henri Bergson and D.H. Lawrence, and can even be glimpsed in the post-structuralist opposition between 'metaphysical closure' and the unthinkable play of difference. All thought is thus a form of alienation, distancing reality in the very act of trying to seize it. Concepts are just pale reflections of the real; but to see concepts as 'reflections' at all is surely very strange. To have a concept is simply to be able to use a word in a particular way; it is not to be *regretted* that the word 'coffee' lacks the grainy texture and rich aroma of the actual thing. There is no 'nameless gap' here between the mind and the world. Having a concept is no more like having an experience than throwing a tantrum is like throwing a party. It is only because we are tempted to think of concepts in empiricist style as 'images' or 'offprints' of the world that we begin to fret about the eternal rift between the two.

The Will for Schopenhauer is quite futile and purposeless, but shields us from a knowledge of its own utter pointlessness by breeding in us a delusion known as the intellect. The intellect obtusely believes life to be meaningful, which is just a cunning ruse on the Will's part to keep on perpetuating itself. It is as though the Will takes pity on our hunger for significance and throws us just enough to be going on with. Like capitalism for Marx, or like the unconscious for Freud, the Schopenhauerian Will includes its own dissemblance within itself, known to a gullible humanity as reason. Such reason is just a superficial rationalizing of our desires, but believes itself to be sublimely disinterested. For Immanuel Kant, the world revealed to us by 'pure' (or theoretical) reason is just an assemblage of mechanistic causal processes, as opposed to the realm of 'practical' reason, or morality, where we know ourselves to be free, purposive agents. But it is difficult for us to subsist comfortably in this duality, so Kant looks to aesthetic experience as a way of bridging it. In the act of aesthetic judgement, a piece of the external world momentarily appears to have some kind of purposive point to it, thus assuaging our rage for meaning.[3]

The antithesis in Schopenhauer between intellect and will is a version of the later vexed opposition between theory and ideology. If theory informs us that reality lacks all immanent significance, then we can only act purpose-fully by suppressing this gloomy knowledge, which is one meaning of 'ideology'. All action, as we have seen with Nietzsche and Althusser, is thus a sort of fiction. If for Althusser we cannot act and theorize simultaneously, for Schopenhauer we have a problem even in walking and talking at the same time. Meaning depends on a certain oblivion of our true condition, and has its roots sunk deeply in non-meaning. To act is to lose the truth at the very point of trying to realize it. Theory and practice, intellect and will, can never harmoniously coincide; and Schopenhauer must therefore presumably hope that nobody who reads his philosophy will be in the least affected by it, since this would be exactly the kind of instance of theory transforming our interests which he is out to deny.

There is another paradox about Schopenhauer's writing, which it is worth touching upon briefly. Is that writing the product of the intellect or the will, of 'theory' or 'ideology'? If it is a product of the Will, then it is just one more expression of that Will's eternal pointlessness, with no more truth or meaning than a rumbling of the gut. But it cannot be a work of the intellect either, for the intellect is hopelessly estranged from the true nature of things. The question, in other words, is whether the claim that reason is inherently falsifying is not a species of performative contradiction, denying itself in the very act of assertion. And this is one of the many vexed issues which Schopenhauer will bequeath to his more celebrated successor, Friedrich Nietzsche.

The reality of things for Nietzsche is not Will but power; but this leaves reason in much the same situation as it was with Schopenhauer. Reason for Nietzsche is just the way we provisionally carve up the world so that our powers may best flourish; it is a tool or servant of those powers, a kind of specialized function of our biological drives. As such, it can no more submit those drives to critical scrutiny than can the Schopenhauerian intellect take the measure of the Will which propels it. Theory cannot reflect critically on the interests of which it is the expression. 'A critique of the faculty of knowledge', Nietzsche proclaims, 'is senseless: how should a tool be able to criticise itself when it can only use itself for the critique?'[4] The fact that Nietzsche's own philosophy would appear to do just that is one of the several paradoxes he presents us with.

The mind, then, is just an editing and organizing of the world for certain pragmatic ends, and its ideas have no more objective validity than that. All reasoning is a form of false consciousness, and every proposition we utter is without exception untrue. (Untrue to *what*, and in contrast with what, are tricky logical problems raised by Nietzsche's work.) Our thought moves within a largely unconscious framework of needs, interests and desires founded in the kind of material animals we are, and our truth claims are entirely relative to this context. The whole of our knowledge, as the philosopher Martin Heidegger will later argue, goes on within some practical, pre-reflective orientation to the world; we come to self-consciousness as beings already prejudiced, engaged, interested. Indeed the word 'interested' means literally 'existing in the midst of'; and nobody can exist anywhere else. For Nietzsche and Heidegger as for Marx, we are practical beings before we are theoretical ones; and in Nietzsche's view the notion of intellectual disinterestedness is itself just a concealed form of interest, an expression of the rancorous malice of those too craven to live dangerously. All thought is 'ideological' to the core, the outward mark of struggle, violence, dominion, the clash of competing interests; and science and philosophy are no more than crafty devices by which thought covers over its own unsavoury sources. Like Marx, Nietzsche is out to bring down reason's credulous trust in its own autonomy, scandalously unmasking the blood and toil in which all noble notions are born, the baseness and enmity at the root of our most edifying conceptions.

If reason is a kind of delusion, however, it is a necessary one – for without its deceptive reductions and simplifications we would never be able to survive. It is not true in Nietzsche's view that there is a truck bearing down on me at sixty miles per hour. For one thing, discrete objects such as trucks are just convenient fictions, ephemeral spin-offs of the ubiquitous will to power of which all apparently solid, separate substances are secretly composed. For another thing, the words 'I' or 'me' are equally spurious, fashioning a deceptively ongoing identity out of a bundle of centreless powers, appetites and actions. 'Sixty miles per hour' is just an arbitrary way of chopping up space and time into manageable chunks, with no ontological solidity whatsoever. 'Bearing down' is a bit of linguistic interpretation, wholly relative to the way the human organism and its perceptions have historically evolved. Even so, Nietzsche would not be cruel or cavalier enough to suggest that I shouldn't bother leaping out of the way. Since it is unlikely that I shall be around much longer if I give too much thought to these abstruse matters while the truck is thundering up, the statement is true in the pragmatic sense that it serves my survival and well-being.

The concept of ideology, then, is everywhere at work in Nietzsche's writings, even if the word itself is not; and it is operative in two different senses. The first is the one we have just seen – the view that ideas are simply deceptive rationalizations of passions and interests. There are analogies to this, as we have noted, in the Marxist tradition, at least as far as *particular* ideas are concerned. Nietzsche universalizes to thought as such what for Marxism is true of specific forms of social consciousness. But the alternative meaning of ideology in Nietzsche also finds some warrant in Marxist theory, and this is the conception of it as 'otherworldliness'. Ideology in this sense in Nietzsche's philosophy is that static, dehistoricized realm of metaphysical values ('soul', 'truth', 'essence', 'reality' and the rest) which offers a false consolation for those too abject and unmanly to embrace the will to power – to accept that struggle, disunity, contradiction, domination and ceaseless flux are really all there is. Ideology in this sense is equivalent to metaphysics – to the spuriously eternal verities of science, religion and philosophy, refuge of the 'nihilists' who spurn the joy and terror of endless becoming. The true world (of metaphysics)', Nietzsche comments, using the word 'true' sardonically, 'has been erected on a contradiction of the real world';[5] and his thought is here strikingly close to *The German Ideology*. In the teeth of such anodyne otherworldliness, Nietzsche speaks up instead for 'life': 'life itself is *essentially* appropriation, injury, overpowering of what is alien and weaker; suppression, hardness, imposition of one's own forms, incorporation, and at least, at its mildest, exploitation....'[6] 'Life', in other words, bears an uncanny resemblance to the capitalist market place, of which Nietzsche's own philosophy, among other things, is an ideological rationalization.

The belief that all thought is ideological, a mere rationalizing expression of interests and desires, springs from a social order in which a conflict between sectoral interests is uppermost. It is thus, one might claim, an ideology all of its own. If this is obvious enough in the case of Thomas Hobbes, it is rather less so in the apparently 'radical' version of this case promoted by much postmodernist theory, which is deeply in debt to the work of Nietzsche. That case, put in slightly parodic form, runs somewhat as follows. There is no such thing as truth; everything is a matter of rhetoric and power; all viewpoints are relative; talk of 'facts' or 'objectivity' is merely a specious front for the promotion of specific interests. The case is usually coupled with a vague opposition to the present political set-up, linked to an intense pessimism about the hope for any alternative. In its radical American form, it occasionally goes along with the belief that anything, including life in a Siberian salt-mine, is probably preferable to the current American way of life. Those who expound it will tend to be interested in feminism and 'ethnicity' but not in socialism, and to use terms like 'difference', 'plurality' and 'marginalization' but not 'class struggle' or 'exploitation'.

That there is something in this position is surely clear. We have seen too much of the shifty self-interestedness of the 'disinterested' to be much impressed by it; and we are generally right to suspect that appeals to see the object as it really is can be decoded as invitations to see it as our rulers do. One of the ideological victories of the liberal tradition has been to equate objectivity with disinterestedness, forging a powerful internal bond between the two. We can only get the world straight if we absolve ourselves of particular interests and predilections, viewing it as it would appear if we were not there. Some of those properly sceptical of this fantasy have then thrown out the baby of objectivity with the bathwater of disinterestedness; but this is simply because they have been gullibly convinced that the only viable meaning of 'objectivity' is the one pedalled by this Arnoldian heritage. There is no reason to grant this tradition such implicit credence: the term 'objectivity' has some perfectly workable meanings, as anyone who tried to give it up for six months would quickly discover. The author of *The Drowned and the Saved*, a memoir of the Nazi concentration camps, writes in his preface that he will try to discuss the subject with as much objectivity as he can muster. The author is Primo Levi, supremely non-disinterested victim of Auschwitz; and if Levi wishes to find out what really went on in the camps, it is because he is concerned to prevent them from happening again. Without needs and interests of some kind, we would see no point in getting to know anything in the first place. Capitalist society is a battleground of competing interests, and cloaks this incessant violence in the guise of disinterested ideas. Those postmodernists who quite properly see through this illusion often enough end up pitting against it a 'radical' version of the very market-place behaviour it conceals. In espousing a rich plurality of contending viewpoints and idioms as a good in itself, they turn an idealized version of that market-place reality against the monistic certitudes which help to hold it in place, thus seeking to undermine one part of capitalist logic with another. It is then no wonder that their 'radical' politics are a little strained and bleak, or at the worst (one thinks of Jean Baudrillard and Jean-François Lyotard) entirely vacuous.

The claim that the whole of our thought moves within the frame of certain practical, 'primordial', pre-reflective interests is surely just. But the concept of ideology has traditionally meant a good deal more than this. It is not just out to affirm that ideas are inscribed by interests; it draws attention to the ways in which *specific* ideas help to legitimate unjust and unnecessary forms of political domination. Statements like 'It's just coming up to three o'clock' are certainly traced through with social interests, but whether they are 'ideological' or not depends on their functioning within particular power-structures. The postmodernist move of expanding the concept of interests to encompass the whole of social life, while valid enough in itself, then serves to displace attention from these concrete political struggles, collapsing them into a neo-Nietzschean cosmos in which throwing off an overcoat is secretly just as much a matter of conflict and domination as overthrowing the state. If *all* thought is 'interested' to its roots, then – so it can be argued – the kinds of power-struggles to which, say, socialists and feminists have traditionally drawn attention have no very special status. A 'scandalous' vision of the whole of society as one restless will to power, one irresolvable turmoil of embattled perspectives, thus serves to consecrate the political *status quo*.

What this move involves, in effect, is the conflating of two quite difference senses of 'interest'. On the one hand, there are those 'deep' sorts of interest which structure our very form of life and provide the very matrix of our knowledge – the interest we have, for example, in viewing time as moving forwards rather than backwards or sideways, which we can hardly imagine ourselves out of. On the other hand there are interests like wanting to explode a small nuclear weapon over Fidel Castro's holiday villa, which we can quite easily imagine ourselves out of. The effect of running these two kinds of interests together is to 'naturalize' the latter by lending them something of the ineluctable status of the former. It is true that the mind cannot critically examine a sort of interest which is fundamentally constitutive of it – that this really would be a case of trying to haul ourselves up by our own bootstraps. It is not true, however, that an interest in blasting Fidel Castro into eternity cannot be submitted to rational critique; and the effect of the postmodernist expansion of 'interest', as in the work of Michel Foucault, is to elide this vital distinction.

A prime instance of this gambit can be found in the work of the American neo-pragmatist Stanley Fish. Fish argues that the whole of our so-called knowledge comes down to belief; that these beliefs, at least while we are experiencing them, are ineluctable, in the sense that I cannot choose not to believe what I believe; and that 'theory', far from being capable of making a difference to our beliefs, is just a rhetorically persuasive style of articulating them.[7] It is not hard to recognize in this case traces of the Schopenhauerian relation between intellect and Will, or the Nietzschean priority of power over reason. But it is curious, for one thing, to claim that all knowledge is a question of belief. For the philosopher Ludwig Wittgenstein, it would make no sense to say that I *believe* that I have two hands, any more than it would make sense to say that I *doubted* it. There is simply no context here, usually at least, in which the words 'belief' or 'doubt' could have force. If, however, I wake up after an operation in which there was a risk that one of my hands might be amputated, and the patient in the next bed is brutal enough to enquire whether I still have two hands, I might take a cautious peep under the bedclothes at these heavily bandaged objects and reply: 'I believe so'. Here there *would* be a context in which the term 'belief' would have real force; but it is idle otherwise to think that this kind of knowledge involves 'believing' anything at all.

By ranking all of our beliefs on the same level, as forces which grip us ineluctably, Fish takes up a reactionary political stance. For the effect of this drastic homogenizing of different modes and degrees of belief, as in the case of interests, is to naturalize beliefs such as 'Women should be treated as servants' to the status of 'beliefs' like: 'Vienna is the capital of Austria'. The superficially 'radical' appeal of the case is that the latter kind of proposition is no metaphysical truth but merely an institutional interpretation; its reactionary corollary is that the former sort of belief is made to appear quite as immune to rational reflection as the claim about Vienna.

Fish has thus set the situation up to prove in advance his claim that theoretical reflection can make no whit of difference to what beliefs we actually have. For this claim is otherwise distinctly implausible, involving as it does an untenably strong denial of the ways in which critical thought quite commonly helps to modify or even transform our interests and desires. I may come to see that my current interests are in fact unreasonable, serving as they do to obstruct the more valid interests of others; and if I am feeling suitably heroic I may alter or abandon them accordingly. This may happen in particular if my attention is drawn to certain genetic or functional aspects of my beliefs – where they spring from, and what social effects they breed – of which I was previously ignorant. None of this, of course, is likely to occur if the model for all belief is something like 'Snow is white', and Fish's case is thus pointlessly self-confirming.

Perhaps the problem is that subjecting beliefs to rational critique would seem to demand occupying some 'transcendental' vantage-point beyond them. Michel Foucault had little time for such chimeras; but this does not appear to have prevented him from holding that imprisoning homosexuals is not the most enlightened way of relating to them. The view that critical reflection entails locating oneself in some metaphysical outer space, sublimely absolved from all interests of one's own, is just a tedious bugbear with which those who wish for their own ideological reasons to deny the possibility of such reflection seek to rattle those who do not. And the assumption that without such a God's-eye view we are left with nothing but an array of partial perspectives, any one of which is as good as any other, is simply a kind of inverted metaphysics. Those who imagine that if truth is not absolute then there is no truth at all are simply closet transcendentalists, helplessly in thrall to the very case they reject. As Richard Rorty has pointed out, absolutely nobody is a relativist, in the sense of believing that any view of a particular topic is as good as any other.[8]

Certainly Fish himself is not in this sense a relativist; but he does seem to think that critically examining one's beliefs involves catapulting oneself into outer space. It would mean that

> the individual who was constituted by historical and cultural forces [would have to] 'see through' these forces and thus stand to the side of his own convictions and beliefs. But that is the one thing a historically conditioned consciousness cannot do, conduct a rational examination of its own convictions ... it could only do that if it were not historically conditioned and were instead an acontextual or unsituated entity ...[9]

The self for Fish, as much as for the most shamelessly vulgar Marxism, is the helplessly determined product of history, a mere puppet of its social interests; and there is then nothing between such iron determinism on the one hand and a plainly vacuous transcendentalism on the other. We are either totally constrained by our social contexts, or not constrained at all. In a typical postmodernist sleight of hand, *all* of our beliefs are made to appear as fundamentally constitutive of the self as the 'belief' that I have two hands, so that it follows as logically that reason is unable to round upon them as it does that the eye cannot see itself seeing something. But this is only because Fish's relentlessly monistic vision of things expels all contradiction from both self and world, terrified as it is of the slightest whiff of ambiguity or indeterminacy. Cultural contexts are assumed to be unitary, so that, say, a product of the white South African ruling class must inevitably endorse the doctrine of apartheid. But the South African social context is of course complex, ambiguous and self-contradictory, composed of precious liberal and radical traditions as well as of racist ones; and an upper-class white in those conditions may thus find the racist values 'naturally' bred in him at war with a critical stance towards them. Faced with this argument, Fish will take a smart step backwards and point out that the individual in question is then the determined product of *this* whole conflictive situation, unable to think himself outside his inexorably constraining political ambivalence; but this will not retrieve the fatal concession he has then made to a radical case. For a radical does not need to deny this in the least; he or she just wants to claim that we can submit interests and beliefs, whether our own or others, to critical scrutiny. There is no need to imply that this is done from outside the framework of any belief whatsoever. Perhaps further reflection will then lead the South African to be critical of his own ambivalence, and so come to oppose apartheid wholeheartedly. Fish's case fails because it grants far too much to the political left he is out to discredit. As long as we are able to bring down apartheid, we are really not terribly bothered about the fact that we can only accomplish this project from the standpoint of some belief system or other; in fact it never occurred to us to deny it. Fish wants to worst the political left in order to protect the American way of life; but rather than critically engage with the left's case, he tries in a hubristic gesture to undercut it completely by denying that emancipatory critique can ever get off the ground. But this is only because he has surreptitiously subsumed all interests and beliefs to the status of those which are indeed so utterly constitutive of the self, so fundamentally the grounds of its very historical possibility, that the case proves itself. It is as though my belief that Indian tea is more pleasant than Chinese – a belief I hold loosely, provisionally and indifferently – is imbued with all the immutable force of the Kantian categories.

Unlike Fish, Marxism does not hold that the self is an impotent reflex of its historical conditions. On the contrary, what constitutes a human subject *as* a subject is precisely its ability to transform its own social determinants – to make something of that which makes it. Men and women, as Marx observed, make their own history on the basis of anterior conditions; and both parts of the statement, constituting and constituted, must be allowed equal weight. An historical being is one ceaselessly 'out ahead' of itself, radically 'excessive' and non-self-identical, able within certain definite constraints to pose its own existence as problematic. And it is exactly in this structural gap or lag between the actual and the possible that emancipatory critique can take hold. For Fish, however, radicalism is an impossible enterprise; for either my critical observations on the current power-system are intelligible to that system, in which case they are simply one more move within it and thus not radical at all; or they are not, in which case they are so much irrelevant noise. Ironically, Fish is a sort of 'ultra-leftist' who believes that all 'true' radicalism is some unimaginable anarchism, some 'alternative universe' logic wholly at variance with the present; and he therefore suffers from what Lenin rebuked as an infantile disorder. But of course it is *definitive* of any effective radicalism that it engages with the terms of the given system, precisely in order to subvert it. If it did not, then there would be no question of subversion at all. Nobody can ever really disagree with Stanley Fish – for either he understands what you say, in which case you are not disagreeing with him at all; or he does not, in which case your views belong to some problematic wholly incommensurable with his own. And such incommensurability rules out the possibility of both agreement and disagreement.

What Fish's position at all costs must deny, in other words, is the notion of immanent critique. If he were to countenance for a moment what Karl Marx did to the bourgeois political economists, his case would fall instantly to the ground. For Marxism regards rationality neither as some ahistorical absolute, nor as the mere reflex of current powers and desires. Instead, it seeks to occupy the categories of bourgeois society from within, in order to highlight those points of internal conflict, indeterminacy and contradiction where its own logic might be led to surpass itself. It is just this strategy which Marx adopted with the bourgeois economists, with whom he most certainly shared a categorial logic; unless he and Adam Smith are both in some sense talking about capitalism, then there is no sense in which Marx's case constitutes a *critique* of Smith's. But only some rhetorical ultra-leftism could then imagine that Marx and Smith are much of a muchness, and the former is not 'truly' radical at all. If this is the view of a Fish, it was certainly not the view of the bourgeois political economists, and neither is it the view of US Steel. Postmodern thought would seem to have fallen for the sterile antithesis that 'reason' must either stand wholly on the inside of a form of life, guiltily complicit with it, or lurk at some illusory Archimedean point beyond it. But this is to assume that this form of life is not somehow inherently contradictory, comprising at once beliefs and interests wholly 'internal' to it, and other forms of discourse and practice which run counter to its ruling logic. The much-vaunted 'pluralism' of postmodern theory is curiously monistic on this score. Radical political thought, in the best deconstructive manner, seeks to locate itself neither wholly inside nor wholly outside the given system, but, so to speak, in that system's very internal contradictions, in the places where it is non-identical with itself, in order to elaborate from them a political logic which might ultimately transform the power-structure as a whole. Marxism takes with the utmost seriousness bourgeois society's talk of freedom, justice and equality, and enquires with *faux* naivety why it is that these grandiloquent ideals can somehow never actually enter upon material existence. Fish, of course, will then remind us yet again that all *this* implies some vantage-point of belief, which we cannot occupy and not occupy simultaneously; but it is hard to know who exactly ever thought we could. The last thing Marxism has ever credited is the fantasy that truth is somehow unhistorical.

It is worth adding that Fish's assumption that in order to criticize my beliefs and desires I must stand entirely to one side of them is a hangover from Kantian puritanism. For Kant, moral self-reflection or practical reason must be wholly independent of interest and inclination; for Aristotle, by contrast, a certain critical reflection of one's desire is actually a potential within it. Part of what is involved for Aristotle in living virtuously – living, that is to say, in the rich flourishing of one's creative powers – is to be motivated to reflect on precisely this process. To lack such self-awareness would be in Aristotle's view to fall short of true virtue, and so of true happiness or well-being. The virtues for Aristotle are organized states of desire; and some of these desires move us to curve back critically upon them. Aristotle thus deconstructs Fish's rigorous antithesis of interests and critical thought – an antithesis which crops up in Fish's work as no more than a negative form of Kantianism.

It is clear enough, then, what a 'radical' pragmatism or neo-Nietzschean-ism finally comes down to. It comes down to a shamefaced apologia for the Western way of life, more rhetorically suasive than some explicitly redneck propaganda on behalf of the Pentagon. We begin with a proper dismissal of disinterestedness, a suspicion of objectivity and an apparently hard-nosed insistence on the realities of incessant conflict, and end up playing obediently into the hands of Henry Kissinger. In some such styles of thinking, a transcendentalism of truth is merely ousted by a *transcendentalism of interests*. Interests and desires are just 'givens', the baseline which our theorizing can never glimpse behind; they go, so to speak, all the way down, and we can no more inquire where they actually come from than we could usefully ask the Enlightenment ideologues about the sources of their own Olympian rationality. In this sense, very little has changed from the days of Thomas Hobbes, even if such a standpoint is now commonly associated with political dissent rather than with supporting the absolutist state. Marxism, by contrast, has one or two things to say about the conditions which actually generate our social interests – and says it in a highly 'interested' way.

What is projected by postmodernism as a universally valid relation between knowledge and interests is in fact fairly specific to the bourgeois epoch. For Aristotle, as we have seen, the reflective decision to fulfil a desire is part of that desire itself; and our desires can thus become *reasons* for action. We can speak in this sense of 'mindful desire' or 'desiring mind', in contrast with a later thinker like Kant, for whom our desires and moral decisions must be kept rigorously separate.[10] Once a desire has become a reason for action, however, it ceases to remain identical with itself; it is no longer simply some blind unquestionable cause, but enters into our *discourse* and undergoes significant transformation. For some postmodernism, however, interests and desires would appear to be curiously self-identical; it is Aristotle who emerges in this light as more deconstructive than the deconstructionists. Those who regard reason as no more than the instrument of interests, in a time-hallowed bourgeois tradition, sometimes seem to assume that it is self-evident what exactly our interests are. The problem is promoting them, not defining them. A strange new kind of positivism thus comes to birth, for which it is now desires and interests, no longer brute sense-data, which can be taken as obvious. But we do not of course always spontaneously know what is in our best interests, since we are not transparent to ourselves. Reason is not only a way of pragmatically promoting our desires, but of working out what desires we actually have, and how valid, enhancing and productive they are in relation to the desires of others. It is in this sense that the classical concept of reason is intimately tied to the concept of social justice. We have an interest, as Kant remarked, in reason – an interest in clarifying our real interests. And this is another sense in which reason and passion are not simply to be counterposed as opposites.

Reason is commonly thought to be on the side of disinterestedness and totality, seeing life steadily and seeing it whole. Remove this faculty, and all we appear to be left with is a clash of sectoral standpoints, no one of which can be judged more valid than another. We have noted already that such relativism is no more than a will o' the wisp: nobody in fact believes it for a moment, as an hour's casual observation of their behaviour will readily attest. But the idea persists that reason is a global affair of seeing things dispassionately in the round, whereas interests are stubbornly local and particular. Either we are so deeply 'in the midst' of things, embroiled in this or that specific preoccupation, that we could never hope to grasp our situation as a whole; or we can strive to judge this maelstrom of partial viewpoints from the outside, only to discover that we are standing in empty space. This, in effect, is the double bind genially offered us by a whole array of contemporary theorists (Hans-Georg Gadamer and Richard Rorty may serve as suitably diverse instances), who place under prohibition any attempt to launch a critique of a whole way of life.[11] (Whether this case follows from a cogent or tendentious reading of the later Wittgenstein is a controversial issue; certainly the later Wittgenstein greeted the whole form of life known as Great Britain with undisguised disapproval.) Once again, an apparently radical case veers on its axis here into a covertly conservative one: a 'materialist' stress on the rootedness of our ideas in practical interests, offensive to a social order which considers thought to be nobly neutral, is also a grim *caveat* that any attempt to grasp society as a totality involves a chimerical transcendentalism. Both emphases follow logically enough from a Nietzschean reading of the world.

We have seen already something of the radical riposte to this position. It is not as though there are some theorists who find themselves spontaneously thinking in grandly global terms, while other more modest, less megalomaniac commentators prefer to stick to the irreducibly plural and concretely particular. It is rather that there are certain kinds of concretely particular social interests which could not hope to realize their ends without passing over at some point into a critical inquiry into the structure of society as a whole. To forestall this alarming possibility you have simply to argue, like Margaret Thatcher or Ernesto Laclau, that 'society as a whole' does not exist. It is not that such stubbornly particular interests 'leave themselves behind', so to speak, in this shift to a more global analysis, abandoning their own partisan perspectives for some grandly disinterested view. It is rather that without such more structural theorizing they cannot even be in effective possession of themselves. Some more general kind of critique is constrained by the very logic of these specific concerns. Thus it is that an oppressed group or class – women, the proletariat, ethnic minorities, colonized peoples and the rest – may come to recognize that without grasping something of their own material location within a wider system, they will never be effectively able to realize their highly specific interest in emancipation. Most Western theorists who deny or fail to see this point are located in material situations known as Western universities, where there is no compelling reason, much of the time at least, to bother one's head about such rebarbative abstractions or 'terroristic totalities' as imperialism. Others are not quite so lucky. In this sense it is false to counterpose local interests to global totality; any theory of the latter is quite as 'interested' as a campaign to relocate an airport. To speak simply of a 'plurality of interests', ranging from black inner-city populations to model aircraft buffs, then merely obscures this crucial point.

If there are no rational grounds on which to adjudicate between competing social interests, then the condition we are left with is a violent one. Either I just have to fight you for my position, or I deploy that more subtle form of domination, enthusiastically urged by Fish, which is sophistical rhetoric. This vision of embattled viewpoints slogging it out, each striving to linguistically outdo the other, is very masculinist. It is also politically obtuse: for the fact is that, under capitalist conditions, no *universal* engagement of opposed positions can even get off the ground. It is possible to see a radical interest as just one among many in the theoretical marketplace; but though this is true enough in one sense, it is misleading in another. For the 'interest' of the radical is just to bring about the kind of social conditions in which all men and women could genuinely participate in the formulation of meanings and values, without exclusion or domination. The liberal pluralist is not wrong in seeing such an open dialogue of differences as a desirable goal; he or she is just mystified to think that it could ever be adequately conducted in a class-divided society, where what counts as an acceptable interest in the first place is determined by the ruling power. Such participatory, socialist democratic institutions could be created only once such a power has been overthrown, and along with it the species of sophistical 'mental violence' espoused by a Stanley Fish. As to what meanings and values might result from this comradely encounter of differences, the radical has absolutely nothing to say, since his or her whole political commitment is exhausted in the effort to bring about its historical conditions of possibility.

The most illustrious inheritor of the tradition of Schopenhauer and Nietzsche is Sigmund Freud. Like his precursors. Freud is out to demonstrate the fitfulness and fragility of reason, its dependence upon some more fundamental set of forces. The place radically 'other' to reason which Schopenhauer names Will is for Freud the unconscious; but the unconscious can be seen just as well as a *deconstruction* of the opposition between reason and instinct, rather as Nietzsche sometimes sees the intellect as a faculty internal to the will to power. The rational ego is a kind of organ or outcropping of the unconscious, that piece of it which is turned to the external world; and in this sense our ideas have their complex roots in the bodily drives. Indeed the impulse to knowledge is itself for Freud secretly libidinal, a sublimated form of sexual curiosity to which he gives the name 'epistemophilia'. To know, for Freud as for Nietzsche, is inseparable from the will to dominate and possess. The very distinction between knowing subject and knowable object, the ground of all epistemology, has its basis in our infantile life: under the sway of the so-called pleasure principle, the small infant expels certain objects from itself in fantastic form, thus constituting an external world, and 'introjects' certain others to form the basis of an ego. All of our later knowledge will be carried on within the frame of these more primary attachments and aversions: our ideas move within the context of desire, and there is no thought or perception without its admixture of unconscious fantasy. For Freud, all cognition contains miscognition, all illumination is overshadowed by a certain blindness. Wherever we uncover meaning, then we can be sure to find non-meaning at its root.

Seen in this light, Freud's writings are faithful to the central contention of the tradition we are examining – that the *mind itself* is constituted by a chronic distortion or alienation, and that 'ideology' is thus its natural habitat. False consciousness is no accident which afflicts the intellect in the form of passing prejudice; it is not the result of mystification or false social interests. On the contrary, it was there from the very beginning, lodged deep within the structure of our perceptions. Desire infiltrates our routine projects, causing them to swerve, falter, miss the mark. False consciousness is thus less some specific body of belief than, in Freud's own phrase, the 'psycho-pathology of everyday life'.

In this sense, we might say that Freud's theory of ideology (though the term itself is hardly present in his work) is of an Althusserian cast. Indeed we have seen already that it is from Freud himself, via the detour of Lacan, that Althusser derives his notion of ideology as 'lived relations', which exist largely at the level of the unconscious and involve an inescapable structure of miscognition. Just as in Althusser's thought the subject of ideology exists only through ignorance of its true conditions, so the paradox of Freud, as we have seen, is that the subject comes into being only on the basis of a massive repression of its own unconscious determinants. Oblivion is thus our 'natural' mode, and remembering is simply forgetting to forget. The ground of all our insight, then, is some primordial opaqueness to ourselves: the unconscious produces the ego, but must necessarily be absent from it if the ego is to function effectively. Much the same can be said in Althusser's case about the relations between subject and society, where the latter operates as the 'absent cause' of the former. And this, on the surface at least, is exceedingly gloomy news. If our knowledge is just a function of our self-opacity, how can we hope to achieve the kinds of insights which might set us free? How can there be a 'truth of the subject', if the subject loses itself in the very act of emerging into being?

We can put the problem in different terms. Psychoanalysis is a discourse which strives to engage reflectively with the arational; and as such it suggests that ultimate impossibility of all 'ideology critique'. For to the extent to which such a discourse is 'rational', it opens up a disabling gap between itself and its object; and to the extent to which it simply reproduces the language of desire, it would seem to forfeit all claims to uncovering its hidden mechanisms. The critique of ideology will always be dogged by this impasse or *aporia*, in which to 'understand' the slippery signifiers it examines is to be in that instant eluded by them. The Freud who doubted that there was ever any getting to the bottom of a dream, who pointed to the role of the analyst's own desires ('countertransference'), and who came in later life to speculate that the theoretical constructs of the analyst were perhaps as much convenient fictions as the fantasies of the patient, appears to have been conscious enough of the baffling nature of his own enterprise. But there is also another Freud, whose trust in the ultimate efficacy of reason runs somewhat counter to this scepticism. To put the matter in Marxist terms: if Freud is 'Althusserian' in his awareness of the chronic miscognitions of everyday life, he also shares something of the Enlightenment view of such false consciousness of the early Marx and Engels. And the exemplary Freudian text for this 'enlightened' critique of ideology is his late enquiry into religion, *The Future of an Illusion.*

Religion, in Freud's opinion, fulfils the role of reconciling men and women to the instinctual renunciations which civilization forces upon them. In compensating them for such sacrifices, it imbues an otherwise harsh, purposeless world with meaning. It is thus, one might claim, the very paradigm of ideology, providing an imaginary resolution of real contradictions; and were it not to do so, individuals might well rebel against a form of civilization which exacts so much from them. In *The Future of an Illusion*, Freud contemplates the possibility that religion is thus a socially necessary myth, an indispensable means of containing political disaffection; but he considers this possibility only to reject it. In the most honourable Enlightenment tradition, and despite all his elitist fear of the insensate masses, Freud cannot bring himself to accept that mystification must be an eternal condition of humanity. The idea that a minority of philosophers like himself may acknowledge the unvarnished truth, while the mass of men and women must continue to be the dupes of illusion, is offensive to his rational humanism. Whatever good historical purpose religion may have served in the 'primitive' evolution of the race, the time has now come to replace this myth with the 'rational operation of the intellect', or with what Freud terms 'education in reality'. Like Gramsci, he holds that the secularized, demythologized world view which has so far been largely the monopoly of the intellectuals must be disseminated as the 'common sense' of humanity as a whole.

To dismiss this hope as the dream of some dewy-eyed rationalist would be to evade the courage and challenge of Freud's text. For no modern thinker is more bleakly aware of the extreme precariousness of human reason – of the grim truth, as he comments in this work, that 'arguments are of no avail against (human) passions', and that 'even in present-day man purely reasonable motives can effect little against passionate impulsions'.[12] For all his wary scepticism of the claims of reason, however, Freud has the imagination to ask himself whether unreason must always inevitably reign. The intellect, he remarks, may be powerless in comparison with the instinctual life; but though its voice is a 'soft' one, it does not rest until it has gained a hearing. 'The primacy of the intellect', he writes, 'lies, it is true, in a distant future, but probably not in an *infinitely* distant one' (238). Nothing, he claims, can in the long run withstand reason and experience, and the affront which religion offers to both is all too palpable. In the teeth of his own conservative alarm at the smoulderingly rebellious masses, Freud remains loyal to the *democratic* kernel of a mystified Enlightenment rationality. There is no doubt, in this work at least, as to whether it is such rationality, or a sceptical view of it, which is on the side of political progressivism.

Religion for Freud is a sublimation of our lowly drives to higher spiritual ends; but so in fact is 'culture' or civilization as a whole. 'Having recognised religious doctrines as illusions', he writes, we are at once faced by a further question: may not other cultural assets of which we hold a high opinion and by which we let our lives be ruled be of a similar nature? Must not the assumptions that determine our political regulations be called illusions as well? and is it not the case that in our civilisation the relations between the sexes are disturbed by an erotic illusion or a number of such illusions? (216)

Once one embarks on this line of thought, where will it end? Could it not, Freud muses, extend to reasoning and observation themselves? What if science itself were just another such sublimation? And what of the science known as Freudian psychoanalysis? The concept of sublimation is clearly getting out of hand, and Freud no sooner raises these embarrassing questions than he closes them peremptorily off. Lacking the means for undertaking so comprehensive a task, he modestly informs us, he will concentrate instead on the topic in hand.

Freud closes down the discussion, in short, just before it manoeuvres him into his own version of the Marxist doctrine of base and superstructure. In orthodox Marxist fashion, he informs us elsewhere that the basic motivation of social life is economic: civilization is just a cumbersome device for inducing men and women to do what they spontaneously detest, namely work. We are all naturally bone idle, and without this superstructure of sanctions and cajolements we would just lie around all day in various interesting states of *jouissance*. This is not, of course, exactly Marx's own point: the legal, political and ideological superstructure of society, for him at least, is a consequence of the *self-divided* nature of the economic 'base' in class conditions – of the fact that economic exploitation needs to be socially legitimated. It does not just follow from the universal injunction to labour. But Freud is aware that labour, at least in this kind of society, entails the renouncing of instinctual gratification; and the 'superstructure' of civilization, or 'culture', must therefore either coerce or cajole us into buckling down to the business of material reproduction. Freud's thought here is impeccably Gramscian: the means by which society is perpetuated, so he informs us, are 'measures of coercion and other measures that are intended to reconcile men (to their material destiny) and to recompense them for their sacrifices. These latter may be described as the mental assets of civilisation' (189). Or – in Gramsci's own terms – the institutions of hegemony. Culture for both thinkers is an amalgam of coercive and consensual mechanisms for reconciling human subjects to their unwelcome fate as labouring animals in oppressive conditions.

The problem in Freud's view is that such hegemonic processes can quickly become self-defeating. We sublimate our otherwise anti-social instincts into cultural ideals of one kind or another, which serve to unify a race of predatory egoists who would otherwise be at each other's throats. But these ideals can then become tyrannically excessive in their demands, demanding more instinctual renunciation than we can properly manage and so causing us to fall ill of neurosis. Moreover, this hegemony is threatened as soon as it becomes clear that some are being forced into more renunciation than others. In this situation, Freud comments, a 'permanent state of discontent' will persist in society and may lead to 'dangerous revolts'. If the satisfaction of the minority depends on the suppression of the majority, then it is understandable that the latter will begin to manifest a 'justifiable hostility' to the culture which their labour makes possible, but in which they have too meagre a share. A crisis of hegemony will consequently ensue; for hegemony is established by men and women *internalizing* the law which governs them, and in conditions of flagrant inequality 'an internalisation of the cultural prohibitions among the suppressed people is not to be expected' (191). 'It goes without saying', Freud adds, 'that a civilisation which leaves so large a number of its participants unsatisfied and drives them into revolt neither has nor deserves the prospect of a lasting existence' (192).

The mechanism by which the law of society is internalized is known as the superego. The superego is the voice of authority within us all, no longer an externally imposed power but the very ground of our personal conscience and moral idealism. Once power has inscribed itself within the very form of our subjectivity, any insurrection against it would seem to involve a *self-transgression*. To emancipate ourselves from ourselves – the whole purpose of Freud's therapeutic project – is a much more difficult affair than throwing off some merely external model of dominion. In the formation of the superego or Name-of-the-Father, power comes to entwine itself with the roots of the unconscious, tapping something of its awesome, implacable energy and directing this force sadistically against the ego itself. If political power is as recalcitrant as it is, then it is partly because the subject has come to love and desire the very law which subjugates it, in the erotic perversion known as masochism. 'The suppressed classes', Freud writes, 'can be emotionally attached to their masters; in spite of their hostility to them they may see in them their ideals' (193); and this, psychically speaking, is one secret of the tenacity of political domination.

Making the law our own, however, will not resolve the problems of civilization. Our appropriation of it will always be a partial, ambivalent affair – which is to say in Freudian parlance that the Oedipus complex is never fully dissolved. If we love and desire the law, we also nurture an intense animosity towards it, rejoicing in seeing this august authority brought low. And since the law itself is cruel, sadistic and tyrannical, it drives our aggression back upon ourselves and ensures that for every renunciation of satisfaction we are plunged deeper into neurotic guilt. In this sense, the power which sustains civilization also helps to undo it, stoking up within us a culture of lethal self-hatred. The law is obtuse as well as brutal: it is not only vengeful, paranoid and vindictive, but utterly insensitive to the fact that its insanely excessive demands could not possibly be fulfilled. It is a form of high-minded terrorism, which will simply rub our noses in our failure to live up to it rather than show us how to placate it. Before the law we are always in the wrong: like some imperious monarch, the superego 'does not trouble itself enough about the facts of the mental constitution of human beings. It issues a command and does not ask whether it is possible for people to obey it.'[13] This fanatical power is out of control, driving men and women to madness and despair; and Freud, who regarded the law as one of his oldest enemies, sees it as one aim of psychoanalysis to temper its death-dealing rigour.

It might be thought that men and women would naturally be driven to rebel against any authority as cruel as the superego. If they do not commonly do so, it is because in Freud's view the superego has its roots in the id or unconscious, closer to the unconscious than is the ego itself. Our submission to the law, in other words, is spurred on by strong instinctual forces, which bind us libidinally to it. The paradox, then, is that the very unconscious energies which fuel the superego's despotism are also those which drive us to embrace it; and this can be seen as deconstructing the Gramscian opposition of coercion and consent. What makes the law so coercive – the powerful unconscious impulsions behind its brutality – belong with the erotic drives which lead us to consent to it.

If 'culture' in Freud's eyes is a matter of sublimation, compensation and imaginary resolution, then it is really synonymous with one influential concept of ideology. But Freud's view of civilization is also ideological in a different sense. For him, as much as for Thomas Hobbes or Jeremy Bentham, there is an eternal enmity between the ruthlessly self-gratifying individual and the demands of society. Men and women are naturally self-seeking, dominative and aggressive, monstrous predators who can be dissuaded out of mutual injury only by the prohibitions of authority, or by the bribery of some alternative yield of pleasure. Freud has little or no conception of human society as nourishing as well as constraining – as a place of reciprocal self-fulfilment as well as a mechanism for keeping us from each other's throats. His view of both individual and society, in short, is classically bourgeois: the individual as an isolated monad powered by its appetites, society as some mere contractual device without which libidinal anarchy would be let loose. Given this cynical market-place morality, it is hardly surprising that the 'culture' which is meant to regulate and reconcile individuals is revealed as alarmingly fragile in contrast to their insatiable lust to plunder and possess. Freud's psychoanalytic theory is not finally dissociable from the politics of his social class, and like bourgeois political economy is inscribed at key points by these prejudices. It universalizes a particular view of 'man' to global status; and much the same can be said of the later version of the theory which is the school of Jacques Lacan. Whatever striking insights Lacan's work has undoubtedly to offer, there is surely no doubt that its view of the human subject as a mere effect of some inscrutable Other, its scorn for the whole concept of political emancipation, and its contemptuous dismissal of human history as little more than a 'sewer', has had its part to play in that jaundiced, disenchanted post-war *ethos* which goes under the name of the 'end of ideology'.

Whatever Freud's final trust in human reason, he is plainly not a rationalist as far as psychoanalytic *practice* goes. He does not believe that a patient could ever be cured simply by offering him a theoretical account of his ills. To this extent, Freud is at one with Marx: the point is not to interpret the world, but to change it. Neurosis is to be dispelled not by displacing its 'falsity' with some intellectual truth, but by tackling the material conditions which give birth to it in the first place. For him as for Marx, theory is pointless unless it comes to intervene as a transformative force within actual experience. For Marx, the opposite of an oppressive ideology is not in the end theory or an alternative ideology, but political practice. For Freud, the alternative to psychic disorder is the scene of analysis itself, within which the only truth that matters is that which gets constructed in the interplay between analyst and analysand. Like political practice, the scene of analysis is an active 'staging' or working through of conflicts, a 'theatricalizing' of certain urgent real-life issues in which the practical relations of human subjects to those problems is crucially transfigured. Both revolutionary practice and the scene of analysis involves the painful construction of a new identity on the ruins of the old, which is to be recollected rather than repressed; and in both cases 'theory' comes down to an altered practical self-understanding. Marxism and Freudianism have due respect for analytic discourse, in contrast to those modern irrationalisms which can afford the luxury of not needing to know. But for both creeds, the proof of emancipatory theory lies in the performance; and in this process theory and practice never form some neatly symmetrical whole. For if theory is a material intervention, it will alter the very practice it takes as its object and so stand in need of transformation itself, in order to be equal to the new situation it has produced. Practice, in other words, becomes the 'truth' that interrogates theory; so that here, as in the play of transference and countertransference between analyst and patient, it is never easy to say who exactly is analysing whom. A 'successful' theoretical act is one which substantially engages with practice and thus ceases to remain identical with itself, ceases to be 'pure theory'. Similarly, an ideological practice is no longer identical with itself once theory has entered it from the inside; but this is not to say that it now attains to a truth of which it was previously just ignorant. For theory can only successfully intervene in practice if it elicits what glimmerings of self-understanding the practice *already* has. If the analyst is a 'pure' theoretician, then she will be incapable of deciphering *this particular* form of mystified speech; and if the neurotic patient were not already unconsciously in search of some self-understanding, there would be no neurosis in the first place. For such disturbances, as we saw earlier, are ways of trying to encompass a real dilemma, and so contain their own kind of truth.

If neurosis contains this more 'positive' element, then so for Freud does an ideological illusion like religion. He distinguishes in *The Future of an Illusion* between 'delusions', by which he means psychotic states of mind in outright contradiction with reality, and 'illusions', which for all their unreality express a genuine wish. An illusion, for example, may be false *now*, but might be realized in the future; a middle-class woman may fantasize that a prince will arrive to marry her, and in the odd case may prove prophetic. What characterizes such illusions in Freud's view is their 'forward-looking' perspective, which is to say that they are essentially modes of wish-fulfilment. 'Thus we call a belief an illusion', he writes, 'when a wish-fulfilment is a prominent factor in its motivation, and in doing so we disregard its relations to reality, just as the illusion itself sets no store by verification' (213).

We need only substitute the term 'ideology' for 'illusion' here to read the statement as impeccably Althusserian: it is not a matter of verifying or falsifying the representation in question, but of grasping it as encoding some underlying desire. Such illusions are indissolubly bound up with reality: 'Ideology', comments Slavoj Žižek, 'is not a dreamlike illusion that we build to escape an insupportable reality; in its basic dimension it is a fantasy-construction which serves as a support for our 'reality' itself: an 'illusion' which structures our effective, real social relations and thereby masks some insupportable, real, impossible kernel ...'[14] As Althusser might put the point: in ideology, social reality is *invested* in the imaginary, interwoven with fantasy throughout its entire fabric; and this is very different from conceiving of it as a chimerical 'superstructure' erected over a solidly real 'base'. It is also, we may note, different from conceiving of it merely as a 'screen', which interposes itself between reality and ourselves. The reality and its appearances or fantasmal forms are much more closely intermeshed than any such imagery would imply. Real and imaginary are given in ideology together – which is why Žižek can argue that 'the only way to break the power of our ideological dream is to confront the Real of our desire which announces itself there.' If 'disinvesting' ourselves of an ideological viewpoint is as difficult as it usually is, it is because it involves a painful 'decathecting' or disinvestment of fantasy-objects, and thus a reorganization of the psychical economy of the self. Ideology clings to its various objects with all the purblind tenacity of the unconscious; and one important hold that it has over us is its capacity to yield enjoyment. Beyond the field of ideological signification, as Žižek points out, there is always a kind of non-signifying 'surplus' which is enjoyment or *jouissance*; and this enjoyment is the last 'support' of ideological meaning.[15]

Illusion, then, is by no means in Freud's view a purely negative category. Indeed it is a good deal less negative than Marx's early conception of ideology. If ideology is a condition of reality suffused and supported by our unconscious desires, as well as by our anxiety and aggression, then it conceals a utopian kernel. Illusion adumbrates within the present some more desirable state of affairs in which men and women would feel less helpless, fearful and bereft of meaning. It is thus radically double-edged, anodyne and aspiration together; and Frederic Jameson has argued that this is true of all artefacts in class society. Ideologies, cultural formations and works of art may well operate as strategic 'containments' of real contradictions; but they also gesture, if only by virtue of their *collective* form, to possibilities beyond this oppressive condition.[16] On this argument, even such 'degraded' modes of gratification as pulp fiction encode some frail impulse to a more durable fulfilment, and thus dimly prefigure the shape of the good society. Surprisingly, then, Freud's concept of illusion turns out to be at one with the notion of ideology developed by the later Frankfurt school. For Herbert Marcuse, the culture of class society is at once a false sublimation of social conflict and – if only in the very structural integrity of the work of art – a utopian critique of the present. Walter Benjamin's study of nineteenth-century Parisian society reminds us of Michelet's slogan that 'every epoch dreams its successor', and finds a buried promise of happiness and abundance in the very consumerist fantasies of the Parisian bourgeoisie. Ernst Bloch, in his *Principle of Hope* (1954–5), unearths glimmerings of utopia from that most apparently unpromising of all materials, advertising slogans.

To examine the unconscious dimensions of ideology is at once hopeful and cautionary. If ideology is interwoven with fantasy, then this is one reason for its formidable power; but such fantasies are never easily containable within the present, and point in principle beyond it. Utopia would be a condition in which Freud's 'pleasure principle' and 'reality principle' would have merged into one, so that social reality itself be wholly fulfilling. The eternal war between these principles rules out for Freud any such reconciliation; but the unreality of utopia is therefore also the impossibility of any total identification between our libidinal drives and a given system of political power. What thwarts utopia is the ruin of dystopia too: no ruling class can be wholly victorious. Freud has little to say directly of ideology; but it is very probable that what he points to as the fundamental mechanisms of the psychical life are the structural devices of ideology as well. Projection, displacement, sublimation, condensation, repression, idealization, substitution, rationalization, disavowal: all of these are at work in the text of ideology, as much as in dream and fantasy; and this is one of the richest legacies Freud has bequeathed to the critique of ideological consciousness.

The belief that human existence is basically a matter of interests, and thus 'ideological' to the core, gathers pace in the late nineteenth and early twentieth centuries, as a crisis of capitalism calls its ruling rationality into question.[17] As the capitalist system lurches nearer to global imperialist warfare, the faith in an absolute reason which typified its more 'classical' phase begins inexorably to collapse. Early twentieth-century Europe is awash with symbolism and primitivism, with a return to myth and a cult of unreason; it is shot through with strains of Wagner and Nietzsche, apocalypse and the dark gods. Indeed it is remarkable how much supposedly avant garde thinking today simply reinvents the *fin de siècle*, with its intimations of some primeval chaos lurking beneath the rational forms of society.

In his *Treatise of General Sociology* (1916), produced in the midst of the first world war, the Italian sociologist Vilfredo Pareto argues that the non-rational element in human behaviour greatly outweighs the rational. (No doubt this seemed an eminently rational case at the time, given a quick glance at the newspapers.) In Pareto's view, there are certain relatively invariable 'sentiments' in human life, the expression of which he terms 'residues'; and these provide the primary determinants of our action. Residues become encoded in turn in 'derivations', meaning the sorts of non-logical or pseudo-logical arguments (appeals to custom, tradition, authority and so on) which we use to justify our sentiments. So derivation is really a word for ideology, but a word which applies right across the board of our discourses. Ideas are just specious rationalizations of unchanging human motives; and politics, which for the right-wing Pareto is always funda-mentally elitist even in so-called democratic societies, is the art of acquainting oneself with the 'sentiments' and 'derivations' of the masses in order to manipulate them in the right direction. At an historical moment when mass revolutionary forces were stirring, this case had a certain political urgency about it. Bourgeois rationality is being challenged by emergent social powers, and must drop its mask of disinterestedness: it must ac-knowledge instead that all ideas are a brand of sophistical rhetoric, and hope that its own rhetoric will outdo that of its antagonists.

Ideas for Pareto may be false and unscientific, but still fulfil a useful role in sustaining social unity; and in this he is at one with the political philo-sopher Georges Sorel. In his *Reflections on Violence* (1906), Sorel counters what he sees as the dreary positivism of the Second International with his own peculiarly poeticized brand of Marxism. As a revolutionary syndicalist, Sorel places the general strike at the centre of his political programme; but what practical goals such a strike might achieve is for him a secondary matter. The general strike is a *myth*: it exists as an image or enabling fiction which will unify the proletariat, organize their political consciousness and inspire them to heroic action. 'Use must be made', Sorel writes, 'of a body of images which, *by intuition alone*, and before any considered analyses are made, is capable of evoking as an undivided whole the mass of sentiments which corresponds to the different manifestations of the war undertaken by Socialism against modern society. The Syndicalists solve this problem perfectly, by concentrating the whole of Socialism in the drama of the general strike....'[18] The general strike is a Romantic symbol, distilling in one flash of intuition a whole complex reality; it is a pre-reflective, pre-discursive image which allows for what Sorel, following his mentor Henri Bergson, calls 'integral' rather than analytic knowledge.

Sorel thus represents the point at which a Nietzschean pragmatism inrupts into the Marxist tradition. Political ideas are no longer to be assessed as scientifically correct or erroneous: they must be grasped instead as vital organizing principles, unifying forces which are 'true' in so far as they engender the 'noblest and deepest sentiments' in the working class and spur them to revolutionary action. They are thus conveniently proof against all rational argument. For Sorel as for the Nietzsche he admired, ideas are practical, provisional ways of cohering our experience so that our powers may best flourish. What matters is the *élan* of an image rather than the exactitude of a theory; and to this extent Sorel 'aestheticizes' the process of socialist revolution. The notion of the general strike, he remarks, produces 'an entirely epic state of mind'; and if such imagery is needed it is because there is something 'obscure' and 'mysterious' about socialism which resists all representation. 'No rational induction', Sorel writes in typical obscurantist fashion, 'will ever dispel the mystery which envelopes Socialism';[19] and the same is true of the process of proletarian revolution itself, which 'must be conceived as a catastrophe, the development of which beggars description'.[20] Socialism, in short, is a kind of 'sublimity', defying all discursive analysis; and its content must thus be conveyed in the immediacy of a mythical image rather than by the circumlocutions of science. Much influenced by this Sorelian irrationalism, the German critic Walter Benjamin wrote in his essay on surrealism of the need to 'expel moral metaphor from politics and to discover in political action a sphere reserved one hundred percent for images'.[21]

The essentially practical bent of Sorel's theories (he began life as an engineer) has a superficial radical appeal. But few thinkers more graphically reveal the dangers of pragmatism in radical thought. The intellectuals are not concerned about whether the ideas for which the workers struggle and perhaps die are true, or even whether they are practically efficacious; they are simply convenient ways of generating the kinds of consciousness which the intellectual deems desirable. The irresponsibility of such a stance is at one with Sorel's aestheticist glorification of revolutionary violence as an end in itself. His thinking powerfully influenced Antonio Gramsci, but helped breed a more sinister progeny too. The Romantic cult of will, action and violence, the sub-Nietzschean delight in the theatrical and heroic, the apocalypticism and poetic mysticism – all of these rendered Sorel's thought more than palatable to fascism. Indeed it is in fascism that one current of ideas we are tracing – the 'mythification' of thought, its reduction to a mere instrument of deeper forces – finds its fullest expression.

The relationship between myth and ideology is not easy to determine.[22] Are myths the ideologies of pre-industrial societies, or ideologies the myths of industrial ones? If there are clear parallels between the two, there are also significant points of difference. Both myth and ideology are worlds of symbolic meaning with social functions and effects; but myth is arguably the more capacious term, revolving as it does on the great 'metaphysical' questions of birth, sexuality and death, of sacred times, places and origins. Ideologies are generally more specific, pragmatic forms of discourse, which may encompass such mighty issues but bring them to bear more directly on questions of power. Myths are usually more concerned with how the aardvark got its long nose than with how to spot a communist. They are also typically pre-historical or dehistoricizing, fixing events in some eternal present or viewing them as infinitely repetitive; ideologies, by contrast, may and often do dehistoricize, but the various nineteenth-century ideologies of triumphal historical progress hardly fit this bill. (One may argue, however, that such ideologies of history are historical in their content but immobilized in their form; certainly Claude Lévi-Strauss sees 'history' as simply a modern myth.)

Myths may not legitimate political power as directly as ideologies, but in the manner of Pierre Bourdieu's *doxa* they can be seen as naturalizing and universalizing a particular social structure, rendering any alternative to it unthinkable. They can also be regarded in the style of a Lévi-Strauss as providing imaginary resolutions to real contradictions, and thus resemble ideology in this way too.[23] Some ideological discourses may harness bodies of myth to their purposes, as with Nazism or *The Waste Land*; one might think also of Bertolt Brecht's uses of folk legend in his literary works. Rather than simply identifying myth and ideology, then, it seems safer to speak of those aspects of ideologies which are mythical and those which are not. A myth is not just any old falsehood: we would not describe as a myth the claim that Everest can be scaled in forty minutes at a brisk trot. To qualify as mythical, the belief would have to be widely shared and reflect some significant psychological investment on the part of its adherents. The claim that 'science has the solution to all of humanity's problems' would probably fill this bill, and reveals, moreover, the element of *idealization* which most mythologizing entails. Mythical figures or events are those imbued with an aura of specialness: they are privileged, exemplary, larger-than-life phenomena which distil in peculiarly pure form some collective meaning or fantasy. We can thus speak of 'the myth of Jimi Hendrix', as we would not speak of the myth of Jimmy Carter. Myth is thus a particular *register* of ideology, which elevates certain meanings to numinous status; but it would be a mistake to imagine that all ideological language involves this sort of allure. Like ideology, myth need not involve falsity: there is nothing false about the myth of Jimi Hendrix, unless it implies a belief in his divinity. Nor need myths be mystificatory, in the sense of breeding deceptive effects in the service of a dominant power. The myth of England as a sleeping giant about to arise and throw off its shackles has served the cause of political emancipation in its time. Finally, we may note that whereas myths are typically narratives, ideology does not invariably assume such a form.

This, however, raises an important issue. Do politically oppositional movements live ineluctably in myth, or should we strive – as in that dream of Enlightenment from Kant to Freud – for a future condition in which men and women will face the world without such opiates, confident in their dignity as rational beings? Let us consider the example of the mythologies of Irish nationalism. It is possible to make a number of severe criticisms of this body of belief. At its most extreme it is a form of essentialism, trusting to some pure essence of Irishness (identical with the Gaelic and Catholic) which must be preserved free of contamination from alien influences. In this view, Ulster Protestants would not figure as truly Irish at all. In its crudest manifestations, this essentialism merges into outright racism. Irish nationalism tends to sponsor a cyclical, homogenizing reading of history, in which there is an heroic continuity of anti-imperialist struggle and in which almost all of the ills of Ireland can be laid at Britain's door. All battles are the same battle, all victories and defeats effectively identical. It thrives on an irresponsible, masochistic, quasi-mystical cult of martyrdom and blood-sacrifice, for which failure sometimes appears more efficacious than success. It is notoriously masculinist, furnished with a pantheon of virile, seven-foot-tall young heroes allotted pseudo-religious status. It trades in sexist stereotypes about 'Mother Ireland', to whom these heroes are eternally wedded, and whom they will fertilize with their life-giving blood. It is incurably nostalgic and sentimental, fetishizes the cause of national unity regardless of its social content, and is markedly churlish and atavistic in its attitude to the 'modern'.

It is clear enough that no self-respecting liberal would be caught associating with this barbarous creed. There are, however, two lines of defence which may be launched in its name, neither of which need deny the real criticisms listed above. The first defence is that this blanket condemnation fails to perceive the rational kernel within the mythical shell. It overlooks the fact that this mythology projects in luridly exaggerated form a number of uncomfortable home truths which the British would prefer to ignore, and of which their 'enlightened' rejection of such doctrines is in part a political rationalization. Many of Ireland's problems have indeed had their source in the colonial connection with Britain. For all the mythological *machismo*, Irish men and women have indeed displayed remarkable courage over the centuries in their struggle for national liberation. 'National unity' may certainly be something of a fetish, but are the British who hold this view therefore prepared to hand over the Home Counties to Dublin? There is truth in the charge of masochism and cultic self-sacrifice; but it is also true that Irish republicans have sometimes preferred to spill their own blood rather than that of others. Irish nationalist beliefs are certainly often nostalgic and atavistic, contemptuous of modernity; and looking at modernity, who can blame them? The myths of Irish nationalism, however retrograde and objectionable, are not pure illusions: they encapsulate, in however reductive, hyperbolic a form, some substantial historical facts. They are not just benighted nonsense, as the decent-minded liberal might tend to suspect.

But there is a more fundamental line of defence to be run here. For is not any such critique of the myths of an oppressed people bound to be launched from an aridly intellectualist viewpoint? Men and women engaged in such conflicts do not live by theory alone; socialists have not given their lives over the generations for the tenet that the ratio of fixed to variable capital gives rise to a tendential fall-off in the rate of profit. It is not in defence of the doctrine of base and superstructure that men and women are prepared to embrace hardship and persecution in the course of political struggle. Oppressed groups tell themselves epic narratives of their history, celebrate their solidarity in song and ritual, fashion collective symbols of their common endeavour. Is all this to be scornfully dismissed as so much mental befuddlement? Yet if such mythological consciousness on the part of the oppressed is valid and unavoidable, is it not in uneasy collusion with mystification? When Walter Benjamin wrote that 'myth will persist as long as a single beggar remains',[24] it was this politically negative sense of mythology that he had in mind.

We seem, in short, to be faced with two equally unpalatable alternatives. On the one hand, there is the Enlightenment hope that men and women may come to outgrow mythology altogether; but this would seem to involve a barren rationalism. On the other hand, we may accept that the masses need their myths, but that this is to be sharply distinguished from the theorizing of the intellectuals. In which case, as the work of a Sorel or Althusser may be thought to attest, we have simply swapped an anaemic intellectualism for a cynical opportunism or elitism. There is, however, a useful distinction enforced by Frank Kermode in his *The Sense of an Ending* between 'myth' and 'fiction'. Fiction, in Kermode's view, is a symbolic construct ironically aware of its own fictionality, whereas myths have mistaken their symbolic worlds for literal ones and so come to naturalize their own status.[25] The dividing line between the two is notably blurred, since fictions have a tendency to degenerate into myths. Political demonstrators who chant, 'The workers united shall never be defeated' may actually believe this, which is cause for alarm. For it is not true that the workers united will never be defeated, and it is irresponsible to suggest that it is. But it is unlikely that most people who chant this slogan regard it as some valid theoretical proposition. It is clearly a piece of rhetoric, designed to foster solidarity and self-affirmation, and to 'believe' in it is to believe in it *as such*. It is perfectly possible to believe in it as a piece of political rhetoric but not to believe in it as a theoretical proposition – a situation of believing and not believing simultaneously which somewhat complicates the drastically simplistic phenomenology of belief typical of some contemporary neo-pragmatist thought. To place one's credence in the slogan as rhetorically valid is to perform a fictional act, whereas to take it literally is to fall victim to a myth. And it is in this sense that rationalism and elitism are not, after all, the only political alternatives.

7

DISCOURSE AND
IDEOLOGY

WE HAVE seen that the concept of ideology embraces, among other things, the notion of reification; but it can be argued that it is a reification all of itself. Nobody has ever clapped eyes on an ideological formation, any more than on the Freudian unconscious or a mode of production. The term 'ideology' is just a convenient way of categorizing under a single heading a whole lot of different things we do with signs. The phrase 'bourgeois ideology', for example, is simply shorthand for an immense range of discourses scattered in time and space. To call all of these languages 'bourgeois' is of course to imply that they have something in common; but that common element need not be thought of as some invariable structure of categories. It is probably more useful here to think along the lines of Ludwig Wittgenstein's doctrine of 'family resemblances' – of a network of overlapping features rather than some constant 'essence'.

Much traditional talk of ideology has been couched in terms of 'consciousness' and 'ideas' – terms which have their appropriate uses, but which tend to nudge us unwittingly in the direction of idealism. For 'consciousness' too is a kind of reification, an abstraction from our actual forms of discursive practice. It belongs to what we might call the linguistic revolution of the twentieth century that we have shifted from thinking of words in terms of concepts to thinking of concepts in terms of words. Instead of holding in empiricist vein that words 'stand for' concepts, we now tend to see 'having a concept' as the capacity to use words in particular ways. A concept is thus more of a practice than a state of mind – though we have seen that Louis Althusser risks bending the stick too far in this direction, *reducing* concepts to social practices. But there is a third way between thinking of ideology as disembodied ideas on the one hand, and as nothing but a matter of certain behaviour patterns on the other. This is to regard ideology as a discursive or semiotic phenomenon. And this at once emphasizes its materiality (since signs are material entities), and preserves the sense that it is essentially concerned with *meanings.* Talk of signs and discourses is inherently social and practical, whereas terms like 'consciousness' are residues of an idealist tradition of thought.

It may help to view ideology less as a particular *set* of discourses, than as a particular set of effects *within* discourses. Bourgeois ideology includes this particular discourse on property, that way of talking about the soul, this treatise on jurisprudence and the kind of utterances one overhears in pubs where the landlord wears a military tie. What is 'bourgeois' about this mixed bunch of idioms is less the *kind* of languages they are than the effects they produce: effects, for example, of 'closure', whereby certain forms of signification are silently excluded, and certain signifiers 'fixed' in a commanding position. These effects are *discursive,* not purely formal, features of language: what is interpreted as 'closure', for example, will depend on the concrete context of utterance, and is variable from one communicative situation to the next.

The first semiotic theory of ideology was developed by the Soviet philosopher V.N. Voloshinov in his *Marxism and the Philosophy of Language* (1929) – a work in which the author boldly proclaims that 'without signs there is no ideology'.[1] In his view, the domain of signs and the realm of ideology are coextensive: consciousness can arise only in the material embodiment of signifiers, and since these signifiers are in themselves material, they are not just 'reflections' of reality but an integral part of it. 'The logic of consciousness', Voloshinov writes, 'is the logic of ideological communication, of the semiotic interaction of a social group. If we deprive consciousness of its semiotic, ideological content, it would have absolutely nothing left.'[2] The word is the 'ideological phenomenon *par excellence*', and consciousness itself is just the internalization of words, a kind of 'inner speech'. To put the point differently, consciousness is less something 'within' us than something around and between us, a network of signifiers which constitute us through and through.

If ideology cannot be divorced from the sign, then neither can the sign be isolated from concrete forms of social intercourse. It is within these alone that the sign 'lives'; and these forms of intercourse must in turn be related to the material basis of social life. The sign and its social situation are inextricably fused together, and this situation determines from within the form and structure of an utterance. We have here, then, the outline of a materialist theory of ideology which does not simply reduce it to a 'reflex' of the economic 'base', but grants the materiality of the word, and the discursive contexts in which it is caught up, their proper due.

If language and ideology are in one sense identical for Voloshinov, they are not in another. For contending ideological positions may articulate themselves in the same national language, intersect within the same linguistic community; and this means that the sign becomes 'an arena of class struggle'. A particular social sign is pulled this way and that by competing social interests, inscribed from within with a multiplicity of ideological 'accents'; and it is in this way that it sustains its dynamism and vitality. Voloshinov's work thus yields us a new definition of ideology, as the struggle of antagonistic social interests at the level of the sign.

Voloshinov is the father of what has since come to be called 'discourse analysis', which attends to the play of social power within language itself. Ideological power, as John B. Thompson puts it, is not just a matter of meaning, but of making a meaning *stick*.[3] Voloshinov's theories are taken forward in the work of the French Althusserian linguist Michel Pêcheux, notably in his *Language, Semantics and Ideology* (1975). Pêcheux wishes to go beyond the celebrated Saussurean distinction between *langue* (the abstract system of language) and *parole* (particular utterances) with the concepts of 'discursive process' and 'discursive formation'. A discursive formation can be seen as a set of rules which determine what can and must be said from a certain position within social life; and expressions have meaning only by virtue of the discursive formations within which they occur, changing significance as they are transported from one to the other. A discursive formation thus constitutes a 'matrix of meaning' or system of linguistic relations within which actual discursive processes are generated. Any particular discursive formation will form part of a structured totality of such phenomena, which Pêcheux calls 'interdiscourse'; and each discursive formation is embedded in turn in an ideological formation, which contains non-discursive practices as well as discursive ones.

Every discursive process is thus inscribed in ideological relations, and will be internally moulded by their pressure. Language itself is a 'relatively autonomous' system, shared by worker and bourgeois, man and woman, idealist and materialist alike; but precisely because it forms the common basis of all discursive formations, it becomes the medium of ideological conflict. A 'discursive semantics' would then examine how the elements of a specific discursive formation are linked to form discursive processes with reference to an ideological context. But the position of a discursive formation within a complex whole, which includes its ideological context, will typically be concealed from the individual speaker, in an act of what Pêcheux calls 'forgetting'; and it is because of this oblivion or repression that the speaker's meanings appear obvious and natural to him. The speaker 'forgets' that he or she is just the function of a discursive and ideological formation, and thus comes to misrecognize herself as the author of her own discourse. Rather as the Lacanian infant identifies itself with its imaginary reflection, so the speaking subject effects an identification with the discursive formation which dominates it. But Pêcheux leaves open the possibility of a 'dis-identification' with such formations, which is one condition of political transformation.

The work of Voloshinov and Pêcheux has pioneered a varied, fertile strain of discourse analysis.[4] Much of this work examines how the inscription of social power within language can be traced in lexical, syntactic and grammatical structures – so that, for example, the use of an abstract noun, or a switch of mood from active to passive, may serve to obscure the concrete agency of a social event in ways convenient for ruling ideological interests. Other studies involve analysis of the distribution of speech opportunities within conversation, or the ideological effects of oral narrative organization. While sometimes solemnly labouring the obvious, wheeling up the big guns of linguistic analysis to despatch the inconsiderable gnat of a dirty joke, this brand of investigation has opened up a new dimension in a theory of ideology traditionally concerned with 'consciousness' rather than linguistic performance, 'ideas' rather than social interaction.

A quite different style of thought about language and ideology came to characterize avant-garde European thought in the 1970s. For this current of inquiry, associated with the French semiotic journal *Tel Quel*, ideology is essentially a matter of 'fixing' the otherwise inexhaustible process of signification around certain dominant signifiers, with which the individual subject can then identify. Language itself is infinitely productive; but this incessant productivity can be artificially arrested into 'closure' – into the sealed world of ideological stability, which repels the disruptive, decentred forces of language in the name of an imaginary unity. Signs are ranked by a certain covert violence into rigidly hierarchical order; as Rosalind Coward and John Ellis put it, 'ideological practice ... works to fix the subject in certain positions in relation to certain fixities of discourse.'[5] The process of forging 'representations' always involves this arbitrary closing off of the signifying chain, constricting the free play of the signifier to a spuriously determinate meaning which can then be received by the subject as natural and inevitable. Just as for Pêcheux the speaking subject 'forgets' the discursive formation which sets him in place, so for this mode of thought ideological representation involves repressing the *work* of language, the material process of signifying production which underlies these coherent meanings and can always potentially subvert them.

This is a suggestive conjuncture of linguistics, Marxism and psychoanalysis, involving an enriched materialism which examines the very constitution in language of the human subject. It is not, however, without its difficulties. Politically speaking, this is a latently libertarian theory of the subject, which tends to 'demonize' the very act of semiotic closure and uncritically celebrate the euphoric release of the forces of linguistic production. It occasionally betrays an anarchic suspicion of meaning as such; and it falsely assumes that 'closure' is always counterproductive. But such closure is a provisional effect of any semiosis whatsoever, and may be politically enabling rather than constraining: 'Reclaim the night!' involves a semiotic and (in one sense of the term) ideological closure, but its political force lies precisely in this. The left-semiotic hostility to such provisionally stabilized signifiers comes at times perilously close to the liberal's banal suspicion of 'labels'. Whether such closure is politically positive or negative depends on the discursive and ideological context; and this mode of analysis is generally too eager to overlook discursive context in its left-academicist contemplation of language as 'text'. It is rarely, in other words, a form of actual discourse analysis; instead, like its philological opponents, it takes 'language as such' as its object of enquiry, and thus fails to escape a certain left formalism and abstraction. Jacques Derrida and his progeny are primarily interested in the sliding of the Mallarmean signifier, rather than in what gets said during the tea-break in the Hilton kitchens. In the case of *Tel Quel*, a starry-eyed Western view of the Maoist 'cultural revolution' is naively transplanted to the arena of language, so that political revolution becomes implicitly equated with some ceaseless disruption and overturning. The case betrays an anarchistic suspicion of institutionality as such, and ignores the extent to which a certain provisional stability of identity is essential not only for psychical well-being but for revolutionary political agency. It contains no adequate theory of such agency, since the subject would now seem no more than the decentred effect of the semiotic process; and its valuable attention to the split, precarious, pluralistic nature of all identity slides at its worst into an irresponsible hymning of the virtues of schizophrenia. Political revolution becomes, in effect, equivalent to carnivalesque delirium; and if this usefully reinstates those pleasurable, utopian, mind-shattering aspects of the process which a puritanical Marxism has too frequently suppressed, it leaves those comrades drearily enamoured of 'closure' to do the committee work, photocopy the leaflets and organize the food supplies. What is enduringly valuable about the case is its attempt to uncover the linguistic and psycho-analytic mechanisms of ideological representation – to expose ideology less as some static 'set of ideas' than as a set of complex effects internal to discourse. Ideology is one crucial way in which the human subject strives to 'suture' contradictions which rive it in its very being, constitute it to its core. As with Althusser, it is what produces us as social subjects in the first place, not simply a conceptual straightjacket into which we are subsequently bound.

It is worth pausing to ask of this position, however, whether ideology is always a matter of 'fixation'. What of the consumerist ideologies of advanced capitalism, in which the subject is encouraged to live provisionally, glide contentedly from sign to sign, revel in the rich plurality of its appetites and savour itself as no more than a decentred function of them? It is true that all this goes on within a more fundamental 'closure', one determined by the requirements of capital itself; but it exposes the naivety of the belief that ideology always and everywhere involves fixed or 'transcendental' signifiers, imaginary unities, metaphysical grounds and teleological goals. Post-structuralist thought often enough sets up ideology in this 'straw target' style, only to go on to confront it with the creative ambiguities of 'textuality' or the sliding of the signifier; but five minutes' viewing of a video or cinema advertisement should be enough to deconstruct this rigid binary opposition. 'Textuality', ambiguity, indeterminacy lie often enough on the side of dominant ideological discourses themselves. The mistake springs in part from projecting a *particular* model of ideology – that of fascism and Stalinism – onto the quite different discourses of liberal capitalism. There is a political history behind this error: like the members of the Frankfurt School, certain prominent members of the so-called Yale school of criticism, which has sponsored such notions, have or had political roots of one kind or another in that earlier European context.[6] Ideology, for them as for the end-of-ideology theorists, then comes to signify Hitler or Stalin, rather than Trump Tower or David Frost.

Finally, we may note that this theory of ideology, for all its vaunted 'materialism', betrays an incipient idealism in its heavily subject-centred bias. In its instructive efforts to avoid economic reductionism, it passes over in silence the whole classical Marxist case about the 'infrastructural' bases of ideology, along with the centrality of political institutions. We have seen earlier that we may speak of the institutions of parliamentary democracy themselves as, among other things, an ideological apparatus. The effects of these institutions, to be sure, must 'pass through' the experience of the subject if they are to be ideologically persuasive at all; but there is a certain idealism implicit in taking one's starting-point from the human subject, even if from a suitably 'materialized' version of it. This 'turn to the subject' throughout the 1970s represented at once an invaluable deepening and enriching of classical political theory, and a retreat on the part of the political left from those rather less 'subject-centred' social issues which, in a protracted crisis of the international capitalist system, appeared more than ever intractable.

We have seen that ideology is often felt to entail a 'naturalization' of social reality; and this is another area in which the semiotic contribution has been especially illuminating. For the Roland Barthes of *Mythologies* (1957), myth (or ideology) is what transforms history into Nature by lending arbitrary signs an apparently obvious, unalterable set of connotations. 'Myth does not deny things, on the contrary, its function is to talk about them; simply it purifies them, it makes them innocent, it gives them a natural and eternal justification, it gives them a clarity which is not that of an explanation but of a statement of fact.'[7] The 'naturalization' thesis is here extended to discourse as such, rather than to the world of which it speaks. The 'healthy' sign for Barthes is one which unashamedly displays its own gratuitousness, the fact that there is no internal or self-evident bond between itself and what it represents; and to this extent artistic modernism, which typically broods upon the 'unmotivated' nature of its own sign-systems, emerges as politically progressive. The 'unhealthy' – mythological or ideological – signifier is one which cunningly erases this radical lack of motivation, suppresses the semiotic labour which produced it, and so allows us to receive it as 'natural' and 'transparent', gazing through its innocent surface to the concept or signified to which it permits us magically immediate access. Literary realism, for Barthes and his disciples, is then exemplary of this deceptive transparency – a curiously formalist, trans-historical judgement on everything from Defoe to Dostoevsky, which in the 'wilder' versions of this richly suggestive case becomes an unmitigated disaster which ought really never to have happened.

It is just this spurious naturalization of language which the literary critic Paul de Man sees as lying at the root of all ideology. What de Man terms the 'phenomenalist' delusion, in the words of his commentator Christopher Norris, is the idea that language 'can become somehow consubstantial with the world of natural objects and processes, and so transcend the ontological gulf between words (or concepts) and sensuous intuitions'.[8] Ideology is language which forgets the essentially contingent, accidental relations between itself and the world, and comes instead to mistake itself as having some kind of organic, inevitable bond with what it represents. For the essentially tragic philosophy of a de Man, mind and world, language and being, are eternally discrepant; and ideology is the gesture which seeks to conflate these quite separate orders, hunting nostalgically for a pure presence of the thing within the word, and so imbuing meaning with all the sensuous positivity of natural being. Ideology strives to bridge verbal concepts and sensory intuitions; but the force of truly critical (or 'deconstructive') thought is to demonstrate how the insidiously figural, rhetorical nature of discourse will always intervene to break up this felici-tous marriage. 'What we call ideology', de Man observes in *The Resistance to Theory*, 'is precisely the confusion of linguistic with natural reality, of reference with phenomenalism.'[9] One might find exemplary instances of such a confusion in the thought of the later Heidegger, for whom certain words allow us a privileged access to 'Being'; in the contemporaneous literary criticism of F.R. Leavis; and in the poetry of Seamus Heaney. The flaw of this theory, as in the case of Barthes, lies in its unargued assumption that *all* ideological discourse operates by such naturalization – a contention we have already seen reason to doubt. As often in the critique of ideology, one particular paradigm of ideological consciousness is surreptitiously made to do service for the whole varied array of ideological forms and devices. There are styles of ideological discourse other than the 'organicist' – the thought of Paul de Man, for example, whose gloomy insistence that mind and world can never harmoniously meet is among other things a coded refusal of the 'utopianism' of emancipatory politics.

It belongs to a post-structuralist or postmodernist perspective to see all discourse as traced through by the play of power and desire, and thus to view all language as ineradicably *rhetorical*. We should be properly suspicious of too hard-and-fast a distinction between some scrupulously neutral, purely informative sort of speech act, and those 'performative' pieces of language which are clearly engaged in cursing, cajoling, seducing, persuading and so on. Telling someone the time of day is as much a 'performative' as telling them to get lost, and no doubt involves some inscrutable play of power and desire for any analyst with enough useless ingenuity to pursue the matter. All discourse is aimed at the production of certain effects in its recipients, and is launched from some tendentious 'subject position'; and to this extent we might conclude with the Greek Sophists that everything we say is really a matter of rhetorical performance within which questions of truth or cognition are strictly subordinate. If this is so, then all language is 'ideo-logical', and the category of ideology, expanded to breaking-point, once more collapses. One might add that the production of this effect is precisely part of the ideological intention of those who claim that 'everything is rhetorical'.

It is, however, a simple sleight-of-hand, or sheer intellectual disingen-uousness, to imagine that all language is rhetorical to exactly the same degree. Once again, postmodernist 'pluralism' here stands convicted of violently homogenizing quite different sorts of speech act. The assertion 'It's five o'clock' certainly involves interests of a kind, springing as it does from a particular way of slicing up temporality, and belonging as it does to some intersubjective context (that of telling someone the time) which is never innocent of authority. But it is merely perverse to imagine that such an utterance, in most circumstances at least, is as 'interested' as stating that by five o'clock all historical materialists must be washed in the blood of the Lamb or face instant execution. Someone who writes a doctoral thesis on the relations between race and social class in South Africa is by no means disinterested; why bother, for one thing, to write it in the first place? But such a piece of work normally differs from statements such as 'The white man will never surrender his heritage' in that it is open to being disproved. Indeed this is part of what we mean by a 'scientific' hypothesis, as opposed to a groan of alarm or a stream of invective. The pronouncement 'The white man will never surrender his heritage' *appears* as though it could be disproved, since it could be obtusely taken as a sociological prediction; but to take it this way would of course be wholly to miss its ideological force.

There is no need to imagine that to enforce a working distinction between these two discursive genres is to surrender to the myth of some 'scientific disinterestedness' – a fantasy which no interesting philosopher of science has anyway entertained for the past half-century. The humanist's traditional patrician disdain for scientific enquiry is not rendered particularly more plausible by being dressed up in glamorously avant-garde guise.

If all language articulates specific interests, then it would appear that all language is ideological. But as we have seen already, the classical concept of ideology is by no means limited to 'interested discourse', or to the production of suasive effects. It refers more precisely to the processes whereby interests of a certain kind become masked, rationalized, naturalized, universalized, legitimated in the name of certain forms of political power; and much is to be politically lost by dissolving these vital discursive strategies into some undifferentiated, amorphous category of 'interests'. To claim that all language is at some level rhetorical is thus not the same as to claim that all language is ideological. As John Plamenatz points out in his work *Ideology*, someone who shouts 'Fire!' in a theatre is not engaging in ideological discourse. A mode of discourse may encode certain interests, for example, but may not be particularly intent on directly promoting or legitimating them; and the interests in question may in any case have no crucially relevant relation to the sustaining of a whole social order. Again, the interests at stake may not be in the least 'false' or specious ones, whereas we have seen that, for some theories of ideology at least, this would need to be so for a discourse to be dubbed ideological. Those who today press the sophistical case that all language is rhetorical, like Stanley Fish in *Doing What Comes Naturally*, are quite ready to acknowledge that the discourse in which they frame this case is nothing but a case of special pleading too; but if a Fish is genially prepared to admit that his own theorizing is a bit of rhetoric, he is notably more reluctant to concede that it is a piece of *ideology*. For to do this would involve reflecting on the political ends which such an argument serves in the content of Western capitalist society; and Fish is not prepared to widen his theoretical focus to encompass such embarrassing questions. Indeed his response would no doubt have to be that he is himself so thoroughly a product of that society – which is undoubtedly true – that he is quite unable to reflect on his own social determinants – which is undoubtedly false.

It is via the category of 'discourse' that a number of theorists over recent years have made the steady trek from erstwhile revolutionary political positions to left reformist ones. This phenomenon is generally known as 'post-Marxism'; and it is worth inquiring into the logic of this long march from Saussure to social democracy.

In a number of works of political theory,[10] the English sociologists Paul Hirst and Barry Hindess firmly reject the kind of classical epistemology which assumes some match or 'correspondence' between our concepts and the way the world is. For if 'the way the world is' is itself always conceptually defined, then this age-old philosophical case would appear to be viciously circular. It is a rationalist fallacy, so Hindess and Hirst argue, to hold that what enables us to know is the fact that the world takes the shape of a concept – that it is somehow conveniently pre-structured to fit our cognition of it. As for a Paul de Man, there is no such congruence or internal bond between mind and reality, and so no privileged epistemological language which could allow us untroubled access to the real. For to determine that this language adequately measured the fit or non-fit between our concepts and the world, we would presumably need another language to guarantee the adequacy of *this* one, and so on in a potentially infinite regress of 'metalanguages'. Rather, objects should be considered not as external to a realm of discourse which seeks to approximate them, but as wholly internal to such discourses, constituted by them through and through.

This position – though Hindess and Hirst do not say so, perhaps being nervous or unaware of the fact – is a thoroughly Nietzschean one. There is no given order *in* reality at all, which for Nietzsche is just ineffable chaos; meaning is just whatever we arbitrarily construct by our acts of sense-making. The world does not spontaneously sort itself out into kinds, causal hierarchies, discrete spheres, as a philosophical realist would imagine; on the contrary, it is *we* who do all this by talking about it. Our language does not so much *reflect* reality as *signify* it, carve it into conceptual shape. The answer, then, to *what* exactly is being carved into conceptual shape is impossible to give: reality itself, before we come to constitute it through our discourses, is just some inarticulable *x*.

It is hard to know quite how far this anti-realist case can be pressed. Nobody believes that the world sorts itself into shape, independently of our descriptions of it, in the sense that the literary superiority of Arthur Hugh Clough to Alfred Lord Tennyson is just a 'given' distinction inscribed in reality before time began, grandly autonomous of anything we might come to say about the issue. But it seems plausible to believe that there is a given distinction between wine and wallabies, and that to be unclear on this point might be the occasion of some frustration on the part of someone looking for a drink. There may well be societies for which these things signify something entirely at odds with what they signify for us, or even certain bizarre cultural systems which saw no occasion to *mark* the distinction at all. But this does not mean that they would stock their off-licences with wallabies or encourage children to feed bottles of wine in their zoos. It is certainly true that we ourselves may not distinguish between certain sorts of plant which for another culture are uniquely different. But it would be impossible for an anthropologist to stumble upon a society which registered no distinction between water and sulphuric acid, since they would all be long in their graves.

Similarly, it is difficult to know how hard to press the case that our discourses do not reflect real causal connections in reality – an empiricist doctrine which a good many post-Marxists have rather surprisingly appropriated. It is certainly arguable that the Marxist claim that economic activity finally determines the shape of a society is just a causal relation which Marxists, for their own political reasons, want to construct, rather than a hierarchy already inscribed in the world waiting to be discovered. It is somewhat less persuasive to claim that the apparent causal relation between my lunging at you with a scimitar and your head dropping instantly to the ground is just one discursively constructed for particular ends.

Hindess and Hirst's 'anti-epistemological' thesis is intended among other things to undermine the Marxist doctrine that a social formation is composed of different 'levels', some of which exert more significant determinacy than others. For them, this is merely another instance of the rationalist illusion, which would view society as somehow already internally structured along the lines of the concepts by which we appropriate it in thought. There is, then, no such thing as a 'social totality', and no such thing as one sort of social activity being in general or in principle more determinant or causally privileged than another. The relations between the political, cultural, economic and the rest are ones *we* fashion for specific political ends within given historical contexts; they are in no sense relations which subsist independently of our discourse. Once again, it is not easy to see just how far this case should be extended. Does it mean, for instance, that we cannot in principle rule out the possibility that the Bolshevik revolution was triggered by Bogdanov's asthma or Radek's penchant for pork pies? If there are no causal hierarchies *in* reality, why should this not be so? What is it which *constrains* our discursive constructions? It cannot be 'reality', for that is simply a *product* of them; in which case it might appear that we are free, in some voluntarist fantasy, to weave any network of relations which strikes our fancy. It is clear in any case that what began as an argument about epistemology has now shifted to an opposition to revolutionary politics; for if the Marxist doctrine of 'last-instance' economic determinacy is discarded, then much in traditional revolutionary discourse will need to be radically revised. In place of this 'global' brand of analysis, Hindess and Hirst urge instead the pragmatic calculation of political effects within some particular social conjuncture, which is a good deal more palatable to Mr Neil Kinnock. This theory, coincidentally enough, was sponsored just at the historical point where the radical currents of the 1960s and early 1970s were beginning to ebb under the influence of an aggressive set of assaults from the political right. In this sense, it was a 'conjunctural' position in more senses than it proclaimed.

The thesis that objects are entirely internal to the discourses which constitute them raises the thorny problem of how we could ever judge that a discourse had constructed its object validly. How can anyone, on this theory, ever be wrong? If there can be no meta-language to measure the 'fit' between my language and the object, what is to stop me from constructing the object in any way I want? Perhaps the internal rigour and consistency of my arguments is the litmus test here; but magic and Satanism, not to speak of Thomistic theology, are perfectly capable of constructing their objects in internally coherent ways. Moreover, they may always produce effects which somebody, from some vantage-point somewhere, may judge to be politically beneficial. But if meta-language is an illusion, then there would seem no way of judging that any particular political perspective was more beneficial than any other. The pragmatist move here, in other words, simply pushes the question back a step: if what validates my social interpretations are the political ends they serve, how am I to validate these ends? Or am I just forced back here, aggressively and dogmatically, on asserting my interests over yours, as Nietzsche would have urged? For Hindess and Hirst, there can be no way of countering an objectionable political case by an appeal to the way things are with society, for the way things are is just the way you construct them to be. You must appeal instead to your political ends and interests – which means that it is now these, not the distinction between wine and wallabies, which are somehow sheerly 'given'. They cannot be derived from social reality, since social reality derives from *them*; and they are therefore bound to remain as mysteriously unfathered and self-referential as the work of art for a whole tradition of classical aesthetics.

Where interests derive from, in other words, is as opaque a matter for post-Marxism as where babies come from is for the small infant. The traditional Marxist case has been that political interests derive from one's location within the social relations of class-society; but this for post-Marxism would seem to entail the unSaussurean assumption that our political discourses 'reflect' or 'correspond' to something else. If our language is not just some passive reflection of reality, but actively constitutive of it, then this surely cannot be so. It cannot be that your place within a mode of production furnishes you with certain objective interests which your political and ideological discourses then simply 'express'. There can be no 'objective' interests spontaneously 'given' by reality; once again, interests are what we *construct*, and politics in this sense has the edge over economics.

That social interests do not lie around the place like slabs of concrete waiting to be stumbled over may be cheerfully conceded. There is no reason to suppose, as Hindess and Hirst rightly argue, that the mere occupancy of some place within society will automatically supply you with an appropriate set of political beliefs and desires, as the fact that by no means all women are feminists would readily attest. Social interests are indeed in no sense independent of anything we come to do or say; they are not some given 'signified', which has then merely to discover its appropriate signifier or mode of ideological discourse to come into its own. But this is not the only way of understanding the concept of 'objective interests'. Imagine an objective location within the social formation known as third galley slave from the front on the starboard side. This location brings along with it certain responsibilities, such as rowing non-stop for fifteen hours at a stretch and sending up a feeble chant of praise to the Emperor on the hour. To say that this social location comes readily inscribed with a set of interests is just to say that anyone who found himself occupying it would do well to get out of it, and that this would be no mere whim or quirk on his part. It is not necessarily to claim that this thought would spontaneously occur to a galley slave as soon as he had sat down, or to rule out the odd masochist who took a grisly relish in the whole affair and tried to row faster than the others. The view that the slave, *ceteris paribus*, would do well to escape is not one that springs from some God's-eye viewpoint beyond all social discourse; on the contrary, it is more likely to spring from the viewpoint of the League of Escaped Galley Slaves. There is no interest in question here that nobody could ever conceivably come to know about. When the galley slave engages in a spot of critical self-reflection, such as muttering to himself 'this is one hell of a job', then he might reasonably be said to be articulating in his discourse an objective interest, in the sense that he means that it is one hell of a job not just for him but for anyone whatsoever. There is no divine guarantee that the slave *will* arrive at the conclusion that there might be more agreeable ways of passing his time, or that he will not view his task as just retribution for the crime of existing, or as a creative contribution to the greater good of the empire. To say that he has an objective interest in emancipating himself is just to say that if he *does* feel this way, then he is labouring under the influence of false consciousness. It is to claim, moreover, that in certain optimal conditions – conditions relatively free of such coercion and mystification – the slave could be brought to recognize this fact. He would acknowledge that it was in fact in his interests to escape even before he came to realize this, and this is part of what he is now realizing.

The galley slave might be instructed by the odd discourse theorist he encountered at various ports of call that the interests he had now begun to articulate were in no sense a mere passive reflection of social reality, and he would do well to take this point seriously. He would no doubt appreciate the force of it already, recalling the long years during which he held the view that being lashed to ribbons by the emperor's captain was an honour ill-befitting a worm such as himself, and remembering the painful inner struggle which brought him to his current, more enlightened opinions. He might well be brought to understand that 'oppression' is a discursive affair, in the sense that one condition is identifiable as oppressive only by contrast with some other less or non-oppressive state of affairs, and that all this is cognizable only through discourse. Oppression, in short, is a normative concept: someone is being oppressed not simply if they drag out a wretched existence, but if certain creative capacities they could feasibly realize are being actively thwarted by the unjust interests of others. And none of this can be determined other than discursively; you could not decide that a situation was oppressive simply by looking at a photograph of it. The galley slave, however, would no doubt be churlishly unimpressed by the suggestion that all this meant that he was not 'really' oppressed at all. He would be unlikely to greet such a judgement with the light-hearted playfulness beloved of some postmodernist theorists. Instead, he would doubtless insist that while what was in question here was certainly an interpretation, and thus always in principle controvertible, what the interpretation enforced was the *fact* that this situation was oppressive.

Post-Marxism is given to denying that there is any necessary relation between one's socio-economic location and one's politico-ideological interests. In the case of our galley slave, this claim is clearly false. It is certainly true, as post-Marxism properly insists, that the slave's politico-ideological position is not just some 'reflex' of his material conditions. But his ideological views do indeed have an internal relation to that condition – not in the sense that this condition is the automatic *cause* of them, but in the sense that it is the *reason* for them. Sitting for fifteen hours a day in the third row from the front is what his ideological opinions are *about*. What he says is about what he does; and what he does is the reason for what he says. The 'real' here certainly exists prior to and independent of the slave's discourse, if by the 'real' is meant that specific set of practices which provide the reason for what he says, and form the referent of it. That these practices will be interpretatively transformed when the slave arrives at his emancipatory views is doubtless true; he will be led to theoretically revise those conditions in a quite different light. This is the kernel of truth of the post-Marxist case: that 'signifiers', or the means of political and ideological representation, are always active in respect of what they signify. It is in this sense that politico-ideological interests are not just the obedient, spontaneous expression of 'given' socio-economic conditions. What is represented is never some 'brute' reality, but will be moulded by the practice of representation itself. Political and ideological discourses thus produce their own signifieds, conceptualize the situation in specific ways.

It is only a short step from here – a step which Hindess and Hirst rashly take – to imagining that the *whole socio-economic situation* in question is simply defined by political and ideological interests, with no reality beyond this. Semiotically speaking, Hindess and Hirst have merely inverted the empiricist model: whereas in empiricist thought the signifier is thought to follow spontaneously from the signified – in the sense that the world instructs us, so to speak, in how to represent it – it is now a question of the signified following obediently from the signifier. The situation is just whatever political and ideological discourses define it as being. But this is to conflate economic and political interests just as drastically as the most vulgar Marxism. For the fact is that there are economic interests, such as desiring better pay or conditions of work, which may not yet have achieved *political* articulation. And such interests can be inflected in a whole number of conflicting political ways. As well as merely inverting the relation between signified and signified, Hindess and Hirst thus also effect a fatal semiotic confusion between *signified* and *referent*. For the referent here is the whole socio-economic situation, the interests contained in which are then signified in different ways by politics and ideology, but are not simply identical with them.

Whether 'economics' gives rise to 'politics', or *vice versa* as post-Marxism would hold, the relationship in both cases is essentially causal. Lurking behind the post-Marxist view is the Saussurean notion of the signifier as 'producing' the signified. But this semiotic model is in fact quite inadequate for an understanding of the relation between material situations and ideological discourse. Ideology neither legislates such situations into being, nor is simply 'caused' by them; rather, ideology offers a set of *reasons* for such material conditions. Hindess and Hirst, in short, overlook the *legitimating* functions of ideology, distracted as they are by a causal model which merely stands vulgar Marxism on its head. The relation between an object and its means of representation is crucially not the same as that between a material practice and its ideological legitimation or mystification. Hindess and Hirst fail to spot this because of the undifferentiated, all-inclusive nature of their concept of discourse. Discourse for them 'produces' real objects; and ideological language is therefore just one way in which these objects get constituted. But this simply fails to identify the specificity of such language, which is not just any way of constituting reality, but one with the more particular functions of explaining, rationalizing, concealing, legitimating and so on. Two meanings of discourse are falsely conflated: those which are said to constitute our practices, and those in which we talk about them. Ideology, in short, *goes to work* on the 'real' situation in transformative ways; and it is ironic in one sense that a pair of theorists so eager to stress the activity of the signifier should overlook this. In another sense, it is not ironic at all: for if our discourses are constitutive of our practices, then there would seem no enabling distance between the two in which this transformative labour could occur. And to speak of a transformative labour here implies that something pre-exists this process; some referent, something *worked upon*, which cannot be the case if the signifier simply conjures the 'real' situation into being.

What is being implicitly challenged by Hindess and Hirst is nothing short of the whole concept of representation. For the idea of representation would suggest that the signified exists prior to its signifier, and is then obediently reflected by it; and this, once more, runs against the grain of Saussurean semiotics. But in rightly rejecting an *empiricist* ideology of representation, they mistakenly believe themselves to have disposed of the notion as such. Nobody is much enamoured these days of an idea of representation in which the signified spontaneously puts forth its own signifier; in which some organic bond is imagined to exist between the two, so that the signified can be represented *only* in this way; and in which the signifier in no sense alters the signified, but remains a neutral, transparent medium of expression. Many post-Marxists accordingly abandon the whole term 'representation', while around them the benighted masses continue to speak of a photograph of a chipmunk as 'representing' a chipmunk, or a set of interlinked circles as 'representing' the Olympic games. There is no reason to imagine that the complex conventions involved in associating an image with its referent are adequately explained by the empiricist version of the process, and no need to throw up trying to give an account of the former simply because the latter model has been discredited. The term 'representation' has perfectly valid uses, as the populace, if not some post-Marxists, are well aware; it is just a trickier cultural practice than the empiricists used to think.

The reason why Hindess and Hirst wish to jettison the whole notion of representation is by no means ideologically innocent. They wish to do so because they want to deny the classical Marxist contention that there exists some internal relation between particular socio-economic conditions, and specific kinds of political or ideological positions. They therefore argue either that socio-economic interests are just the product of political and ideological ones, or that the two lie on quite different levels, with no necessary linkage between them. Semiotics, once more, is a kind of politics – since if this is so, then many traditional Marxist theses about the socialist transformation of society being necessarily in the interests of the working class would need to be scrapped. Saussurean linguistics is once more craftily harnessed to the cause of social reformism – a cause rendered more reputable than it might otherwise appear by its glamorous association with 'discourse theory'.

The constructive side of Hindess and Hirst's case is that there are a good many political interests which are by no means necessarily tied to *class* situations, and that classical Marxism has often enough lamentably ignored this truth. Such non-class political movements were gathering force in the 1970s, and the writings of the post-Marxists are among other things a creative theoretical response to this fact. Even so, the move of severing all necessary link between social situations and political interests, intended as a generous opening to these fresh developments, in fact does them a disservice. Consider, for example, the case of the women's movement. It is certainly true that there is no organic relation between feminist politics and social class, *pace* those Marxist reductionists who struggle vainly to funnel the former into the latter. But there is a good case for arguing that there is indeed an internal relation between being a woman (a social situation) and being a feminist (a political position). This is not, needless to say, to claim that all women will spontaneously become feminists; but it is to argue that they *ought* to do so, and that an unmystified understanding of their oppressed social condition would logically lead them in that direction. Just the same is true of the other non-class political currents astir in the 1970s: it seems odd to assert, for example, that there is a purely contingent connection between being part of an oppressed ethnic minority and becoming active in anti-racist politics. The relation between the two is not 'necessary' in the sense of natural, automatic or ineluctable; but it is, in Saussure's terms, a 'motivated' rather than purely arbitrary one even so.

To suggest that someone *ought* to adopt a particular political position may sound peculiarly patronizing, dictatorial and elitist. Who am I to presume that I know what is in someone else's interests? Isn't this just the style in which ruling groups and classes have spoken for centuries? The plain fact is that I am in full possession of my own interests, and nobody can tell me what to do. I am entirely transparent to myself, have an utterly unmystified view of my social conditions, and will tolerate no kind of suggestion, however comradely and sympathetic its tone, from anybody else. I do not need telling by some paternal elitist about what is in my 'objective' interests, because as a matter of fact I never behave in a way which violates them. Even though I eat twelve pounds of sausages a day, smoke sixty cigarettes before noon and have just volunteered for a fifty percent wage cut, I resent the idea that I have anything to learn from anyone. Those who tell me that I am 'mystified', just because I spend my weekends gardening free of charge for the local squire, are simply trying to put me down with their pretentious jargon.

As far as the relation between social interests and ideological beliefs go, we saw in chapter 2 that they were in fact extremely variable. No simple, single homology is at stake here: ideological beliefs may signify material interests, disavow, rationalize or dissemble them, run counter to them, and so on. For the monistic thinking of a Hindess and Hirst, however, there can only ever be one fixed, invariable relation between them: no relation whatsoever. It is true that in their astonishingly repetitive texts the disingenuous word 'necessary' occasionally slides into this formulation: in a whole series of slippages, they glide from arguing that political and ideological forms cannot be conceived of as the *direct* representation of class interests, to claiming that there is no *necessary* relation between the two, to suggesting that there is no connection between them at all. 'There can be no justification', they write, 'for a "reading" of politics and ideology for the class interests they are alleged to represent ... political and ideological struggles cannot be conceived as the struggles of economic classes.'[11] The theoretical strategem is plain enough: feminist, ethnic or ecological politics are obviously not internally related to class interests, in which case neither are socialism or Toryism.

Here, as in almost all of their arguments, Hindess and Hirst theatrically overreact to reductionistic forms of Marxism. Their whole discourse is one prolonged bending of the stick in the other direction, recklessly exaggerating what is otherwise a valuably corrective case. If the relations between ideological forms and social interests are not eternally fixed and given, why should one dogmatically rule out the possibility that some types of ideological discourse may be more closely tied to such interests than others? Why limit one's pluralism in this self-denying way? What self-imposed, *a priori* restrictive practice is at work here? If it is true that there is no 'motivated' relation between being, say, a petty-bourgeois intellectual and opposing fascism, does it follow that there is no such relation either between puritan ideology and the early bourgeoisie, anti-imperialist beliefs and the experience of colonialism, or socialism and a lifetime's unemployment? Are all such relations as arbitrary as being an anti-Semite and an abstract expressionist simultaneously? 'Political practice', they comment, 'does not recognise class interests and then represent them: it constitutes the interests which it represents.'[12] If this means that the 'signifier' of political practice is active in respect of the 'signified' of social interests, modifying and transforming them by its interventions, then it is hard to see why one would want to deny such a case. If it means – to return to our example of the galley slave – that this man has no interests whatsoever relevant to his class position before political discourses moved in to articulate them, then it is clearly false. The slave had indeed a whole cluster of interests associated with his material situation – interests in snatching a little rest from time to time, not gratuitously antagonizing his superiors, sitting behind a somewhat bulkier slave to win a little protection from the sun, and so on. It is just these sorts of material interests which his political and ideological discourse, when he acquires it, will go to work upon, elaborating, cohering and transforming them in various ways; and in this sense material interests undoubtedly exist prior to and independent of politico–ideological ones. The material situation is the *referent* of the slave's political discourse, not the *signified* of it – if by this we are supposed to believe that it is wholly *produced* by it. Hindess and Hirst fear that to deny that the slave's unenviable condition is the product of a politico–ideological language is to imagine that it is then just a 'brute' fact, independent of discourse altogether. But this apprehension is quite needless. There is no non–discursive way in which the slave can decide not to antagonize his superiors; his 'real' situation is inseparably bound up with linguistic interpretation of one kind or another. It is just a mistake to run together *these* kinds of interpretation, inscribed in everything we do, with those specific forms of discourse which allow us to criticize, rationalize, suppress, explain or transform our conditions of life.

We have seen that Hindess and Hirst reject the idea that political interests represent pre–given social or economic ones. They still use the *term* representation; but the signifier now entirely constitutes what it signifies. This means, in effect, that they have come up not with the theory of representation but with a philosophy of identity. Representation or signification depends on a difference between what presents and what is presented: one reason why a photograph of a chipmunk represents a chipmunk is because it is not the actual animal. If the photograph somehow constituted the chipmunk – if, in some Berkeleyan fantasy, the creature had no existence until it was snapped by the camera – it would not act as a representation of it. Much the same goes for Hindess and Hirst's talk of the political/ideological and the social/economic. If the former actually fashion the latter then they are at one with them, and there can be no talk of representation here at all. The two become as indissoluble as a word and its meaning. The semiotic model which governs their thinking here, misleadingly, is thus the Saussurean one between signifier and signified, or word and concept, rather than that between sign and referent.

The upshot of this drastic swerve from economism – which would hold that the political/ideological passively and directly represents class interests – is an overpoliticization. It is now politics, not economics, which reigns supreme. And taken in any crassly literal sense, this case is simply absurd. Are we being asked to believe that the reason some people vote Conservative is not because they are afraid a Labour government might nationalize their property, but that their regard for their property is *created* by the act of voting Conservative? Does a proletarian have an interest in securing better living conditions only because she is already a socialist? On this argument, it becomes impossible to say what politics is actually *about*. There is no 'raw material' on which politics and ideology go to work, since social interests are the product of them, not what they take off from. Politics and ideology thus become purely self-constituting, tautological practices. It is impossible to say where they derive from; they simply drop from the skies, like any other transcendental signifer.

If the working class has no interests derived from its socio-economic conditions, then there is nothing in this class to *resist* its being politically or ideologically 'constructed' in various ways. All that resists my own political construction of the class is someone else's. The working class, or for that matter any other subordinate group, thus becomes clay in the hands of those wishing to coopt it into some political strategy, tugged this way and that between socialists and fascists. If socialism is not necessarily in the workers' interests, since the workers in fact have no interests outside those they are 'constructed' into, why on earth should they bother to become socialists? It is not in their interests *now* to become so, since nothing in their concrete conditions would intimate this; they will become socialists only when their present identities have been transformed by the process of becoming socialist. But how would they ever come to embark on this process? For there is nothing in their conditions now which provides the slightest motivation for it. The future political selves they might attain have no relation whatsoever to their present socio-economic ones. There is merely a blank disjunction between them, as there is for those Humean philosophers for whom what I was at the age of twenty has no relation at all to what I shall be at the age of sixty.

Why, in any case, should someone become a socialist, feminist or anti-racist, if these political interests are in no sense a response to the way society is? (For society, let us recall, is in Hindess and Hirst's view no way at all, until it has come to be politically constructed in a certain manner.) Of course, once Hindess and Hirst begin to *spell out* why they themselves are socialists they will find themselves ineluctably referring to something very like 'the way society is'; but strictly speaking this notion is inadmissable to them.

Radical politics thus becomes a kind of moral option, ungrounded in any actual state of affairs; and these rigorous post-Althusserians accordingly lapse into that humanistic heresy known to Marxism as 'moralism'. Some people, it appears, just are feminists or socialists, as others are UFO buffs; and their aim is to 'construct' other groups or classes in ways which strategically further these interests, despite the fact that there is no 'given' reason why these groups or classes should take the least interest in the project.

Alert to these and other problems, the post-Marxist Ernesto Laclau and Chantal Mouffe offer us in their *Hegemony and Socialist Strategy*[13] a suitably modified version of the Hindess and Hirst case. Laclau and Mouffe entirely endorse Hindess and Hirst's doctrine that, in the words of the former pair, there is 'no logical connection whatsoever' (84) between class position and the political/ideological. This means, presumably, that it is wholly co-incidental that all capitalists are not also revolutionary socialists. Laclau and Mouffe also observe that 'hegemony supposes the construction of the very identity of [the] social agents [being hegemonized]' (58), a formulation which leaves the question of *what* is being 'constructed' here hanging in the air. Either this statement means that there are no social agents at all until the process of political hegemony creates them, in which case hegemony is a circular, self-referential affair, which like a work of literary fiction secretly fashions the reality it claims to be at work upon. Or it means that there *are* existing social agents, but the process of hegemony lends them an entirely different identity all of its own – in which case, as we have seen, it is hard to know why these agents should be in the least motivated to leap the abyss between their current and putative selves.

Whereas Hindess and Hirst would abruptly sever all 'necessary' links between social conditions and political interests, Laclau and Mouffe, while endorsing this move, paint a more nuanced picture. There may be no *logical* relation between these two realms; but that does not mean, *à la* Hindess and Hirst, that political and ideological forms simply bring socio-economic interests into existence, for this, as Laclau and Mouffe shrewdly recognize, is merely to lapse back into the very ideology of identity which post-Marxism seeks to escape. If the various elements of social life – those groups, so to speak, awaiting the event of being hegemonized into a radical political strategy – do not retain a certain contingency and identity of their own, then the practice of hegemony simply means fusing them together into a new kind of closed totality. In that case, the unifying principle of the social whole is no longer 'the economy' but the hegemonizing force itself, which stands in a quasi-transcendental relation to the 'social elements' on which it goes to work. Laclau and Mouffe accordingly insert some cautious qualifications. As we have seen, their position is that hegemony constructs – presumably 'totally' – the very identity of the agents or elements in question; but elsewhere in their text the hegemonic representation 'modifies' (58) or 'contributes to' (110) the social interests represented, which would imply that they exert some weight and autonomy of their own. Elsewhere, in a notable equivocation, they suggest that the identity of the elements is 'at least partially modified' (107) by their hegemonic articulation – a phrase in which everything hangs on that evasive little 'at least'. At another point, the authors claim that once social agents have been politically hegemonized, their identity ceases to be 'exclusively' (58) constituted through their social locations.

The dilemma is surely clear. It seems peculiarly arrogant and appropriative to argue that, say, once a group of oppressed women are 'hegemonized' – made part of some broader political strategy – their identities as they exist now will be entirely submerged in this process. What they will be then has no relation to what they are right now. If this is so, then the hegemonizing process appears every bit as imperious and all-totalizing as 'the economy' was for 'vulgar' Marxism. But if too much weight is accorded to the kinds of interests such women have now, in their 'pre-hegemonized' condition, then – so post-Marxism fears – one is in danger of falling back into an empiricist model of representation, in which political/ideological discourses simply 'reflect' or passively 'represent' pre-constituted social interests. Laclau and Mouffe steer niftily between this particular Scylla and Charybdis, but the strain of the operation betrays itself in the textual inconsistencies of their work. Striving for some middle ground, the authors seek neither a total separation between the two spheres in question, nor a Hindess-and-Hirstian conflation of them. They insist instead on a 'tension' between the two, in which the economic is and is not present in the political, and vice-versa. But their text continues to hesitate symptomatically between the 'extreme' view that the signifier fashions the signified entirely – political hegemony constructs 'the very identity' of social agents – and the more temperate case that the means of politico-ideological representation have an *effect* on the social interests they represent. In other words: the logic of Laclau and Mouffe's *politics* – their proper concern to safeguard the 'relative autonomy' of the specific social interests of women, ethnic groups and so on – is not entirely at one with the logic of a full-blooded post-structuralist *theory* which would recognize no 'given' reality beyond the omnipotent sway of the signifier.

Hegemony and Socialist Strategy is at least unequivocal in its curt rejection of the whole concept of 'objective interests', which it can make no sense of at all. But this is only because it subscribes implicitly to a wholly untenable version of the idea, and then quite understandably goes on to reject it. For Laclau and Mouffe, objective interests means something like interests automatically supplied to you by your place in the relations of production; and they are of course quite right to dismiss this notion out of hand as a form of economic reductionism. But we have seen already that there are more interesting ways of framing the concept. An objective interest means, among other things, a course of action which is in fact in my interests but which I currently do not recognize as such. If this notion is unintelligible, then it would seem to follow that I am always in perfect and absolute possession of my own interests, which is clearly nonsense. There is no need to fear that objective interests somehow exist outside social discourse altogether; the phrase just alludes to valid, discursively framed interests which do not exist for me right now. Once I have acquired such interests, however, I am able to look back on my previous condition and recognize that what I believe and desire now is what I would have believed and desired then if only I had been in a position to do so. And being in a position to do so means being free of the coercion and mystification which in fact prevented me at the time from acknowledging what would be beneficial for me. Note that there is both continuity and discontinuity, identity and difference, at work here: what I am now is not what I was then, but I can see that I *should* have been clamouring then for what I am struggling for now, if only I had understood my circumstances better. This case thus runs counter both to the view that I am always self-identical, always secretly in possession of my own best interests, and to the 'discontinuous' case that what I am now, as a politically self-aware being, has nothing whatsoever to do with what I was when my best interests were unclear to me. In overreacting to the former fantasy, post-Marxism is at grave risk of lapsing into the latter, politically fruitless position.

What makes a political radical attempt to hegemonize one social group rather than another? The answer, surely, can only be because she had decided that the 'given' situation of this group, appropriately interpreted and transformed, is of relevance to the radical project. If monopoly capitalists have no interests independent of the way they are politically articulated, then there would seem no reason at all why the political left should not expend enormous resources of energy in seeking to win them to its programme. The fact that we do not is because we consider that the *given* social interests of this class make them a good deal less likely to become socialists than, say, the unemployed. It is not in the given interests of men to become feminists (although it is certainly in their long-term ones), and this fact has clear political consequences: it means that feminists should not spend too much of their precious political time trying to win men over, though neither should they look the odd gift horse in the mouth. The question of what weight one allots to 'given' interests – or whether they exist at all – is thus of vital relevance to practical politics. If there is no 'necessary' relation between women and feminism, or the working class and socialism, then the upshot would be a disastrously eclectic, opportunistic politics, which simply drew into its project whatever social groups seemed currently most amenable to it. There would be no good reason why the struggle against patriarchy should not be spearheaded by men, or the fight against capitalism led by students. Marxists have no objection to students, having occasionally been in this unenviable condition themselves; but however politically important the intelligentsia may sometimes be, it cannot provide the major troops for the fight against capitalism. It cannot do so because it happens not to be socially located within the process of production in such a way as to be feasibly capable of taking it over. It is in this sense that the relation between certain social locations, and certain political forms, is a 'necessary' one – which is not, to repeat, to assert that it is inevitable, spontaneous, guaranteed or God-given. Such convenient travesties of the case can be left to the fantasies of post-Marxism.

We have seen that a particular brand of semiotics or discourse theory was the vital relay by which a whole sector of the political left shifted its political ground from revolutionism to reformism. That this should have happened just at a time when the former strategy was confronting genuine problems is hardly a coincidence. For all of its undoubted insights, discourse theory provided the *ideology* of this political retreat – an ideology especially alluring to left 'cultural' intellectuals. Hindess and Hirst now espouse a politics which could hardly be dubbed radical at all, while Laclau and Mouffe, if rather more explicitly anti-capitalist, are almost wholly silent in *Hegemony and Socialist Strategy* on the very concept of ideology. In this rarefied theoretical milieu, all talk of social class or class-struggle became rapidly branded as 'vulgar' or reductionist overnight, in panic-stricken reaction to an 'economism' which every intelligent socialist had in any case long left behind. And then, no sooner had this position become the fashionable orthodoxy of sections of the political left, than a sector of the British working class embarked upon the greatest, most protracted piece of industrial militancy in the annals of British labour history ...

With Laclau and Mouffe, what Perry Anderson has called the 'inflation of discourse' in post-structuralist thought reaches its apogee. Heretically deviating from their mentor Michel Foucault, Laclau and Mouffe deny all validity to the distinction between 'discursive' and 'non-discursive' practices, on the grounds that a practice is structured along the lines of a discourse. The short reply to this is that a practice may well be organized like a discourse, but as a matter of fact it is a practice rather than a discourse. It is needlessly obfuscating and homogenizing to subsume such things as preaching a sermon and dislodging a pebble from one's left ear under the same rubric. A way of *understanding* an object is simply projected into the object itself, in a familiar idealist move. In notably academicist style, the contemplative analysis of a practice suddenly reappears as its very essence. Why should we want to *call* a building a 'menu', just because in some structuralist fashion we might examine it along those lines? The fact that there is no necessity for this move (for the Humean Laclau and Mouffe there is no necessity for anything) betrays it as far from innocent. The category of discourse is inflated to the point where it imperializes the whole world, eliding the distinction between thought and material reality. The effect of this is to undercut the critique of ideology – for if ideas and material reality are given indissolubly together, there can be no question of asking where social ideas actually hail from. The new 'transcendental' hero is discourse itself, which is apparently prior to everything else. It is surely a little immodest of academics, professionally concerned with discourse as they are, to project their own preoccupations onto the whole world, in that ideology known as (post-) structuralism. It is as though a theatre critic, on being asked the way, were to instruct you to exit stage-left at the end of the High Street, circumvent the first flat you reach and head for the backdrop of the hills. The neo-Nietzschean language of post-Marxism, for which there is little or nothing 'given' in reality, belongs to a period of political crisis – an era in which it could indeed appear that the traditional social interests of the working class had evaporated overnight, leaving you with your hegemonic forms and precious little material content. Post-Marxist discourse theorists may place a ban on the question of where ideas come from; but we can certainly turn this question back on themselves. For the whole theory is itself historically grounded in a particular phase of advanced capitalism, and it is thus living testimony in its very existence to that 'necessary' relation between forms of consciousness and social reality which it so vehemently denies. What is offered as a *universal* thesis about discourse, politics and interests, as so often with ideologies, is alert to everything but its own historical grounds of possibility.

CONCLUSION

I HAVE tried in this book to outline something of the history of the concept of ideology, and to disentangle some of the conceptual confusions attendent upon it. But in doing so I have also been concerned to develop my own particular views on the issue; and it is to a summary of these that we can finally turn.

The term ideology has a wide range of historical meanings, all the way from the unworkably broad sense of the social determination of thought to the suspiciously narrow idea of the deployment of false ideas in the direct interests of a ruling class. Very often, it refers to the ways in which signs, meanings and values help to reproduce a dominant social power; but it can also denote any significant conjuncture between discourse and political interests. From a radical standpoint, the former meaning is pejorative, while the latter is more neutral. My own view is that both of these senses of the term have their uses, but that a good deal of confusion has arisen from the failure to disentangle them.

The rationalist view of ideologies as conscious, well-articulated systems of belief is clearly inadequate: it misses the affective, unconscious, mythical or symbolic dimensions of ideology; the way it constitutes the subject's lived, apparently spontaneous relations to a power-structure and comes to provide the invisible colour of daily life itself. But if ideology is in this sense primarily performative, rhetorical, pseudo-propositional discourse, this is not to say that it lacks an important propositional content – or that such propositions as it advances, including moral and normative ones, cannot be assessed for their truth or falsehood. Much of what ideologies say is true, and would be ineffectual if it were not; but ideologies also contain a good many propositions which are flagrantly false, and do so less because of some inherent quality than because of the distortions into which they are commonly forced in their attempts to ratify and legitimate unjust, oppressive political systems. The falsity in question, as we have seen, may be epistemic, functional or generic, or some combination of the three.

Dominant ideologies, and occasionally oppositional ones, often employ such devices as unification, spurious identification, naturalization, deception, self-deception, universalization and rationalization. But they do not do so universally; indeed it is doubtful that one can ascribe to ideology any *invariable* characteristics at all. We are dealing less with some essence of ideology than with an overlapping network of 'family resemblances' between different styles of signification. We need, then, to look sceptically upon various essentialist cases about ideology: on the historicist case that it is the coherent world-view of a 'class subject'; on the theory that it is spontaneously secreted by the economic structures of society; or on the semiotic doctrine that it signifies 'discursive closure'. All of these perspectives contain a kernel of truth; but taken in isolation they show up as partial and flawed. The 'sociological' view that ideology provides the 'cement' of a social formation, or the 'cognitive map' which orientates its agents to action, is too often depoliticizing in effect, voiding the concept of ideology of conflict and contradiction.

Ideology in its dominant forms is often seen as a mythical or imaginary resolution of such contradictions, but it would be unwise to overestimate its success in achieving this goal. It is neither a set of diffuse discourses nor a seamless whole; if its impulse is to identify and homogenize, it is nevertheless scarred and disarticulated by its *relational* character; by the conflicting interests among which it must ceaselessly negotiate. It is not itself, as some historicist Marxism would seem to suggest, the founding principle of social unity, but rather strives in the teeth of political resistance to reconstitute that unity at an imaginary level. As such, it can never be simple 'other-worldliness' or idly disconnected thought; on the contrary, it must figure as an organizing social force which actively constitutes human subjects at the roots of their lived experience and seeks to equip them with forms of value and belief relevant to their specific social tasks and to the general reproduction of the social order. But those subjects are always conflictively, precariously constituted; and though ideology is 'subject-centred', it is not *reducible* to the question of subjectivity. Some of the most powerful ideological effects are generated by institutions such as parliamentary democracy; impersonal political processes rather than subjective states of being. The structure of commodity fetishism is likewise irreducible to the psychology of the human subject. Neither psychologistic theories of ideology, nor accounts which view it as the well-nigh automatic effect of objective social structures, are equal to the complexity of the notion. In a parallel way, ideology is never the mere expressive effect of objective social interests; but neither are all ideological signifiers 'free-floating' in respect of such interests. The relations between ideological discourses and social interests are complex, variable ones, in which it is sometimes appropriate to speak of the ideological signifier as a bone of contention between conflicting social forces, and at other times a matter of more internal relations between modes of signification and forms of social power. Ideology contributes to the constitution of social interests, rather than passively reflecting pre-given positions; but it does not, for all that, legislate such positions into existence by its own discursive omnipotence.

Ideology is a matter of 'discourse' rather than of 'language' – of certain concrete discursive effects, rather than of signification as such. It represents the points where power impacts upon certain utterances and inscribes itself tacitly within them. But it is not therefore to be equated with just any form of discursive partisanship, 'interested' speech or rhetorical bias; rather, the concept of ideology aims to disclose something of the relation between an utterance and its material conditions of possibility, when those conditions of possibility are viewed in the light of certain power-struggles central to the reproduction (or also, for some theories, contestation) of a whole form of social life. For some theorists of the notion, ideology is an inherently technical, secular, rationalist mode of social discourse, which has spurned all religious or metaphysical efforts to legitimate a social order; but this view underplays its archaic, affective and traditionalist dimensions, which may enter into significant contradiction with its more 'modernizing' thrust.

No radical who takes a cool look at the tenacity and pervasiveness of dominant ideologies could possibly feel sanguine about what would be necessary to loosen their lethal grip. But there is one place above all where such forms of consciousness may be transformed almost literally overnight, and that is in active political struggle. This is not a Left piety but an empirical fact. When men and women engaged in quite modest, local forms of political resistance find themselves brought by the inner momentum of such conflicts into direct confrontation with the power of the state, it is possible that their political consciousness may be definitively, irreversibly altered. If a theory of ideology has value at all, it is in helping to illuminate the processes by which such liberation from death-dealing beliefs may be practically effected.

NOTES

INTRODUCTION

1. See, for example, the declaration of the Italian postmodernist philosopher Gianni Vattimo that the end of modernity and the end of ideology are identical moments. 'Postmodern Criticism: Postmodern Critique', in David Woods, ed., *Writing the Future*, London 1990, p. 57.

1 WHAT IS IDEOLOGY?

1. For a useful summary of the various meanings of ideology, see A. Naess et al., *Democracy, Ideology and Objectivity*, Oslo 1956, pp. 143 ff. See also Norman Birnbaum, 'The Sociological Study of Ideology 1940–1960', *Current Sociology*, vol. 9, 1960, for a survey of theories of ideology from Marx to the modern day and an excellent bibliography.

2. Emile Durkheim, *The Rules of Sociological Method*, London 1982, p. 86.

3. For the 'end of ideology' ideologists, see Daniel Bell, *The End of Ideology*, Glencoe, Ill., 1960; Robert E. Lane, *Political Ideology*, New York, 1962, and Raymond Aron, *The Opium of the Intellectuals*, London 1957.

4. Edward Shils, 'The concept and function of ideology', *International Encyclopaedia of the Social Sciences*, vol. 7, 1968.

5. Alvin Gouldner, *The Dialectic of Ideology and Technology*, London 1976, p. 4.

6. John B. Thompson, *Studies in the Theory of Ideology*, Cambridge 1984, p. 4. For another general study of ideology see D.J. Manning, ed., *The Form of Ideology*, London 1980.

7. Kenneth Minogue, *Alien Powers*, London 1985, p. 4.

8. M. Seliger, *Ideology and Politics*, London 1976, p. 11. See also his *The Marxist Concept of Ideology*, London 1977.

9. See Michel Foucault, *Discipline and Punish: The Birth of the Prison*, New York 1977.

10. See Emile Beneviste, *Problems in General Linguistics*, Miami 1971.

11. Raymond Williams, *Keywords*, London 1976, pp. 143–4.

12. Richard Rorty, *Contingency, Irony and Solidarity*, Cambridge 1989.

13. Alex Callinicos, *Marxism and Philosophy*, Oxford 1985, p. 134.

14. Göran Therborn, *The Ideology of Power and the Power of Ideology*, London 1980, p. 5.

15. M. Seliger, *Ideology and Politics*, passim.

16. Rosalind Coward and John Ellis, *Language and Materialism*, London 1977, p. 90.

17. Bjørn T. Ramberg, *Donald Davidson's Philosophy of Language*, Oxford 1989, p. 47.

18. 'Belief, Bias and Ideology', in M. Hollis and S. Lukes, eds, *Rationality and Relativism*, Oxford 1982.

19. The latter claim was one of the few parts of my argument to be seriously contested when I delivered a version of this chapter as a lecture at Brigham Young University, Utah.

20. See Sabina Lovibond, *Reason and Imagination in Ethics*, Oxford 1982, and David O. Brink, *Moral Realism and the Foundations of Ethics*, Cambridge 1989.

21. Lovibond, *Reason and Imagination*, p. 36.

22. I.A. Richards, *Principles of Literary Criticism*, London 1924, ch. 35.

23. See Terry Eagleton, *The Ideology of the Aesthetic*, Oxford 1990, pp. 93–96.

24. Louis Althusser, *For Marx*, London 1969, p. 234.

25. See J.L. Austin, *How To Do Things With Words*, London 1962.

26. Paul Hirst, *Law and Ideology*, London 1979, p. 38.

27. Paul de Man, *Allegories of Reading*, New Haven 1979, ch. 1.

28. Denys Turner, *Marxism and Christianity*, Oxford 1983, pp. 22–3.

29. *Ibid.*, p. 26.

30. Raymond Geuss, *The Idea of a Critical Theory*, Cambridge 1981, ch. 1.

31. *Ibid.*, p. 21.

32. Tony Skillen, 'Discourse Fever', in R. Edgley and P. Osborne, eds, *Radical Philosophy Reader*, London 1985, p. 332.

33. Peter Sloterdijk, *Critique of Cynical Reason*, London 1988, ch. 1.

2 IDEOLOGICAL STRATEGIES

1. M. Poster, ed., *Jean Baudrillard: Selected Writings*, Cambridge 1988, p. 172.

2. Slavoj Žižek, *The Sublime Object of Ideology*, London, 1989, p. 28.

3. Raymond Geuss, *The Idea of a Critical Theory*, ch. 1.

4. See Pierre Macherey, *A Theory of Literary Production*, London 1978.

5. See Herbert Marcuse, *One-Dimensional Man*, Boston 1964, and Theodor Adorno, *Negative Dialectics*, London 1973 and *Minima Moralia*, London 1974.

6. Raymond Williams, *Marxism and Literature*, Oxford 1977, p. 132.

7. V.N. Voloshinov, *Marxism and the Philosophy of Language*, New York and London 1973, p. 93.

8. Williams, *Marxism and Literature*, p. 125.

9. Voloshinov, *Marxism and the Philosophy of Language*, p. 92.

10. Williams, *Marxism and Literature*, p. 125.

11. J. Laplanche and J-B. Pontalis, *The Language of Psycho-Analysis*, London 1980, p. 375.

12. See, for example, Jon Elster, *Sour Grapes: Studies in the Subversion of Rationality*, Cambridge 1983, and Herbert Fingarette, *Self-Deception*, Atlantic Highlands, N.J., 1969.

13. Turner, *Marxism and Christianity*, pp. 119–21.

14. I owe some of these points to Jon Elster, 'Belief, Bias and Ideology', in M. Hollis and S. Lukes, eds, *Rationality and Relativism*, Oxford 1982.

15. Karl Marx and Frederick Engels, *The German Ideology*, ed. C.J. Arthur, London 1974, pp. 65–6.

16. See Jorge Larrain, *The Concept of Ideology*, London 1979, p. 62.

17. Louis Althusser, *Lenin and Philosophy*, London 1971, p. 164.

18. See Norman Geras, *Marx and Human Nature, London 1983.*

19. *Althusser, Lenin and Philosophy*, p. 175.

3 FROM THE ENLIGHTENMENT TO THE SECOND INTERNATIONAL

1. See George Lichtheim, 'The Concept of Ideology', in *The Concept of Ideology and other Essays*, New York 1967. See also Hans Barth, *Truth and Ideology*, Berkeley and Los Angeles 1976, ch. 1.

2. For a useful account of this style of thought, see Basil Willey, *The Eighteenth Century Background*, London 1940.

3. For a superbly erudite account of Tracy's life, see Emmet Kennedy, *A Philosopher in the Age of Revolution: Destutt de Tracy and the Origins of 'Ideology'*, Philadelphia 1978.

4. Quoted by Kennedy, *A Philosopher in the Age of Revolution*, p. 189.

5. Quoted in Naess et al., *Democracy, Ideology and Objectivity*, p. 151.

6. For an account of Marx and ideology, see H. Lefebvre, *The Sociology of Marx*, London 1963, ch. 3.

7. Marx and Engels, *The German Ideology*, p. 47. For some interesting comments on this text, see Louis Dupré, *Marx's Social Critique of Culture*, New Haven and London 1983.

8. *Ibid.*, p. 47 (my italics).

9. *Ibid.*, p. 52.

10. Williams, *Marxism and Literature* p. 60.

11. See W.J.T. Mitchell, *Iconology*, Chicago and London 1986, pp. 168 ff.

12. *Ibid.*, p. 173.

13. Marx and Engels, *The German Ideology*, p. 64.

14. *Ibid.*, p. 64.

15. *Ibid.*, p. 53.

16. Marx and Engels, *Selected Works*, vol. 1, London 1962, p. 362.

17. K. Marx, *Capital*, vol. 1, New York 1967, p. 71. For two excellent analyses of Marx's later version of ideology, see Norman Geras, 'Marxism and the Critique of Political Economy', in R. Blackburn, ed., *Ideology in the Social Sciences*, London 1972, and G.A. Cohen, *Karl Marx's Theory of History: A Defence*, Oxford 1978, ch. 5. See also the comments by Franz Jakubowski, *Ideology and Superstructure in Historical Materialism*, London 1976.

18. Callinicos, *Marxism and Philosophy*, p. 131.

19. Etienne Balibar, 'The Vacillation of Ideology', in C. Nelson and L. Grossberg, eds, *Marxism and the Interpretation of Culture*, Urbana and Chicago 1988, p. 168.

20. Larrain, *The Concept of Ideology*, p. 180.

21. Geras, 'Marxism and the Critique of Political Economy', p. 286.

22. John Mepham, 'The Theory of Ideology in *Capital*', *Radical Philosophy*, no. 2, summer 1972.

23. Georg Lukács, *History and Class Consciousness*, London 1971, pp. 83–4.

24. Joe McCarney, *The Real World of Ideology*, Brighton 1980, p. 95.

25. F. Engels, *Anti-Dühring*, Moscow 1971, p. 135.
26. V.I. Lenin, *What Is To Be Done?*, London 1958, p. 23.

4 FROM LUKÁCS TO GRAMSCI

1. Lukács, *History and Class Consciousness*, p. 204.
2. *Ibid.*, p. 204.
3. 'Historicism' in its Marxist sense is elegantly summarized by Perry Anderson as an ideology in which 'society becomes a circular "expressive" totality, history a homogeneous flow of linear time, philosophy a self-consciousness of the historical process, class struggle a combat of collective "subjects", capitalism a universe essentially defined by alienation, communism a state of true humanism beyond alienation' (*Considerations on Western Marxism*, London 1976, p. 70).
4. Bhikhu Parekh, *Marx's Theory of Ideology*, London 1982, pp. 171–2.
5. Like most analogies, this one limps: the Hegelian Idea is really its own creation, whereas the proletariat, far from being self-generating, is for Marxism an effect of the process of capital.
6. Leszek Kołakowski, *Main Currents of Marxism*, vol. 3, Oxford, 1978, p. 270 (my parenthesis).
7. Lukács, History and Class Consciousness, p. 83. For useful discussions of Lukács's thought, see A. Arato and P. Breines, *The Young Lukács*, London 1979, ch. 8, and Michael Löwy, *Georg Lukács - From Romanticism to Bolshevism*, London 1979, part 4.
8. Lukács, *History and Class Consciousness*, p. 52.
9. Gareth Stedman Jones, 'The Marxism of the early Lukács: An Evaluation', *New Left Review*, no. 70, November/December 1971.
10. Nicos Poulantzas, *Political Power and Social Classes*, London 1973, part 3, ch. 2. It should be pointed out that Lukács does in fact hold that there are heterogeneous 'levels' of ideology.
11. See Ernesto Laclau, *Politics and Ideology in Marxist Theory*, London 1977, ch. 3.
12. Lukács, *History and Class Consciousness*, p. 76.
13. *Ibid.*, p. 70.
14. See Lucio Colletti, *Marxism and Hegel*, London 1973, ch. 10.
15. Lukács, *History and Class Consciousness*, p. 54.
16. *Ibid.*, p. 50.
17. *Ibid.*, p. 69.
18. Karl Mannheim, *Ideology and Utopia*, London 1954, p. 87. There are suggestive critiques of Mannheim in Larrain, *The Concept of Ideology*, and in Nigel Abercrombie, *Class, Structure and Knowledge*, Oxford 1980. See also B. Parekh's essay in R. Benewick, ed., *Knowledge and Belief in Politics*, London 1973.
19. Perry Anderson, 'The Antinomies of Antonio Gramsci', *New Left Review*, no. 100, November 1976/January 1977.
20. V.I. Lenin, *Collected Works*, vol. 27, Moscow 1965, p. 464. See also Carmen Claudin-Urondo, *Lenin and the Cultural Revolution*, Hassocks, Sussex, 1977.
21. Williams, *Marxism and Literature*, p. 112. For a historical study of political hegemony in eighteenth- and nineteenth-century England, see Francis Hearn, *Domination, Legitimation, and Resistance*, Westport, Conn., 1978.
22. See my *The Ideology of the Aesthetic*, Oxford 1990, chs 1 and 2.
23. Antonio Gramsci, *Selections from the Prison Notebooks*, Q. Hoare and G. Nowell Smith, eds, London 1971, p. 268.

24. *Ibid.*, p. 376.

25. *Ibid.*, p. 370.

26. *Ibid.*, p. 348.

27. *Ibid.*, p. 365.

28. See on this topic Alberto Maria Cirese, 'Gramsci's Observations on Folklore', in Anne Showstack Sassoon, ed., *Approaches to Gramsci*, London 1982.

29. Quoted in Cirese, 'Gramsci's Observations', p. 226.

30. Gramsci, *Prison Notebooks*, p. 424.

31. *Ibid.*, p. 328.

32. See Nicos Poulantzas, *Political Power and Social Classes*, London 1973, 111, 2. How far Poulantzas levels these charges directly at Gramsci, rather than at Lukács, is somewhat ambiguous.

33. See Chantal Mouffe, 'Hegemony and Ideology in Gramsci', in Chantal Mouffe, ed., *Gramsci and Marxist Theory*, London 1979, p. 192.

34. Gramsci, *Prison Notebooks*, p. 453.

35. *Ibid.*, p. 18.

5 FROM ADORNO TO BOURDIEU

1. See Fredric Jameson, *The Political Unconscious*, London 1981, pp. 114–15.

2. See Theodor Adorno, *Aesthetic Theory*, London 1984.

3. Adorno, *Negative Dialectics*, p. 161.

4. *Ibid.*, p. 150.

5. *Ibid.*, p. 6.

6. See Jürgen Habermas, *The Theory of Communicative Action*, 2 vols, Boston 1984.

7. Quoted by Thomas McCarthy, *The Critical Theory of Jürgen Habermas*, London 1978, p. 273.

8. Quoted in Peter Dews, ed., *Habermas: Autonomy and Solidarity*, London 1986, p. 51.

9. McCarthy, *The Critical Theory of Jürgen Habermas*, p. 56.

10. Quoted *ibid.*, p. 201.

11. Jürgen Habermas, *Knowledge and Human Interests*, Cambridge, 1987, p. 217. Habermas's account of Freud has been in my view justly criticized as excessively rationalistic.

12. *Ibid.*, p. 227.

13. Karl Marx, *Theories of Surplus Value*, vol.1, Moscow n.d., p. 147.

14. See Etienne Balibar and Pierre Macherey, 'On Literature as an Ideological Form', in Robert M. Young, ed., *Untying the Text*, London, 1981.

15. Russell Keat, *The Politics of Social Theory*, Oxford, 1981, p. 178.

16. For excellent accounts of Althusser's thought, see Alex Callinicos, *Althusser's Marxism*, London 1976; Ted Benton, *The Rise and Fall of Structural Marxism*, London 1984; and Gregory Elliott, *Althusser: The Detour of Theory*, London 1987.

17. The essay 'Ideology and Ideological State Apparatuses' can be found in Louis Althusser, *Lenin and Philosophy*, London 1971.

18. For a coruscating account of Western Marxism, see Perry Anderson, *Considerations on Western Marxism*, London 1976.

19. See Louis Althusser, *Essays in Self-Criticism*, London 1976, p. 119.

20. See Barry Barnes, *Knowledge and the Growth of Interests*, London 1977, p. 41.

21. See Edward Thompson, 'The Poverty of Theory: Or An Orrery of Errors', in *The Poverty of Theory*, London 1978.

22. Althusser, *Essays in Self-Criticism*, p. 121.

23. Lacan's essay can be found in his *Ecrits*, London 1977. See also Fredric Jameson, 'Imaginary and Symbolic in Lacan', *Yale French Studies*, 55/56, 1977.

24. Louis Althusser, *For Marx*, London 1969, pp. 233–4.

25. See Colin MacCabe, 'On Discourse', *Economy and Society*, vol. 8, no. 3, August 1979.

26. Althusser, *Lenin and Philosophy*, p. 174.

27. Peter Dews, *Logics of Disintegration*, London 1987, pp. 78–79.

28. See Anderson, *Considerations on Western Marxism*, Ch. 4.

29. Lenin and Philosophy, p. 181.

30. A discrepancy noted by Jacques Rancière in his 'On the Theory of Ideology – Althusser's Politics', in R. Edgley and P. Osborne, eds, *Radical Philosophy Reader*, London 1985.

31. See my 'Base and Superstructure in Raymond Williams', in Terry Eagleton, ed., *Raymond Williams: Critical Perspectives*, Cambridge 1989.

32. Althusser, *Lenin and Philosophy*, p. 169 (my italics).

33. Althusser, *For Marx*, p. 235.

34. Quoted by Jonathan Rée, *Philosophical Tales*, London 1985, p. 59.

35. Clifford Geertz, 'Ideology as a Cultural System', in *The Interpretation of Cultures*, New York 1978. Stuart Hall also adopts this version of ideology in his 'The Problem of Ideology', in Betty Matthews, ed., *Marx: A Hundred Years On*, London 1983.

36. See Althusser's unpublished essay of 1969, 'Théorie, Pratique Théorique et Formation Théorique, Idéologie et Lutte Idéologique', quoted by Elliot, *Althusser*, pp. 172–4.

37. Raymond Boudon, *The Analysis of Ideology*, Oxford 1989, part 1.

38. Dick Howard, *The Politics of Critique*, London 1989, p. 178.

39. Alvin Gouldner, *The Dialectic of Ideology and Technology*, London 1976, p. 30.

40. See Thompson, *Studies in the Theory of Ideology*, p. 34.

41. Jürgen Habermas, *Towards A Rational Society*, Boston 1970, p. 99 (my parentheses).

42. Pierre Bourdieu, *Outline of a Theory of Practice*, Cambridge 1977, p. 192.

6 FROM SCHOPENHAUER TO SOREL

1. Albert O. Hirschman, *The Passions and the Interests*, Princeton New Jersey 1977.

2. *Ibid.*, p. 43.

3. For a fuller account, see *The Ideology of the Aesthetic*, Oxford 1990, ch. 3.

4. Friedrich Nietzsche, *The Will to Power*, New York 1968, p. 269.

5. Friedrich Nietzsche, *The Twilight of the Idols*, London 1927, p. 34.

6. Friedrich Nietzsche, *Beyond Good and Evil*, in Walter Kaufmann, ed., *Basic Writings of Nietzsche*, New York 1968, p. 393.

7. Stanley Fish, *Doing What Comes Naturally*, Oxford 1989.

8. Richard Rorty, *Consequences of Pragmatism*, Minneapolis 1982, p. 166.

9. Fish, *Doing What Comes Naturally*, p. 245.

10. See Jonathan Lear, *Aristotle and the Desire to Understand*, Cambridge 1988, ch. 5.

11. See Christopher Norris, *The Contest of Faculties*, London 1985.

12. Sigmund Freud, *The Future of an Illusion*, in *Sigmund Freud: Civilisation, Society and Religion*, Harmondsworth 1985, p. 225. (All subsequent references are given parenthetically after quotations.)

13. Sigmund Freud, *Civilisation and its Discontents*, in *Sigmund Freud: Civilisation, Society and Religion*, Harmondsworth 1985, p. 337.

14. Slavoj Žižek, *The Sublime Object of Ideology*, London 1989, p. 45.

15. *Ibid.*, p. 125.

16. See Fredric Jameson, *The Political Unconscious*, Conclusion.

17. For a general survey of this period, see H. Stuart Hughes, *Consciousness and Society*, London 1959.

18. Georges Sorel, *Reflections on Violence*, Glencoe, Illinois 1950, p. 140.

19. *Ibid.*, p. 167.

20. *Ibid.*, p. 168.

21. Walter Benjamin, 'Surrealism', in *One-Way Street*, London 1978, p. 238.

22. See B. Halpern, 'Myth and Ideology', in *History and Theory*, no. 1, 1961.

23. See Claude Lévi-Strauss, *Structural Anthropology*, London 1968; and *The Savage Mind*, London 1966.

24. Walter Benjamin, *Gesammelte Werke*, R. Tiedemann and T.W. Adorno, eds, Frankfurt 1966, vol. 5, p. 505.

25. See Frank Kermode, *The Sense of an Ending*, New York 1967, pp. 112–13.

7 DISCOURSE AND IDEOLOGY

1. V.N. Voloshinov, *Marxism and the Philosophy of Language*, New York 1973, p. 9.

2. *Ibid.*, p. 13.

3. Thompson, *Studies in the Theory of Ideology*, p. 132.

4. See, for example, William Labov, *Sociolinguistic Patterns*, Philadelphia 1972; Malcolm Coulthard, *Introduction to Discourse Analysis*, Harlow 1977; M.A.K. Halliday, *Language as Social Semiotic*, London 1978; Gunter Kress and Roger Hodge, *Language as Ideology*, London 1979; Roger Fowler, *Literature as Social Discourse*, London 1981; and Diane Macdonell, *Theories of Discourse*, Oxford 1986.

5. Rosalind Coward and John Ellis, *Language and Materialism*, London 1977, p. 73.

6. See my discussion of this topic in *The Function of Criticism*, London 1984, pp. 100–2.

7. Roland Barthes, *Mythologies*, London 1972, p. 143.

8. Christopher Norris, *Paul de Man: Deconstruction and the Critique of Aesthetic Ideology*, London 1988, pp. 48–9.

9. Paul de Man, *The Resistance to Theory*, Minneapolis 1986, p. 11.

10. See in particular Barry Hindess and Paul Hirst, *Pre-Capitalist Modes of Production* London 1975, and *Mode of Production and Social Formation*, London 1977. John Frow promotes a similar 'semiotic' theory of ideology in his *Marxism and Literary History*, Oxford 1986, pp. 55–8.

11. A. Cutler, B. Hindess, P. Hirst and A. Hussain, *Marx's 'Capital' and Capitalism Today*, vol. 1, London 1977, pp. 222, 236.

12. *Ibid.*, p. 237.

13. Ernesto Laclau and Chantal Mouffe, *Hegemony and Socialist Strategy*, London 1985. (All page references to this work will be given parenthetically after quotations.)

FURTHER READING

For those looking for an excellent book-length introduction to the topic of ideology, Jorge Larrain's *The Concept of Ideology* is difficult to match in historical scope and analytic power. It can be supplemented by the deeply tendentious title essay of George Lichtheim's *The Concept of Ideology and Other Essays*, and by the brief but suggestive essay on ideology contained in Raymond Williams's *Marxism and Literature*. Raymond Geuss's *The Idea of a Critical Theory* is a particularly elegant, rigorous study of the question, with special reference to the Frankfurt School, while John B. Thompson's *Studies in the Theory of Ideology* ranges usefully from Castoriadis to Habermas from a position broadly sympathetic to the latter.

Classic Marxist texts on the subject are Marx and Engels, *The German Ideology*; Marx's chapter on commodity fetishism in *Capital* Volume 1; Georg Lukács's essay on 'Reification and the Consciousness of the Proletariat' in *History and Class Consciousness*; V.N. Voloshinov's *Marxism and the Philosophy of Language*; and Louis Althusser's now celebrated essay on 'Ideology and Ideological State Apparatuses' in *Lenin and Philosophy*.

INDEX

235

Heaney, Seamus 200
Hegel, G.W.F. xii, 3, 78, 94, 99, 151, 161
   The Phenomenology of Spirit 70, 98
Hegemony and Socialist Strategy (Laclau
   and Mouffe) 215, 217, 218
hegemony, concept of 112–17, 120, 122,
   158, 179, 180, 215–17, 228 n21
Heidegger, Martin 3, 164, 200
Helvetius, Claude 66, 160
Hindess, Barry 203–6, 208, 209, 210,
   212–16, 218
Hirschman, Albert 160
Hirst, Paul 22, 203–6, 208, 209, 210,
   212–16, 218
historical materialism 74, 90, 91, 104,
   136, 140
History and Class Consciousness (Lukács)
   94, 95, 98, 100, 102, 103, 104
Hobbes, Thomas 78, 159, 165, 181
Holbach, P. d' 66
Horkheimer, Max, and Theodor
   Adorno, *Dialectic of Enlightenment*
   127
Howard, Dick 154
Hume, David 159, 219

idealism 36, 67, 72, 76, 78, 99, 153, 193,
   199
identity thinking 2, 126, 127, 128
ideology xi, 1–3, 10, 28, 43–5, 48, 49, 51,
   63, 69, 107, 109, 110, 164, 165, 166,
   193, 199, 221, 224
   in Adorno 126, 127, 128
   Althusserian definition of 18–21, 50,
      58, 141, 142, 144, 146–50, 152,
      153, 198
   and Bourdieu 158, 188
   and discourse 16, 29, 135, 194, 195,
      196, 202, 209, 223
   dominant 27, 30, 34–7, 41, 45–7, 56,
      81, 83, 112, 122, 123, 134, 222

end of xii, 4, 5, 38, 39, 42, 154, 182,
   225 n1
Freudian concept of 176, 177, 181,
   185
Gramscian theory of 116, 117, 119
in Habermas 128, 129, 132, 155
in Lukács 3, 59, 87, 99, 100, 101,
   102–3, 105, 106
Marx and 11, 30, 66, 70, 72, 76–80,
   82, 83, 91, 125
and science 64, 65, 66, 67, 95, 111,
   137, 138, 139, 140, 159
see also critique, of ideology; false
   consciousness
imperialism 96, 97, 107, 175
intelligentsia 118, 119, 120, 121, 123
interests
   and definition of ideology 1, 9–10,
      29, 160, 221, 223
   post-Marxist theorization of 212–13,
      217
   postmodernist theorization of 165,
      166, 167, 172–3
irony 11, 40, 60

Jameson, Fredric 126, 184
Jefferson, Thomas 69

Kant, Immanuel 19, 20, 111, 162, 172,
   173, 189
Keat, Russell 136
Kennedy, Emmet 69
Kermode, Frank, *The Sense of an Ending*
   191
Kolakowski, Leszek 99
Korsch, Karl 95

labour 74, 85, 86, 133, 179
   division of 148, 151
   power 95, 125
Lacan, Jacques 142, 144, 145, 176, 182